# CLEVELAND
## ARCHITECTURE
# 1876-1976

# CLEVELAND ARCHITECTURE 1876-1976

Eric Johannesen

The Western Reserve Historical Society

This work was made possible through the assistance of matching research grants from the Warner M. Bateman Memorial Fund of the Cleveland Foundation and the National Endowment for the Humanities. The findings and conclusions presented here do not necessarily represent the views of the Foundation or of the Endowment.

The publication was made possible through a grant from the George Gund Foundation and with the support of the Ohio Arts Council.

Unless otherwise noted, all illustrations are from the History Library of the Western Reserve Historical Society or from photographs by the author.

CLEVELAND ARCHITECTURE, 1876–1976
Copyright © 1979 by The Western Reserve Historical Society
All rights reserved
Manufactured in the United States of America
This is publication number 149 of The Western Reserve Historical Society
FIRST EDITION

**Library of Congress Cataloging in Publication Data**

Johannesen, Eric.
    Cleveland architecture, 1876–1976.

    Bibliography: p.
    Includes index.
    1. Cleveland—Buildings. 2. Architecture—Ohio—Cleveland. 3. Architecture, Modern—19th century—Ohio—Cleveland. 4. Architecture, Modern—20th century—Ohio—Cleveland. I. Title.
NA735.C6J63      720'.9771'32      79-22976
ISBN 0-911704-21-3

# FOREWORD

In 1964, the Western Reserve Historical Society co-published the late Edmund H. Chapman's book, *Cleveland: Village to Metropolis*. He tells well the history of Cleveland architecture for the first three quarters of the nineteenth century, describing buildings that, for the most part, have disappeared.

Left untold was the remarkable story of Cleveland architecture from 1875 to the present, the period of the city's great industrial growth. A large percentage of the structures built during this 100-year period are still standing today. To tell this story was the purpose of the author, Eric Johannesen, regional preservation officer of the Ohio Historic Preservation Office at the Western Reserve Historical Society.

Formerly professor and head of the art department of Mount Union College, Mr. Johannesen had already written books on the architecture of early Ohio colleges and the cities of Toledo and Alliance. Taking leave of absence from the preservation office, he dedicated an entire year to the research and writing project, which was made possible by matching grants from the National Endowment for the Humanities and the Cleveland Foundation. In addition, the George Gund Foundation has provided a generous publication subsidy, assisted by support from the Ohio Arts Council. For all this backing we are especially grateful.

*Cleveland Architecture 1876-1976* gives us a far more comprehensive insight into the building patterns of the city and brings to light many facts which were hitherto unknown. It also affords opportunity to appreciate and better understand the city and some of the forces that helped make it what it is today.

Meredith B. Colket, Jr.
Executive Director
The Western Reserve Historical Society

# CONTENTS

# PREFACE

Although I began this study of Cleveland's architecture knowing that the city could boast many fine buildings and a few superlative ones, by and large I accepted the consensus of critic and layman that anything between New York and Chicago had to be basically conservative and second class. However, the more I saw, the more I realized that perhaps it was the traditional art historian's premises that needed re-evaluation. Art history has generally been treated as a sequence of stylistic developments and revolutionary form-makers. Thus the history of American architecture embraces a procession of styles from the Colonial to the post-Modern, the development of the steel-framed skyscraper, and the work of innovative architects from Thomas Jefferson to Robert Venturi. But architecture is much more than an abstract art. It is also an index of a place's physical and spiritual identity. I found that in dealing with the social and technical currents of the late nineteenth and early twentieth centuries, Cleveland had evolved certain urban forms and structures which made it the peer of any city and superior to most.

Possibly the notion of Cleveland's architectural conservatism stems in part from the fact that stylistically its most visible symbol, the Terminal Tower, was fifteen years out of date when it was completed. Nevertheless, the underlying idea of the Terminal group was staggering. It anticipated the purpose and size of Rockefeller Center (combined with Grand Central), and it required an unprecedented development of the concept of air rights. Cleveland's public buildings were also conservative in style, but at the same time Cleveland was the first city to plan a formal grouping of its public buildings. Furthermore, the basic elements of the grouping plan were all determined locally before Chicago's Daniel Burnham was invited to make his contribution. Cleveland's progressive vision also conceived the suburban industrial research park, and although the suburban garden city was an old idea, it achieved its fullest and most spectacular realization in Shaker Heights, whose conception has been vindicated by its stability more than half a century later. Cleveland has not often excelled in the "biggest" or "the most." For a city of its size, however, its progressiveness, innovation, and vision have been disproportionately great, and this fact was recognized nationally at least throughout the first third of the twentieth century.

Since new ideas and structures do not spring "fully-armed from the head of Zeus," I have attempted to place them in a context which helps to explain them. This means including typical and representative scenes which form the groundwork for the more notable architectural accomplishments. In Cleveland it means at least a reference to the industrial and transportation networks which shaped the city; to the neighborhoods of the manifold immigrant, ethnic, and racial groups which brought it to life; and to some of the chief institutions which nourished it. With a few important exceptions such as Nela Park, Shaker Heights and the Metropolitan Park System, the suburban and metropolitan areas have been accorded a relatively brief treatment, and the main emphasis is on what is now called the "inner city."

My approach to particular structures ranges

rather freely from geographical areas to social context, from functions to architectural styles, building technology, and the work of individual architects. I hope this is not confusing. It is an attempt to deal with the physical history of a complex period in an intelligible way, and more important, to avoid the false simplifications of the linear development of architectural style. The space allotted to the various subjects may surprise some readers. It seemed to me that where a subject (such as the Group Plan) is thoroughly documented elsewhere in easily available sources, it was legitimate to treat that subject concisely in order to allow more space for the unfamiliar and the previously unrecognized.

Nor have I emphasized the architect as an individual creative artist. From the point of view of public need, the architect is a practitioner who provides shelter with practicality, economy, and good looks at a consistent level of quality. Because of the money and the opportunities to build in Cleveland, the city attracted numerous fine practitioners, many of whom have not been noted before even locally. The better architect is the one who brings to this practice a higher degree of imagination and taste. Certain Cleveland architects in this class achieved regional if not national reputations in their own lifetimes and will be even more widely appreciated when their definitive monographs are written. These would certainly include Charles Schweinfurth and the firm of Walker & Weeks, to name only two. Of the greatest architects, the form-makers who create a new language of space, mass, and detail which is prophetic of the general vocabulary of later architects, it is admittedly difficult to point to any in Cleveland.

No one can use the resources of the Western Reserve Historical Society Library, where the bulk of this book was written, without the indispensable assistance of reference librarian Virginia Hawley. In this case, Mrs. Hawley was a valued reader of several chapters of the manuscript in addition to being a cheerful and indefatigable help in searching for sources. In addition, I am indebted to many colleagues at the Historical Society for their support, and especially to John Grabowski for his knowledge regarding the ethnic communities of Cleveland and his assistance in using the library's picture collection. I am grateful to Thomas Fisher for keeping the regional Ohio Historic Preservation Office above water during my absence, and also for bringing to the manuscript the insights of a recent architectural graduate regarding the contemporary scene. I am greatly indebted to Mary-Peale Schofield, who generously allowed me free access to her amazingly complete files on early twentieth century domestic architecture in Cleveland and its suburbs. Ruth Helmuth was most helpful at the Case Western Reserve University archives, as were Scott Feigenbaum, Kevin Vesely, and David Thum at the Cuyahoga County archives. Grace Goulder Izant, Arnold Lewis, Roderick B. Porter, Kermit J. Pike, and John S. Pyke, Jr. read early drafts of several chapters and gave me much needed encouragement as well as invaluable comments on both substance and style. I am particularly appreciative of the continual support of Meredith B. Colket, Jr., executive director of the Historical Society, throughout the project. I am also grateful to many architects for their thoughts and resources, especially Richard Fleischman, Robert C. Gaede, Alfred W. Harris, Jr., Norman Perttula, Alex C. Robinson, John A. Rode, Wallace G. Teare, Peter van Dijk, R. van Petten, and Thomas T. K. Zung.

ERIC JOHANNESEN
1979

# CLEVELAND
## ARCHITECTURE
# 1876-1976

## OHIO STATE BUILDING.

The Ohio State Building, Philadelphia Centennial Exhibition, 1876, Heard and Sons, architects. (*Final Report, Ohio State Board of Centennial Managers*)

# 1876: The Centennial Year

The Centennial was over. David Bailey, a country school teacher from Highland, Ohio, undertook to write a retrospective view of the Exhibition. He noted that in July, 1876, the mercury in Philadelphia was at 98 degrees in the shade. He found Archibald Willard's *Yankee Doodle* "a very spirited piece." His descriptions of the exhibits were almost as complete as those of a guide book, and, in fact, he freely acknowledged his debt to other published sources. Near the end of his account he asked, "And in a hundred years from now? God knows."[1]

David Bailey saw Rutherford B. Hayes, Governor of Ohio and candidate for the Presidency during a visit to Ohio's building at the Exhibition. The building had been erected for the comfort and convenience of the citizens of the State, and according to James D. McCabe's *Illustrated History of the Centennial Exhibition*, it was "the most elegant and substantial of all the State edifices." The entire front, and the first story of twenty feet, were constructed of neatly dressed stone from different Ohio quarries. Between January and May, 1876, detailed drawings of the twenty-one stone courses were made and furnished to the various contributors, and the stone was cut according to these details, transported to Philadelphia and placed in the building. Notwithstanding all the difficulties, the building was finished by May 20, ten days after the opening of the Exhibition, and was the second state building ready for use.[2]

Within sixty days from the closing of the Exhibition, the buildings were to be removed, but the Ohio Board of Centennial Managers considered whether their building should be torn down, or retained as a monument of the resources of Ohio.

They resolved to donate the building to the city of Philadelphia, and Philadelphia accepted the donation. Several other buildings were offered in a similar manner, but only the Ohio State Building was retained. A hundred years later, it was the only state building from the Exhibition still standing on its original site in Fairmount Park. Its architects were Messrs. Heard and Sons.[3]

Charles W. Heard was the apprentice and son-in-law of the Western Reserve builder Jonathan Goldsmith, and he typified the mid-nineteenth century evolution from carpenter to master builder to architect. He was an important Cleveland citizen, active in literary and debating societies, in

The Ohio House, 1876 Centennial Exhibition, Fairmount Park, Philadelphia.

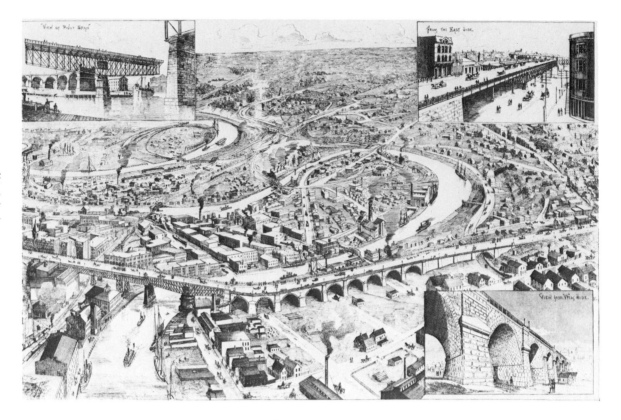

Bird's-Eye View of the Flats in 1878, based on a sketch by F. A. Coburn, architect.

Democratic politics and in the fire department, and was one of the founders of the Cleveland Academy of Natural Science. When Heard died in Cleveland on August 29, 1876, he had witnessed the transformation of the commercial town of the canal era into an industrial city.[4]

By 1876 the physical pattern of what is now known as the "inner city" in Cleveland had been established by the location of the new railroad rights-of-way along the most expedient routes, together with the pre-emption of the flats along the river by commerce and industry. It is not known which side Charles Heard may have taken in the arguments which began as early as the 1860s on controlling air pollution and limiting the growth of industry, but it is apparent that expediency and convenience won. On the other hand, there were no precedents for overall planning in the face of the new pressures for expansion. The city had grown east and west since the mid-century so that the original New England village plan centered on the Public Square was only a small part of the city. Nevertheless the old street patterns were fixed. The original layout of connecting streets between radiating avenues reached as far as Willson (East

55th) Street, while to the east of Willson, in the area annexed from East Cleveland in 1872, it was replaced by a more mechanical grid.

The coming of the railroads had defined certain areas and permanently established their character. The Cleveland and Erie took the easy level route along the lakeshore and prevented its development for residential or public use. The Cleveland and Pittsburgh from the southeast crossed Euclid Avenue at Willson and effectively sealed the fate of Euclid as a residential street. Industrial and commercial establishments stretched all along the railroad right-of-way, and within a few years the great houses of Euclid Avenue were confined to the stretch between Muirson (East 12th) and Case (East 40th) Streets. Likewise, the character of the "Flats" in the Cuyahoga Valley was established by 1876. Transportation depots, commercial warehouses and the new factories made possible by the rail transport of raw materials occupied the whole valley. As the Flats became congested, the wholesale warehouses spread to Superior Avenue and the other streets near the river, so that the old residential district was completely replaced.

The Public Square was now entirely surrounded

by commercial buildings, except on the north side where the Court House and the Old Stone Church stood, and the northeast side occupied by the Federal Building. Charles Heard could go in every direction from the Public Square and find buildings of his design. There were the Old Stone Church and Case Hall, the large public hall and office building on Superior just east of the Federal Building, where Heard's own office was located. Beyond Case Hall was the massive five-story City Hall, Cleveland's most elaborate exercise in the "French" style. On Euclid at Sheriff (East 4th) was the Euclid Avenue Opera House, connected to Heard's Block, his own business building. Farther out Euclid and Prospect Streets were many residences designed by Heard, including those of Hinman Hurlbut, Henry B. Payne, Charles Hickox and George Merwin. To the west toward the flats were more commercial blocks, such as those for Payne and Perry and I. S. Converse, and no doubt many other unknown ones. Finally, the city was dotted with public schools by Heard and his various partners. Among them were the Central High School of 1856 and Eagle Street, Sterling, St. Clair and Rockwell schools.[5]

Charles Heard did not live to see the destruction of his Second Presbyterian Church by fire in October, 1876. A hundred years later the familiar buildir  of Heard's Cleveland were all but gone, and only three of his structures remained in the center city — the Old Stone Church, Sterling School and the Merwin residence.

*above*: Sterling School, East 30th at Carnegie Avenue, 1868, Heard and Blythe, architects.

*left*: Merwin house (Rowfant Club), 3028 Prospect Avenue, Charles W. Heard, architect.

*below*: Old Stone Church, Public Square, 1855, Heard and Porter, architects. (*Martin Linsey*)

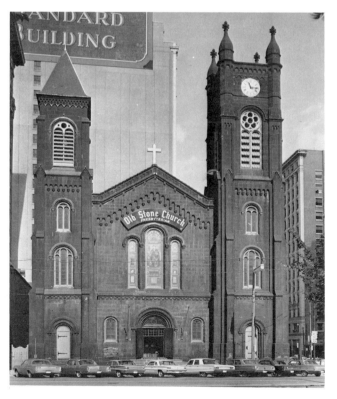

Wilshire Building under construction, 1882, 340 Superior Avenue NW (demolished), John H. Edelman, architect.

# 1876–1890

## The Commercial City

The reasons for the energy and optimism of Cleveland in the decade and a half following the Centennial year are not difficult to find. The combination of canal traffic, lake commerce, and the railroads had made the city a transportation center. The ship building industry flourished; in the years between the end of the Civil War and 1880 over 200 sailing and steam vessels were built. Cleveland, lying equidistant between the iron ore region of Lake Superior and the coal fields of Ohio and Pennsylvania, also seemed destined to become a great manufacturing center. The Cleveland Rolling Mill was producing vast quantities of iron and steel products, including essential steel rails for railroads all over the country. Under John D. Rockefeller, the Standard Oil Company had begun its growth toward a colossal monopoly that produced "unbelievable riches" for its shareholders. Charles F. Brush's development of the arc light and the first practical power station helped to create a new industry. Because of these and other enterprises, the accumulation of vast private fortunes was underway, and these resulted in the building of grand and ostentatious residences.[6]

The population of the city was 160,000 in 1880, of which more than one third were foreign born. To the Germans and Irish, which formed the largest immigrant groups a decade before, were added a large number of Bohemians, while the Poles were beginning to come in increasing numbers for employment in the Newburgh steel mills. In the post-Civil War decades the future of Cleveland as a great city seemed to be assured. A contemporary historian observed that "the era of the laying of her foundation as a city was passed; her institutions were firmly established; she was no longer an experiment but a sure success . . ."[7]

If there was one enterprise symbolizing for its citizens the energy and growth of Cleveland, it was the construction of the Superior Viaduct, to be followed ten years later by the Central Viaduct. Despite the incorporation of both Cleveland and Ohio City (an independent municipality across the river) in 1836 and their merger in 1854, the idea of a high-level bridge between the two cities was not seriously revived until the late 1860s. In 1870 the city council appointed a committee to report on a high-level bridge. There was considerable discussion of alternate proposals, and injunctions and objections caused several alterations and compromises. Finally the state legislature authorized two bond issues, in 1874 and 1876, totalling $2,700,000. The west side masonry arches were contracted for in 1874, and the work begun that autumn. The bridge was completed and dedicated in 1878. Its statistics are impressive. The western approach consisted of ten masonry arches of Berea sandstone, and was 64 feet wide. There were some 2,000,000 cubic feet of masonry in the structure. The river was spanned by an iron drawbridge which opened on a pivot operated by a steam engine and requiring one minute to open or close. The pivot span was 46 feet wide. The bridge carried roadways with pedestrian walks on either side, and after the connection of the West Side street railway in 1880, two streetcar tracks as well. The total length of the structure was 3,211 feet, and the final cost was $2,225,000.[8]

On December 27, 1878, there was a great celebration at the opening of the Viaduct. When the bridge was described in 1886, it was considered,

Superior Viaduct, 1878. B. F. Morse, engineer.

together with the Central Viaduct then under construction, to be unequaled "by any city in the West, and compared with the population, the whole constituted an undertaking of greater importance than Brooklyn Bridge."[9] The comparison was not entirely an idle one. The completion of the Brooklyn Bridge in 1883 had an almost mythic significance for Americans as a symbol of progress, and the reference indicates Cleveland's participation in this faith. Above all, it indicates that the linking of the east and west sides of the Cuyahoga was considered a matter of vital consequence for the future of the

city, and represented an optimistic though not unrealistic estimate of the potential of Cleveland.

The center span of the Superior Viaduct was dismantled following the completion of the new Detroit-Superior High-Level Bridge in 1918. On the west side the seven remaining arches are still suggestive of the scale and expressive power of Roman masonry. The engineer, B. F. Morse, had also been the architect of the Northern Ohio Lunatic Asylum (Cleveland State Hospital), built in 1875. In 1976 the hospital was one of the few remaining large institutional buildings testifying to the social

Northern Ohio Lunatic Asylum, 1875 (demolished 1977), B. F. Morse, architect, John Gill, builder.

consciousness of the Victorian age. Part institution, part fortress, and part prison, with its two central towers dominating the vista at the end of East 93rd Street, it, like the viaduct, inspired awe at the sheer mastery of inert matter.[10]

The decade of the 1880s marked a genuine departure in Cleveland architecture as it did throughout the country. This was recognized by the Cleveland Architectural Club, whose 1900 catalog stated:

> Cleveland's architectural history, up to 1885, was written in the commonplace two, three, four and five story business and office buildings; the frame house, many times contractor designed; the city church, and the public buildings that distinguished the western architectural idea up to that time. Isolated examples, in each of the above lines, stood as monuments to the good taste and architectural ability of their designers, but these were but oases in the predominating desert of architectural nothingness.[11]

The business district north of Superior Avenue and west of Ontario Street was one of the proving grounds for the new architecture. A building recognized by the Cleveland Architectural Club as "marking an epoch" in office construction was the Blackstone Building, which stood at the southwest corner of West 3rd and Frankfort until the 1950s. It was built in 1881 by Jacob B. Perkins, a grandson of General Simon Perkins, early settler in the Western Reserve. Perkins named the building for the most famous of English jurists, Sir William Blackstone, and it was occupied almost entirely by lawyers. The architects were F. A. Coburn and Frank S. Barnum, one of two or three architectural firms that dominated the decade.[12]

The Blackstone was an example of mill construction, a method of fire-resistant wooden interior construction in which solid wooden members without boxed-up hollow spaces were supported directly on girders and masonry walls. On the exterior the building displayed a much greater amount of window space and a heightened definition of the stone and brick supporting piers. The ground story bays were amazingly open for a wood and masonry building. On the interior, the Blackstone contained a four-story light court, one of a series which was to result in some of Cleveland's most notable interiors, culminating in the Arcade less than ten years later. With regard to the style of the building, the traditional categories seem to be almost irrelevant. In spite of the mansard roof, and a number of other style references which could be discovered by those inclined to do so, it seems to make more sense to accept a contemporary judg-

ment on its own terms: "Though no recognized style of architecture has been rigidly followed, the advantages and beauties of the Grecian, Roman, and Gothic have been adopted by our architects, and a system has grown up not referable to any particular period, but a combination of many, which may be described distinctively as American."[13]

A young architect-draftsman in Coburn and Barnum's office may have had an influence on the design of the Blackstone. His name was John H. Edelman, and he is known to have sculptured the bust of Blackstone over the entrance. A Cleveland native, Edelman had lived in Chicago from 1872 to 1876 and again in 1880, where he was the foreman of William LeBaron Jenney's drafting room and later the office foreman of Dankmar Adler. He befriended the younger Louis Sullivan, and in later years Sullivan referred to Edelman as his mentor and credited him with inspiring the concept of "Form follows function." The combination of the mansard roof and the polychrome treatment of the Blackstone was similar to that found in buildings erected in Chicago at the same time by Adler's office, with whom Sullivan was then working. Edelman

Blackstone Building and Power Block, West 3rd Street and Frankfort, 1881 (demolished), Coburn and Barnum, architects. Bust of Blackstone by John Edelman.

Furniture Block, West 3rd Street and Frankfort, 1882 (demolished), Coburn and Barnum, architects.

6th Street, was later expanded in the same style to more than twice its former size. There are iron columns in the basement and first five floors, and wooden posts on the sixth. Such interior structural iron posts had been used in Cleveland at least since 1855. Architecturally, the most striking feature of the facade is the arrangement of the windows into two arcades, the first embracing the first two floors, and the second the next three floors. The arches contain fanlights with radiating mullions, and the whole arrangement creates an extremely light and open effect altogether unprecedented in Cleveland.

A second building by Cudell and Richardson had been erected two years earlier for the George Worthington Company, one of Cleveland's pioneer wholesale hardware companies.[17] It might almost have been a sketch for the Root, McBride Building, as it has the same arrangement of two multi-story ranks of windows, but the effect is not quite as bold.

Throughout the area bounded by West 3rd and West 9th Streets, Superior and Lakeside Avenues, a number of these early commercial structures still remained in the 1970s. Some of them dated back to the earlier period of the bracketed Italianate style (1850–1875), and their relatively flat fronts and individual windows with ornamental hoodmolding were quite different from corresponding features of the new buildings.

Other commercial buildings in the 1880s style were located outside the downtown: on Lorain Avenue and West 25th Street on the West Side, on Euclid Avenue near the East 55th Street intersection of the Pennsylvania Railroad, and as far out as the end of the Woodland Avenue street railway line, some four miles to the southeast of the Public Square. The store of Otto F. Lohmann, apothecary, at Woodland and East 84th Street, was occupied in 1885.[18] Mr. Lohmann was a German immigrant who had come to Cleveland in 1866 and established his business as a druggist and apothecary in 1869. While Lohmann's Block is a more typical building of the day and does not exhibit the same structural experimentation, it serves as a good example of the general style tendencies common to many smaller commercial buildings.

Fireproof construction was a major goal of the architecture of the 1880s, and two hotels completed only a year apart made this feature a part of their advertising. The Stillman, erected on Euclid Avenue near East 12th Street in 1884, was an eight-story structure with 200 rooms for residential apartments. Architecturally it was not memorable, for the

designed the Wilshire Building in Cleveland, which stood on Superior Avenue and displayed ornament said to have been by Sullivan.[14]

Across the street from the Blackstone, another block by Coburn and Barnum was erected the following year.[15] It was occupied by Vincent, Barstow & Company as a warehouse and retail store for fine furniture. Six stories instead of five, the Furniture Block was evidently designed in the same idiom to complement the Blackstone. The same open bays and sturdy expression of the piers were used, and while the general effect of openness was not quite so great, the definition of the masonry piers was, if anything, more pronounced, and the whole had a more rational simplicity.

Farther to the north and west of the Monumental Park (Public Square) were more utilitarian commercial and warehouse structures. Two of the most important were designed by F.E. Cudell and J. N. Richardson, another of the more important firms of the decade. In 1884 the warehouse building of Root and McBride, a wholesale dry goods firm, was completed on West 6th Street and Lakeside.[16] The original building, with 115 feet of frontage on West

architect was unable to cope with the problem of unifying an eight-story facade, contenting himself with the addition of various layers of architectural styles. However, its advertising claimed: "The construction renders it absolutely fireproof, the roof being of tile and cement upon a framework of steel, while all the floors and partitions are of iron and tile, making it incombustible throughout. The safety of guests in no hotel in this country or Europe is no more secure against the ravages of fire."[19]

When the Hollenden Hotel opened in 1885, it was the first large hotel east of the Square for travelers as well as permanent residents. It was built by a corporation headed by Liberty E. Holden, whose wealth had been acquired in real estate and mining interests, and who had bought the *Plain Dealer* the year before. His associate in both the newspaper and hotel enterprises was Charles H. Bulkley. For many years the Hollenden was Cleveland's legendary hotel, having as guests five Presidents, heads of foreign governments, politicians and entertainment celebrities. The interior was noted for its paneled walls, mahogany fittings and specially designed furniture. The Hollenden boasted incandescent electric lights and 100 private baths in addition to its fireproof construction. A number of additions and renovations were made over the years, but the original building was a massive eight-story block with open ground floor bays in the new style. There

*above left*: Root and McBride Warehouse (Bradley Building), West 6th Street and Lakeside, 1884, Cudell and Richardson, architects.

*above right*: The George Worthington Company, 802 West St. Clair, 1882, Cudell and Richardson, architects. (*Cuyahoga County Archives photo by David Thum*)

*below*: Lohmann's Block, Woodland Avenue at East 84th Street, 1885, Andrew Mitermiler, architect.

11

Hollenden Hotel, 1885 (demolished), George F. Hammond, architect.

were also ranks of projecting bay windows at the center and the ends of each facade, similar to those which are such a feature of the Chicago Style. The great pyramidal roof which rose from the corner gave an eclectic chateau-like appearance to an otherwise modern building. The Hollenden was designed by George F. Hammond, a young Boston architect who moved to Cleveland at the time of this commission and later planned some of the city's more important buildings.[20]

The masterpiece of commercial building by Cudell and Richardson was the Perry-Payne, built in 1888–1889. Henry B. Payne, prominent lawyer and railroad executive, erected the building, giving it his own name and that of his wife, the daughter of early merchant Nathan Perry, Jr. Payne had been a Congressman and sat on the commission that decided the disputed Hayes-Tilden election in 1876. The building was occupied primarily by shipping and iron ore company offices.[21]

The Perry-Payne Building is an eight-story office building of masonry and iron construction. The external stone and brick piers diminish from twenty-four to eighteen inches throughout the eight stories. The interior structure consists of iron posts with the floors and roof constructed of tile and concrete. In spite of the fact that the exterior walls are still masonry load-bearing, they have been opened up to a remarkable degree, especially on the first two floors. It is clear that the facade is a logical extension of Cudell and Richardson's work in the Root & McBride and Worthington Buildings. Originally there was a great inner court with a glass roof, but it has been floored over. It is said that builders, architects, and other visitors came to Cleveland from a considerable distance to inspect the building, its structure and its light court.[22]

Lobby, Hollenden Hotel. (*American Architect and Building News*)

Interior court, Perry-Payne Building.

## Euclid Avenue

Henry B. Payne lived in a home designed by Charles Heard on Euclid Avenue. His neighbors were the president and other partners of the Standard Oil Company, the developer of the arc light and practical electric power, the president of the Cleveland Rolling Mill Company, railroad financiers, shipping and iron ore executives, bankers and vessel owners. Euclid had been a fine residential street from its inception, but by the 1870s retail business was beginning to encroach, moving eastward from the Square. Between East 12th and East 40th Streets, however, was the section which came to be known as "Millionaire's Row." Large houses stood well back on wide, spacious lawns, and trees lined the roadway, making it for Clevelanders and many visitors "the most beautiful street in the world." Between 1882 and 1886 the avenue was repaved with Medina sandstone. There were still mansions from the Greek Revival period, as well as Gothic Revival and Tuscan villas from the fifties and sixties, when the street reached its heyday in the 1880s, and a handful

Perry-Payne Building, 740 Superior Avenue, 1889, Cudell and Richardson, architects.

of great new mansions lifted its architectural character above the ordinary.

One house from the earlier Civil War period should be mentioned, because it was the only nineteenth century mansion still surviving from "Millionaire's Row" in 1976. The home was built by Anson Stager, general superintendent of the Western Union Telegraph Company, probably in 1863, and later owned by T. Sterling Beckwith, founder of Beckwith, Sterling & Company.[23] With its mansard roofs and hooded windows, the house was a free interpretation of the Second Empire style. Originally it had a charming arcaded veranda and porte-cochere, which gave an air of informality even to such a large house.

In the first years of the post-Centennial period, residences continued to be built on a fundamentally conservative plan. The Rufus K. Winslow house, built on Euclid Avenue in 1878 for the lake vessel owner whose office was down on the Old River Road (West 11th Street), was basically a symmetrical Italianate house. However, the underlying form was tarted up with pointed windows, clustered colonnettes, crocketted gable dormers, diamond

13

*above*: Stager-Beckwith house (University Club), 3813 Euclid Avenue, ca. 1863.

*below left*: Rufus K. Winslow house, Euclid Avenue, 1878 (demolished), Levi T. Scofield, architect.

*below right*: Drawing of a Victorian House, ca. 1876, Levi T. Scofield.

panes, stained glass, and a Gothic porte-cochere, to make it one of Cleveland's most outstanding examples of high Victorian Gothic. After a period of disrepute, the term Victorian is once again recognized as conveying something definite—a picturesque outline, somewhat coarse or exaggerated proportions, a profusion of ornamental detail, and in general, an impression of solid middle-class substance.

The architect of the Winslow house was Levi T. Scofield, (1842-1917), a Cleveland architect whose major works were public buildings and monuments, including the State Asylum in Columbus (1869), the Mansfield Reformatory (1884), the Cleveland Central High School (1878), the Ohio Monument at the Columbian Exposition of 1893, and Cleveland's Soldiers and Sailors Monument completed in 1894. Scofield's residential work has not been completely studied, but the majority of the plans in a large collection of existing drawings are residences which are basically Victorian in character. The Winslow house is similar in most details, excepting only the upper part of the tower, to one of these drawings, which is unidentified as to name or location.[24]

The real revolution in residential architecture occurred, interestingly enough, within a year of the date of the Blackstone. It was heralded by the immense mansion begun in 1883 by Sylvester T.

Sylvester T. Everett house, Euclid Avenue, 1883 (demolished), Charles F. Schweinfurth architect.

*below*: side elevation.

Everett, banker, mine owner, railway promoter and financier. The house was designed by Charles F. Schweinfurth, the premier residential architect of Euclid Avenue, having designed no less than fifteen of the Euclid mansions over the years. Schweinfurth (1856-1919) began his career in New York, and there is sufficient evidence to make it plausible that he was an apprentice in the office of Henry H. Richardson as a very young man. Later he worked for seven years in the office of the Supervising Architect of the Treasury in Washington, D. C. Apparently Schweinfurth came to Cleveland, which he was to make his home, for the specific purpose of executing the Everett commission, although it is unclear exactly how he happened to be chosen. From 1883 to 1886 he maintained an office with his brother Julius, who then returned to practice in Boston.[25]

The Richardsonian character of the Everett house was undeniable. Its calculated asymmetries and bold sculptured forms, together with the rock-faced stonework and polychrome effects, must have created a sheer external presence that was somewhat overwhelming. On the interior, the rooms were finished in the most lavish and expensive woodwork, and the great staircase ascended past a semi-circular balcony where Mrs. Everett welcomed her guests to the third floor ballroom.

What is the reason for the sudden appearance of such a mansion, larger and more costly than any previous residence in Cleveland? Although it shows the influence of H. H. Richardson, and its architect was New York-trained, these facts alone are not sufficient as explanation. By comparision, the Stager-Beckwith and Winslow houses were simply enlarged dwellings, while this was a fortress palace. The answer may be that Sylvester T. Everett was a representative of a new phenomenon in American industry. Stager was a company official, Beckwith a businessman, and Winslow a ship owner. Everett, on the other hand, was a financier.

Samuel Andrews house, Euclid Avenue, 1885 (demolished).

The years since the Civil War had seen the great push toward the West. Neither the transcontinental railroads which facilitated this expansion, nor the development of the resources of the West, would have been possible without the investment and speculation of Eastern capitalists and corporations. These projects required far greater sums of money than could be realized without relying on corporate enterprise. At the same time, competition threatened small individual businessmen, who responded by the formation of trusts and mergers. The classic example of this process is the centralization of the various components of the oil producing and refining group formed by John D. Rockefeller of Cleveland. It was in 1882 that Rockefeller's group established a trust which placed the stocks of many concerns in the hands of a few trustees, and a few years later that a holding company was formed under the Standard Oil Company of New Jersey.[26]

These forces created a new type of businessman, and this was the world in which Sylvester T. Everett moved. Everett was a native of Trumbull County and began his banking career as a messenger boy and collection clerk with a Cleveland firm at the age of fourteen. At thirty he was manager of the banking house which later became Everett, Weddell & Company. He founded the National Bank of Commerce and was an organizer of the Union National Bank. After twenty years in banking he devoted himself to other interests, becoming a director of the Cleveland Rolling Mill Company and a developer of street railways and railroads. He was the chief promoter of the Valley Railway, and promoted, financed, and built the country's first successful electric street railway in Akron. Everett had mining investments in several states, and mining and ranch properties in Colorado. [27] A man involved in these kinds of activities required a mansion which would express his wide financial interests and would later serve as the place to entertain other captains of industry and finance, such as Andrew Carnegie and J. P. Morgan, as well as four presidents: Grant, Hayes, McKinley and Taft. Everett clearly knew what he wanted, and he found in Schweinfurth the man who could give it to him.

It is a truism that men like Everett saw themselves as a new aristocracy, as "barons of industry." Schweinfurth and others (such as Henry Ives Cobb in the Potter Palmer mansion in Chicago, 1882) found in the Romanesque idiom an architectural equivalent for the ambitions and achievements of this new breed of industrialist-financier. This was not a conscious program so much as a happy meeting of the right clients and the right architects at the right time. The rusticated castle-like style was simply an alternative to the French chateaux which Richard Morris Hunt was simultaneously building for the Vanderbilts. The first masterpiece of that style, the W. K. Vanderbilt house in New York, had just been completed in 1881.

John D. Rockefeller's own home on Euclid Avenue was in the older style, but he had purchased it in 1868, two years before the Standard Oil Company was even formed. The home of Samuel Andrews, however, was built in 1882–1885 and partook of the new baronial manner. Andrews was one of the original partners of the firm which became Standard Oil, and thus shared in some of the early profits of the industry. However, he sold his shares in the company to Rockefeller in 1874 and did not reap the phenomenal riches that others did. The building of Andrews' mansion seemed "a gesture of bravado." The house had between eighty and a hundred rooms, an immense central hall, carved staircases and woodwork, stained glass, and five separate apartments for the financier's daughters. Not surprisingly, it was soon found that the plan of the mansion made it impossible for servants to function efficiently. Andrews' hope of entertaining Queen Victoria never came to pass, and the house was soon closed. It came to be known as "Andrews' folly," standing vacant for twenty-five years until its demolition in 1923.[28]

The "bigness" of the Andrews house amused an Irish journal in 1883:

> Not long since we had Mr. Vanderbilt's hideous construction paraded before our eyes; and now Cleveland, Ohio, takes up the running. . . . An American gentleman who has seen the interior of the house at Cleveland, and who happens also to have casually dropped in at 'the principal palaces of Europe,' is of the opinion that none of them can beat the Ohio product. And fancy! all this dazzling splendour—exceeding that of Windsor, or Versailles, or the Winter Palace—has been procured by the easy, steady, oleaginous flow of oil![29]

Andrews' house shared the same bluntness, the same asymmetrical massing, the same towered silhouette, the same rusticated stonework and carved effects, and above all the same expression of ambition, that differentiated the Everett house from its predecessors. Even though the former might be called Victorian Gothic and the latter Richardsonian Romanesque, their characteristic similarities as baronial houses of the 1880s are more compelling than their differences.

The same is true of the Charles F. Brush mansion, built in 1884 and exhibiting nominally Northern Renaissance characteristics. Its own particular stylistic details are the curious stocky porch columns, the parapet gables, the gable dormers, and especially the domed cupola on the side tower. The architect was George H. Smith, whom Brush would retain five years later for an even grander commission. The house was demolished after Brush's death in 1929, in accordance with the specifications in his will.[30]

Like the Andrews house, the Brush house showed similarities to Schweinfurth's Everett house in its scale, its irregularity and its rustication. Perhaps even more important is the expressiveness which these qualities evoked. By comparison, the early Victorian houses seem quiet and chaste. Furthermore, the play of stylistic details indicates that this was the first period of true "eclecticism." The earlier revivals—Greek, Gothic, and Italianate—had been genuine vernacular idioms in America. In the new houses, the importance of the individual architect as designer, together with the many alternatives open to the client, become apparent. Thus the decade of the 1880s produced a residential architecture for the wealthy class which was distinctly different in character from nineteenth century residential architecture up to that time.

Charles F. Brush house, Euclid Avenue, 1884 (demolished), George H. Smith, architect.

The fashionable church of the nabobs of Euclid Avenue was St. Paul's Episcopal Church, located on "Millionaire's Row" at the corner of East 40th Street. "Horse-drawn carriages with liveried servants deposited the cream of society at its doors." Among the vestrymen were J. H. Devereux, president of the Cleveland, Columbus & Cincinnati Railroad, Zenas King, president of the King Iron Bridge & Manufacturing Company, and Andros B. Stone, president of the Cleveland Rolling Mill Company. St. Paul's had sold the property at its downtown location on the corner of East 4th Street in 1874. The new church, claimed to be "the largest and most imposing in the city," was erected in 1875–1876. The style was Victorian Gothic, and the new structure, constructed of Berea sandstone, was designed by Gordon W. Lloyd of Detroit.[31] The unique 120-foot tower consists of four slender turrets with crocketed pinnacles, surrounding an octagonal louvered belfry. Also notable are the Gothic porches over the front and side stoops. On the interior, the proportions of the aisled nave and the Gothic chancel appear low, but the open, decorated wood trusses create the general effect of an English parish church. In 1927 St. Paul's congregation moved to Cleveland Heights. The Euclid Avenue building was purchased by the Catholic Diocese in 1931 and rededicated as St. Paul's Shrine of the Blessed Sacrament.

St. Paul's Episcopal Church (Shrine of the Blessed Sacrament), Euclid Avenue at East 40th Street, 1876, Gordon Lloyd, architect.

Less than ten years after the completion of St. Paul's, the wide-reaching influence of Henry H. Richardson's Romanesque revival on church design had begun to spread over the country. In January, 1884, the interior of the Old Stone Church (First Presbyterian) on the Square was gutted by a fire that started in the nearby Park Theatre and also destroyed the connecting Wick Block. The original church had been designed by Heard and Porter in the earlier Romanesque Revival and erected in 1855. After a great deal of agonizing discussion involving in part the opportunity to sell the valuable site at a considerable profit, the church decided to rebuild within the old walls. A guarantee by Mrs. Samuel Mather and others to cover the deficits at least to $10,000 helped to sway the decision. This was the first of many projects on which Mrs. Mather and Charles Schweinfurth were to be connected. The redesigned and rebuilt interior was opened in

December, 1884, and the narrative states that the members were "dazzled by a scene of magnificence far exceeding their highest expectations."[32]

There is more than a hint of similarity between the remodeled interior of the Old Stone Church and the interior of Richardson's Trinity Church in Boston. The key motif is a semicircular arch with wooden tie beams at the base, resting on a pair of arched braces. In Boston's Trinity (1873–1877), with which Schweinfurth would have been acquainted, the main arch covers the greater portion of the width of the nave, and the braces rest on the side walls. In the rebuilt interior of Old Stone Church, the complete motif is placed between the two longitudinal trusses which support the roof. These are treated as a false clerestory, and the whole is apparently supported on a second set of arched braces. At the entrance end, the arched windows of the original facade are embraced by one great semicircular arch. The decorative scheme of painted and frescoed walls, executed by Julius Schweinfurth, together with stained glass windows by John LaFarge and Louis C. Tiffany, created the same general effect of Byzantine splendor as Richardson's Trinity Church.[33]

The remodeled interior of the Old Stone Church must be compared with that of the new Calvary Presbyterian Church, built in 1888–1890. Three months before the fire at Old Stone, a small Gothic stone chapel had been dedicated at the Calvary Mission on Euclid at East 79th Street. The chapel was established by Dr. Hiram C. Haydn of the Old Stone Church to serve the area east of 55th Street, and shared its ministry with Old Stone. In 1888 the cornerstone was laid for the new Romanesque church adjoining the chapel, and it was dedicated in 1890.[34] On the interior of Calvary Presbyterian, the scheme used in Old Stone was elaborated further by Schweinfurth. Each set of arches is supported by slender clustered columns making a traditional three-aisled division of the nave, although the seating is arranged in the curved auditorium fashion. The side aisles have additional arched bracing, with a pierced plate between the braces and the hammerbeam of the upper brace.

The effect of these two interiors is to create an increasingly light and airy atmosphere which belies the fortress-like character of the massive exterior walls, towers, and Romanesque arches. In this respect, the new eclecticism of the period, achieved by combining different styles and spatial effects, was expressed in the churches as well as the homes of Euclid Avenue.

18

Old Stone Church, interior rebuilt 1884, Charles F. Schweinfurth, architect.

Calvary Presbyterian Church, Euclid Avenue at East 79th Street, 1890, Charles F. Schweinfurth, architect.

## Neighborhood Buildings—I

The stretch of Prospect Avenue parallel to Euclid was lined with houses only slightly less grand. South of Sibley Street (Carnegie Avenue), however, these gave way to relatively modest wooden structures. Of the occasional brick houses, an outstanding one built by Jacob Goldsmith was still standing in 1976. Goldsmith was a partner in the firm of Koch, Goldsmith, Joseph & Company, wholesale clothiers founded in 1873, and a continuation of the firm of Koch, Kauffman & Loeb established in 1841. Goldsmith moved into the mansion on East 40th Street in 1880, and subsequently the house was occupied by the Jewish Infants Orphan Home and later the Universal Negro Improvement Association.[35] Although not on the scale of the Euclid Avenue mansions, the Goldsmith house is still impressive. The general arrangement is conservative, consisting of a central hall flanked by rooms of approximately equal size. Each of the four main rooms has a fireplace whose full height chimneypiece detail is carved in the Eastlake style. In the polychrome treatment of the exterior stone and brick, the rigorous articulation of the facade by projecting piers, and the eclectic gable design, the style of the house is quite characteristic of its date.

Jacob Goldsmith was a director of the Jewish Orphan Asylum which erected a new home on Woodland Avenue in 1888. He was also a member of

Jacob Goldsmith house, 2200 East 40th Street, 1880, attributed to Cudell and Richardson.

its Committee on Buildings and Grounds, and its Committee on Finances.[36] These facts give credence to the suggestion that his own residence was planned by the same architects as the asylum building, Cudell and Richardson. Called "one of the most important Jewish charities," the Orphan Asylum (not to be confused with the Jewish Infants Orphan Home) was founded in 1868. It "became a model institution in operation, in the development of personnel and in the molding of character and responsibility."[37] The asylum complex included a large main building, a school to the west, and a number of utilitarian outbuildings. The location on Woodland Avenue near East 55th Street was at the eastern edge of the Jewish settlement at that time. The large three-story brick main building, with a five-part facade, had concave-convex gables and a central tower with a bell-shaped roof, all of which suggest a definitely Dutch or Northern character. The arched entrance portico on coupled Ionic columns showed considerable sophistication and an awareness of European architecture.

John N. Richardson (1837–1902) was a native of Scotland, while Frank (Franz) E. Cudell (1844–1916) was born at Herzogenrath near Aix-la-Chapelle (Aachen), Germany, and lived there until he emigrated at the age of twenty-two. Employed briefly in the New York office of Leopold Eidlitz, one of America's leading nineteenth century architects, Cudell came to Cleveland in 1867 and formed a

Jewish Orphan Asylum, Woodland Avenue, 1888 (demolished), Cudell and Richardson, architects.

partnership with Richardson in 1870. Cudell's younger brother Adolph went on to Chicago, where he was the senior partner of Cudell and Blumenthal. Architects of fashionable Aldine Square on the South Side, which had a distinctly European feeling, their masterpiece was the Cyrus H. McCormick mansion (1875), based on the recently completed Pavillon Richelieu of the Louvre.[38] Whether one argues from the buildings to biography or from biography to the buildings, it is clear that Frank Cudell was steeped in Gothic, German, and Dutch architecture (the municipal boundaries of Aachen are on the frontiers of Holland and Belgium).

This is equally evident if we look back for a moment at three churches designed by Cudell and Richardson over a decade earlier than the Orphan Asylum. It is a ticklish question whether they should be categorically labeled "Victorian Gothic," or whether the European experience of the architects was truly a determining factor. In any case, what is called Victorian Gothic embodied elements from Italy, Germany, and France far more than did the earlier Gothic Revival, which was predominantly English in origin.

The two churches designed for the Catholic Diocese were erected for German-speaking congregations. The first Bishop of Cleveland had been opposed to the institution of distinctively foreign language parishes but was finally persuaded of their necessity. St. Joseph's parish was organized in 1858, the second German church on the East Side. The cornerstone of the Cudell and Richardson building was laid in 1871, and a newspaper account stated that "this will be the first clere-story church ever built in this city." The structure was dedicated in 1873, but the steeple was not completed until 1899. Adjoining the church on the north is a friary for the Franciscan Fathers in charge of the parish, erected in 1893.[39]

The facade of St. Joseph's is the most characteristically German of Cudell and Richardson's churches. It incorporates a westwork, typically found in Carolingian and Romanesque churches, which rises the full height of the center bay and includes three entraces and a steep hipped roof. The interior, however, is a three-aisled hall with an aisle arcade, a blind triforium, and the clerestory, an arrangement which was more typical of the French Gothic. The three-sided apse has tall clerestory windows which flooded the interior with light.

St. Stephen's was the second parish created to serve the German-speaking Catholics on the West Side, after "St. Mary's on the Flats," which is no

St. Joseph's Roman Catholic Church, Woodland Avenue and East 23rd Street, 1873, Cudell and Richardson, architects.

longer in existence. Founded in 1869, the parish occupied a small brick church for six years. The cornerstone of the present church was laid in 1873. The first services were held in 1876, but work continued on the interior for five years, and the edifice was dedicated in 1881. The large cruciform building, 165 feet long and 74 feet wide, is constructed of Amherst stone and undoubtedly has the most massive and permanent appearance of the three Cudell and Richardson churches.[40] On the interior there is no clerestory, the aisle arcade is taller, and the proportion of open space to the supporting columns is much greater, giving the general effect of a hall church. The height of the ceiling is 75 feet, comparable with some of the early cathedrals of Europe. Although not as tall as the greatest of them, it is nonetheless impressive for a Midwestern parish church.

St. Stephen's Roman Catholic Church, West 54th Street, 1873–1881, Cudell and Richardson, architects.

Franklin Circle Christian Church, 1875, Cudell and Richardson, architects.

Inasmuch as these churches were all begun and presumably designed within a three-year period, and in the absence of documentary evidence, there is no point in attempting to discern a stylistic sequence in them. Furthermore, the third one, the Franklin Circle Christian Church, was built for a different faith, the Disciples of Christ. The Cleveland congregation of this native American denomination was formed in 1842. Among its renowned ministers was James A. Garfield, later President of the United States. The present church, built in 1874–1875, is in some ways the most picturesque of the three churches, which is partly due to its site facing Franklin Circle.[41] The most unusual feature is the central facade tower with its gabled roof. Together with the shallow transepts, a second square tower on the east side, and a later Bible School annex (1915) built at an angle to the church, the structure achieves a unique configuration. The Disciples' auditorium is less liturgical in form than the other two, as would be expected. Both the shallow transepts and the balcony over the narthex are framed with tripartite Gothic arches on slender foliated columns. The Catholic Gothic style has been adapted for the space requirements of a Protestant preaching denomination.

In spite of their differences, these three buildings suggest that Cudell, who is credited with their design, found his youth in Aachen an unforgettable influence. If it is too fanciful to say that he was essentially a "Gothic" architect, it is completely consistent to realize that he was also responsible for the Worthington, Root & McBride, and Perry-Payne buildings, in which the striving for "Gothic" structure and light was expressed in modern terms.

Franklin Circle, then known simply as the Circle, was the geographical and social focus of Franklin Avenue, the West Side equivalent of Euclid Avenue. Six radiating streets came together at the circle, which had been laid out in 1836 when the west side of the Cuyahoga River was an independent village, Ohio City. In 1857 the circle was fenced, and a fountain and a wooden pavilion were installed. In 1872 Franklin Street was put through the circle. Opposite the church and nearby on Franklin was a veritable enclave of the Rhodes and Hanna clan. There were the houses of Daniel P. Rhodes, his sons Robert and James Ford Rhodes, and his son-in-law Marcus A. Hanna. Dan Rhodes was the founder of the large iron ore and pig iron company which became the M. A. Hanna Company in 1885. The family homes had been established on Franklin since the 1860s and early 1870s, so their architecture belongs to the earlier era. Only the picturesque Robert Rhodes house remains, housing the Cuyahoga County Archives.

Beyond the Circle very few brick or stone houses existed. Four blocks west on Franklin stands one house from the 1880s which is notable in spite of the spurious "haunted house" publicity which has surrounded it, the so-called "Franklin Castle." It was built by Hannes Tiedemann, a vice president of the Savings and Trust Company located on Euclid near East 3rd Street. Founded in 1883, the company was one of the first banking institutions organized in Ohio under the law permitting the establishment of trust companies. Thus it was among the city's financial institutions which were instrumental in making vast industrial expansion possible.[42]

Tiedemann's house was built in 1881, according to the best available evidence, so it seems to have been almost exactly contemporary with the Everett and Andrews houses and the Standard Oil trust. Architecturally it is not as ambitious as the Euclid Avenue mansions and is more nearly characterized by what is generally called "Queen Anne" style. Standing on a very narrow lot and presenting a narrow facade to the street, the house still achieves a

Hannes Tiedemann House, 4308 Franklin Avenue, 1881.

degree of monumentality because of the heavily rusticated stonework, the cylindrical tower at the southeast corner, the stone porch stoop with its balustrade, and the stone brackets and dormers.

The neighborhood around the Circle which formed the center of the old Ohio City, bounded roughly by Detroit Avenue and West 25th, Monroe, and West 45th Streets, was the home of varied economic and social groups in the late nineteenth century. The wealthy lived on Franklin Avenue and some of the streets to the north. South of Franklin were the smaller homes of tradesmen, artisans, factory laborers and brewery employees. Most of their houses were in the common vernacular building style, either frame with a simple gabled outline and a small stoop or side porch, or brick with stone lintels over doors and windows. Although the name "Ohio City" was revived in the 1970s, the majority of the existing houses were built after 1854, the date of the merger with Cleveland. Many houses were in the Italianate, Eastlake and Queen Anne styles, with ornamental detail rendered in the jigsaw and lathe of the carpenter-builder. The building lots were very narrow, but it is significant that the ideal of the detached house was retained; there were no row houses in the manner of eastern cities like Philadelphia or Baltimore. It is also important that individual ownership was the general rule. There were few renters, and the era of the speculative builder who put up blocks and blocks of identical houses was still over the horizon. Most of the houses were planned by carpenter-builders, sometimes calling themselves architects, or by the owners themselves.[43]

The original inhabitants of the neighborhood were chiefly Irish and German. The Irish had settled there since the 1830s, some of them having been laborers on the Ohio Canal in 1826. By the 1870s they had entered diverse trades and businesses. German immigrants had arrived first in 1830 and settled along Lorain Street. The first large migration took place in 1854, however, following the political upheavals in Europe, and a second wave arrived in 1882 as a result of the depressed economic conditions of the 1870s.

In the early 1880s this German-Irish neighborhood was the location of a mission to discover whether conditions would warrant the establishment of a Catholic college and preparatory school in Cleveland. The Fathers of the Jesuit German Province of Buffalo took charge of St. Mary's parish on West 30th Street for this purpose in 1880. When

St. Ignatius College (St. Ignatius High School), West 30th Street and Carroll, 1888–1891.

Nineteenth century houses in old Ohio City area, Bridge Avenue near West 30th Street.

24

the project was approved, St. Ignatius College opened in 1886 in a plain two-story frame structure. Two years later, the north wing of the present five-story brick building was erected with a frontage of 80 feet on Carroll Avenue. The southern wing, stretching 200 feet on West 30th, was added in 1890–1891. The unfinished wall at the south end of the building clearly indicates that the original design was conceived as a symmetrical building twice the completed size, with the tower at the center of the facade. The plans for the building are said to have been prepared by Brother Wipfler of the Jesuits, who was sent from Europe for this purpose.[44]

The building, which became St. Ignatius High School after the college was separated and became John Carroll University in 1923, is an unusually fine example of the High Victorian Gothic style, the only distinguished one surviving in Cleveland apart from the churches. Its ornamental brick and stone banding displays the polychromatic use of materials advocated by John Ruskin, the principal philosopher of the style. In this respect the building is similar to many other American examples, although it was erected ten years after the style was at its height. However, certain details, specifically the corner turrets and eyelet dormers of the main tower, give St. Ignatius High School a definitely Germanic flavor appropriate to its occupants, its architect, and its neighborhood.

An institution indispensable to the large German and Bohemian communities was the brewery. Although rarely housed in buildings of notable architectural style, brewery structures have been recognized as being among "the most distinctive and unusual industrial architecture to be found on this continent."[45] In the nineteenth century beer was considered a commonplace and healthful beverage and the true temperance drink. Brewing was a local industry and most of the product of a brewery was generally sold in the immediate area. As a strictly functional building, the brewery might not be considered especially subject to architectural treatment, particularly in nineteenth century terms. A single building might contain the brew-house, malt-house, storehouse, boiler and engine rooms, and an ice-making plant. Nevertheless, a statement written in 1903 noted: "It is not sufficient that the brewery should be equipped with all the latest apparatus and machinery, but due consideration should also be made to good taste and to the wealth of the owners by a handsome architectural construction and with an eye for the beautiful."[46]

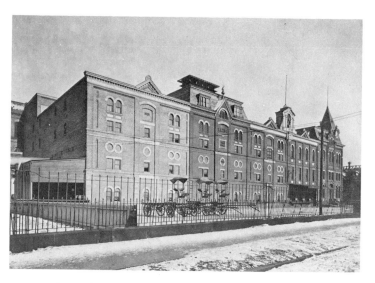

Leisy Brewery, Vega Avenue, 1884 (demolished), Andrew Mitermiler, architect.

Isaac Leisy mansion, Vega Avenue, 1892 (demolished), Andrew Mitermiler, architect.

The largest in Cleveland was the Isaac Leisy Brewery, a West Side landmark until its demolition in the early 1970s. Founded in 1873, the Leisy Brewery underwent a large expansion in 1884, when the "substantial, modernly-appointed structures, with up-to-date equipment," were constructed on Vega Avenue.[47] The main facade was over 200 feet long, and the entire plant occupied half a city block. Its masonry walls were marked by a series of engaged piers alternating with arched windows. Essentially conservative in style, its stone and brickwork displayed some of the same coloristic effects found in other buildings of the decade. Leisy's Brewery was planned by Andrew Mitermiler (1840–1896), a Bohemian-born architect who also designed several other breweries, Bohemian and German social halls and institutions, and Lohmann's Block, mentioned earlier. Mitermiler's advertisement of 1886 stated: "He is recognized as a thoroughly representative member of the distinctive American school of architecture, and has solved and still is successfully solving the complex problem of how to best utilize the minimum of the building area with the maximum of accommodation and architectural beauty of design."[48]

In the tradition of family ownership and management, the residence of Isaac Leisy was built next to the brewery. Comparing it to the Euclid Avenue mansions, a newspaper article called the three-story stone house, which had two octagonal towers and a carriage entrance with marble pillars, the "most baronial" of the houses of the period. Completed in 1892, it too was designed by Mitermiler.[49]

The German influence was also reflected in an important Victorian Gothic church begun in this decade. The Church of St. Michael the Archangel, the outgrowth of a mission established in 1881 to minister to the increasing numbers of German Catholics, was the largest and claimed to be the most artistically notable church in the Cleveland Diocese. For many years it was the largest church in Cleveland, with a capacity of 1,500 persons. The groundbreaking took place on June 19, 1888, and the church, completed five years ahead of schedule, was dedicated on November 2, 1892. Its final cost was $148,000.[50]

Measuring approximately 100 feet by 170 feet, the imposing building is constructed of random, rock-faced stone masonry. The east facade on Scranton Road has two towers whose spires reach to 180 feet and 232 feet respectively. On the interior, the vestibule, nave, and side aisles are groin-vaulted, with a multiplicity of ribs. The nave columns are clustered colonettes with naturalistic foliated capitals. The church is furnished with over fifty polychrome statues, many of them imported from Germany. The plans by architect Adolph Druiding of Chicago were selected by Bishop Gilmour from a number submitted at the request of the pastor, Father Joseph M. Koudelka. Druiding was also the architect of St. Patrick's Church in Toledo, which was then a part of the Cleveland Diocese, and there are striking resemblances in the design of the two churches, especially in the treatment of the columns and vaulting.

It remained for the Poles to raise one of the most extravagant churches of the decade, St. Stanislaus. The first "considerable" Polish immigration took

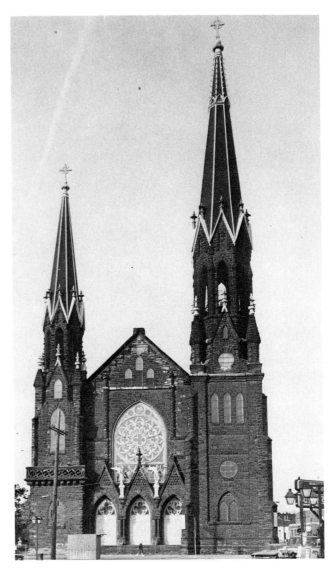

St. Michael the Archangel Roman Catholic Church, Scranton Road at Clark, 1892, Adolph Druiding, architect.

place when the owners of the Newburgh steel mills sought new workers. The Cleveland Rolling Mill Company, originally manned by Welsh, Irish, and Scottish workmen, resulted from a reorganization of Stone, Chisholm & Jones, Newburgh iron-makers, in 1863. In the late 1870s and increasingly after the strikes precipitated by the death of founder Henry Chisholm in 1881, large groups of Polish workers were recruited by the mill owners as they arrived in New York. Many Poles emigrated to escape from political and religious suppression, and while many intended to return to work for the future of the Polish nation, few actually did. They settled in

26

Cleveland in the area south of Broadway between East 55th and East 77th Streets, where they built and owned their own houses much like other immigrant groups.[51]

The first Polish masses were said in 1873, and the parish of St. Stanislaus was formed in 1877. After several years in a small two-story church near the site of the present building, an expanded church was needed and the foundations were laid in 1886. The ambitious pastor Father Kolaszewski planned a grandiose edifice, and in fact the account of the dedication in November, 1891, stated that the cost was $250,000. According to an Engineering News Record Index, the equivalent building cost in 1970 would have been something like $4,880,000. At the time St. Stanislaus was admittedly one of the poorest parishes in the diocese.[52]

The architect of St. Stanislaus was William H. Dunn, who had worked earlier in the office of Levi Scofield, and who later served for a time as city building inspector. St. Stanislaus was apparently one of his independent commissions. The large brick church is yet another example of Victorian Gothic, based in part on East European prototypes. Originally spires on the two facade towers reached to 232 feet, but they were destroyed in a windstorm in 1909 and the upper stages rebuilt in their present form as crowned belfries. The greater part of the expense was lavished on the interior, however. A three-aisled Gothic church like many others, its nave and aisle ceilings, basically four-part vaults, are further elaborated with radiating ribs. The stained glass windows, combining pictorial art with abstract floral and geometric designs, incorporate a comprehensive and complete iconographic scheme, unlike the partially finished programs of many churches. But the major glory is to be found in the carved wooden furnishings, rivalled only by some parts of St. Stephen's. The central altarpiece is an architectural construction, with many major and minor polychrome figures mounted in the niches of a framework which culminates in a steepled superstructure. Other altars and saints occupy the transepts and aisles and adorn the columns of the nave. The richness of the total impression bespeaks a love of craftsmanship and ornamental effect that is unknown to later generations.

The cost of St. Stanislaus can be better appreciated when it is realized that the Central High School, a three-story sandstone Victorian Gothic structure with a tall clock tower, cost $74,000 when it was erected in 1877–1878. During these years the

The main altar, St. Stanislaus Roman Catholic Church, 1891, William H. Dunn, architect. (*A People 100 years: St. Stanislaus*)

Cleveland public schools gained a national reputation under Superintendents Andrew J. Rickoff (1867–1882) and B. A. Hinsdale (1882–1886), former president of Hiram College. The Board of Education generally employed a regular school architect, and in the 1860s Charles Heard had designed most of the school buildings; his successor in the 1870s was his son-in-law Walter Blythe. However, the Central High School, located on East 55th Street, was designed by William Dunn's mentor, Levi T. Scofield. Scofield's design was chosen from among those submitted by six different architects and incorporated a new plan devised by Superintendent Rickoff, in which the classrooms were arranged around a central well extending from the large main hall to the roof. The entire front of the third story contained a general assembly room seating 1,000 persons, and the style of the school was described as "South German Gothic of the thirteenth and fourteenth centuries."[53]

Central High School, East 55th Street, 1878 (demolished), Levi T. Scofield, architect.

Broadway School, Broadway at 79th Street, 1881, Levi T. Scofield, architect. (*Cleveland City Directory*)

Another school designed by Scofield was begun the following year, 1879, and completed in 1881. Located on Broadway at Worley Avenue in the Polish neighborhood, it contained eighteen large classrooms and "numerous recitation rooms." The Broadway School was still standing in 1976 thanks to its purchase for use as the parochial school of Holy Name parish in 1944, when it was remodeled to provide classrooms and living quarters for the teaching Sisters. The two schools exhibited many style similarities. The obvious ones were a tall central tower (the height achieved on Broadway by a steep mansard roof), wide gabled attic dormers, and especially the entrance frontispiece on stocky medieval columns. Like Central High, Broadway School had its classrooms grouped around a central well lighted by a skylight in the roof; according to a study made in 1916 schools of this plan "were considered triumphs of school architecture and commissions from all over the country came to see them."[54] By the time of the study, however, that use of space was considered uneconomical and the plan abandoned.

## The East End

The 1880s also witnessed events which led to the development of the area later known as University Circle. Just east of Doan's Corners (Euclid and East 105th Street) was a tract of seventy-five acres of farm land owned by Jeptha H. Wade. Wade was one of the founders of the Western Union Telegraph Company, its first general agent, and the builder of the first transcontinental telegraph line. An associate of such men as Sylvester Everett, Henry B. Payne and Amasa Stone, he lived just across the street from St. Paul's Episcopal Church on Euclid Avenue. In 1881, Wade offered the land along Doan Brook to the City Council as a gift, under conditions which were refined after fifteen months of discussions. Accepted in 1882, the land was to be known "forever by the name of Wade Park." An area known as the "College Reservation" was not included in the gift, but ten years later it was also donated to be used as the site for an art gallery.[55]

Across Euclid Avenue from Wade Park, the Liberty Holden homestead was purchased in 1881 for the site of the Case School of Applied Science and Adelbert College of Western Reserve University. The western part of the land was reserved for Case School and the eastern part for Western Reserve.

The Case School, founded in 1880 by Leonard Case, Jr., became the fourth institution for higher technical education in the country. Case had inherited not only his father's estate but also his civic and philanthropic spirit, and his endowment of the scientific school was in the best traditions of the family. The Case building was begun almost immediately and was occupied in September, 1885. Unfortunately the building was gutted by fire in October of the following year, and the facilities of Adelbert College were used while it was being rebuilt. It reopened in 1888, but the reconstruction was done as economically as possible, and the building never regained the intention of its original design. The original architect had been John Eisenmann, Professor of Civil Engineering at Case School, but his plans have not survived. The reconstruction was done under the supervision of another architect and neither the exterior nor the interiors were particularly distinctive.[56]

In the same year as the founding of the Case School, the removal of Western Reserve College from Hudson, Ohio, where it had been established since 1826, began to be seriously considered. The need for an urban university had been discussed off and on since the closing of the abortive Cleveland University in the West Side Pelton Park (Lincoln Park) area in 1854. It was foreseen that the classical curriculum of Western Reserve and the rising demand for the engineering training that could be provided by Case School would be mutually complementary, and the two schools could collaborate in common interests. Dr. Hiram C. Haydn, a trustee of the college, pastor of the Old Stone Church, and later a president of Western Reserve University, entered into the negotiations which persuaded Amasa Stone to offer $500,000 to the college on the conditions that Cleveland citizens provide the site for its location and that the name be changed to Adelbert College. Stone, railroad president, bridge engineer, steel executive, and father-in-law of John Hay, had shown no apparent interest in educational institutions. However, attracted by the idea of a memorial to his son, Adelbert, who was drowned at the age of twenty-one, he agreed to provide the college building, which was erected in 1881–1882.[57]

Because Amasa Stone supervised the erection of the building himself and then donated it to the college, there are no college records of the construction. For at least thirty years it was thought that John Eisenmann was also the architect of Adelbert College. However, the original plans for Adelbert Hall were rediscovered in 1976 and established the fact that the architect was Joseph Ireland, a native of New York who practiced in Cleveland from 1865 to 1885, when he returned to the East. Ireland had designed the old Society for Savings building (1866) on Public Square, the Geauga County Courthouse (1870) in Chardon, Ohio, and the Euclid Avenue residence of Daniel P. Eells, who was among the trustees who had arranged the purchase of the land for the Case School and Western Reserve. Amasa Stone, Dan Eells, and Joseph Perkins had also employed Ireland as architect for the National Bank Building on Superior Avenue in 1867.[58]

The architectural design of Adelbert exhibits the eclecticism of the age, displaying a mixture of elements from the Victorian Gothic, Queen Anne, and Romanesque styles. Some of the ornamental details are very similar to those on the Eells house. Red horizontal banding in the buff sandstone provides the characteristic polychromy of the 1880s. Originally the entrance tower was taller and topped by a steeple; it was truncated in a renovation of 1901. At the same time the entrance was changed to provide the present divided stairway, and con-

Adelbert College (Adelbert Hall), Western Reserve University, 1881–1882, Joseph Ireland, architect. (*Case Western Reserve University Archives*)

siderable interior renovation was done. The plan of Adelbert is in effect that of a large public school building similar to the Broadway School. The rooms are arranged around a central stairwell with a skylight. The east side of the second and third floors, respectively, contain a large assembly hall and a museum room. In its structure Adelbert is another of the innovative fireproof buildings of the time. The external supporting walls are of stone and the interior partition walls of brick. The floors are constructed of iron beams carrying tile arches and cement. This construction accounts for the fact that there is no perceptible sagging in the forty foot span of the chapel ceiling, nor in the branching flights of wooden stairs which soar up through three stories in the central hall. In a recent renovation the roof skylight was cleaned and restored, again permitting a shaft of daylight to penetrate and enliven the interior.

Western Reserve University was first incorporated in 1884 by the Medical Department of Western Reserve College, which refused to use the name of Adelbert. Adelbert College meanwhile continued as an independent institution "affiliated with the university." Popularly known as the Cleveland Medical College, the medical school had occupied a handsome Greek Revival building on East

9th and St. Clair since 1845. The expanded needs of medical teaching required a larger facility, and plans were underway for a new building on the same site. After many meetings with Professor Edward E. Morley, the eminent mathematician, physicist, and chemist, architects Cudell and Richardson in 1884 designed a four-story pressed brick and terra cotta building[59]. However, following a great fire in the "Flats" in September, 1884, at the lumber yard of the principal donor of the new building, John L. Woods, further planning was delayed until he could provide the funds agreed upon.[60] In late 1884 or early 1885 new plans were drawn by architects Coburn and Barnum for a three-story sandstone structure in the Romanesque style. The old building was razed in April, 1885, and the new one begun in May. There were some delays in construction, and the building was not fully occupied until September, 1887. It was used by the School of Medicine until 1924 and demolished in 1929.

The interior plan was based on the arrangement of the old building, with amphitheaters, dissection room, museum, faculty room, library and stairways in the same position in both, although the area of the new building was twice as great and the cubic content about three times greater. Two amphitheaters and a large lecture room occupied a third of the structure. Frederick Waite has pointed out that because of the changing methods of medical teaching, the interior arrangement would have been far different if the building had been planned only five years later.[61]

On the facade of rusticated brown sandstone the three great round arches on the first story, seven on the second, and fourteen on the third, together with the lack of applied ornament, are reminiscent of Richardsonian buildings of the same period. The absolute plainness of the stone arches, without capitals or carved moldings, might lead one to suspect an acquaintance with Richardson's Marshall Field Wholesale Store in Chicago (1885–1887), whose simplicity has made it a staple landmark in American architectural history. However, Coburn and Barnum's plans were approved on February 12, 1885, while the commission for the Field Store did not reach Richardson's office until April of the same year.[62]

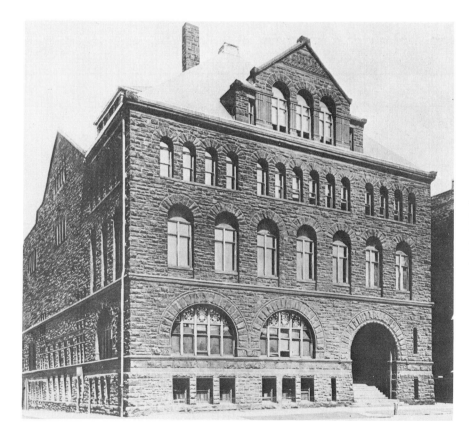

Western Reserve Medical School, East 9th Street and St. Clair, 1885–1887 (demolished), Coburn and Barnum, architects. (*Case Western Reserve University Archives*)

31

The Arcade, 1890, John Eisenmann and George H. Smith, architects.

# 1890: The Year of the Arcade

Between the Centennial year and 1890 the groundwork was laid for a distinctively American architecture. There was no longer any "regional" architecture—transportation and the communication of ideas moved too swiftly for that. The conjunction of technology, taste, and social and economic forces made certain developments inevitable, and these were manifest in Cleveland as elsewhere in the nation. In no sense whatsoever could the architecture of Cleveland in this period be called provincial. Oil, steel, and the railroads had created the money and power which traditionally form the necessary base for the evolution of an ambitious architecture. The effects were most apparent in the homes, offices, and institutions built for the wealthy industrialist-magnates themselves. These circumstances also attracted talented architects, who in turn participated in the era's ferment of ideas.

One characteristic linked the greatest mansion and the poorest immigrant house. This was the commitment to the detached, one-family house, which European critics found to be one of the most distinguishing traits of American architecture. But while it is sometimes supposed that there was a distinctive architectural character to the various immigrant neighborhoods, no convincing evidence has yet been adduced to this effect. The new populations were determined to become American as soon as possible, and while Old World customs and some craft traditions continued, the people built in the local style of the time, whatever it might be. Lorain Street buildings are indistinguishable from Broadway or Woodland Avenue buildings of the same date. Only in the churches, which were the social centers, is there some suggestion of national styles. Even so, most of this is due to the coincidence that the German and Eastern European immigration took place at the same time that the architecture of those nations was a standard source for the late Victorian architect. While Cudell was actually from Germany, the Central High School by Scofield was also "South German Gothic." The specific eclecticism of building a Byzantine church for a Russian community, or a Syrian design for a synagogue, came after the turn of the century.

The dominant mode of the period was a generalized sort of eclecticism, compared to the more "archaeological" eclecticism of the twentieth century. This meant that historical styles and details could be freely combined, but always with the aim of creating something new which would be distinctively "American." The competent architect was well-versed in all kinds of historical detail, which makes the tracing of an architect's work by "style" almost meaningless. One has only to set Coburn and Barnum's Blackstone Building next to their Medical School to realize this.

There were no design secrets. Publications like the *Inland Architect* and the *American Architect* assured that the new developments were known everywhere immediately. A poll in the *American Architect* in 1885 named Richardson's Trinity Church the "best building in the country," thereby guaranteeing its impact. It is also interesting that a French publication of 1886, *L'Architecture Américaine*, included two Cleveland illustrations (compared to fifteen and twenty-one for Chicago and New York respectively). One was the Euclid Avenue home of Charles W. Bingham, an executive in the pioneer hardware firm, by Peabody and Stearns of Boston. The other was an unidentified dining-room buffet by Levi T. Scofield.[1]

There was no fundamental discrepancy between the free stylistic adventures and technological experiments with new building materials, for in the minds of the architects both served the end of creating a new architecture. A traditional concept of architectural history, that there was an extreme polarity between nineteenth century engineering and architecture, leading on one hand to "truthful" structure and the other to Beaux-Arts design, is no longer borne out by the facts. While the engineer and the architect had certainly developed separate professions by this time, B.F. Morse, Coburn and Barnum, George H. Smith, John Eisenmann, and Cudell and Richardson were among those who combined skills of the engineer and the architect, and who were moving toward an architectural expression of the possibilities of new structural materials. The fact that the Case School of Applied Science and Western Reserve University were planned as complementary institutions shows the awareness of the need for interaction between science and the arts.

The Bingham house and St. Paul's Church, and the first of a series of office buildings by Burnham and Root that was under way in 1889, were among the relatively few Cleveland buildings designed by out-of-town architects. The business directory of 1889–1890 lists thirty-six Cleveland architects. A few were foreign-born, and they reflected the predominance of Germans and Bohemians in this generation. The extent to which their origins affected the nature of their buildings is moot. That two architects, Schweinfurth and Cudell, came from architectural families is also an interesting—but largely irrelevant—sidelight. Perhaps more significant are the facts that Schweinfurth was apparently a direct acquaintance of Richardson, that Cudell passed briefly through the office of Eidlitz, and that Sullivan's mentor Edelman worked in Cleveland for a time.

One of the obsessions of the architects of the period was fireproof construction, and it was pursued especially in institutional and public buildings, whether in traditional materials or new ones. This was combined with a trend toward monumentality, which was a natural result of the increasing first-hand knowledge of European architecture. At the same time, another consistent aim was the provision of lighter, more open structure, and this was attempted in wood and masonry even before iron and steel became commonly and economically available. It can hardly be coincidental that a city located in the region with the

greatest number of cloudy days in the United States developed a veritable affair with the light court. Nor is it surprising that the Perry-Payne Building and the public schools attracted widespread attention for this reason, and that the idea culminated in 1890 in the city's greatest structure.

The Cleveland Arcade brought together the economic, technological and esthetic developments of the previous decade. It has no peer in the United States, and it has been compared with the Galleria Vittorio Emmanuele in Milan, which although larger, is not as structurally adventurous.

Erected at a cost of $867,000, the Arcade opened on Memorial Day in 1890. It had been built by a company of which Stephen V. Harkness, one of the original partners of the Standard Oil Company, was president, and Charles F. Brush vice president. Other heavy investors were John D. Rockefeller and Louis H. Severance, the treasurer of Standard Oil. Brush and John L. Severance had their offices in the Arcade for years. Shortly after the opening, the advantages of an arrangement of stores which was, in fact, "an Oriental bazaar" were extolled:

> The great dry goods stores of Chicago and New York have really been for a long time bazaars, and much of their success is due to the fact that they brought together in one focus everything which the general purchaser could require, including lunch and candies. Arcadia is in fact the same thing, only more systematically planned and more economically conducted, and is the reaction of the small dealers against the omnivorous dry goods palaces, in which millions are concentrated, and against which they could make no head when isolated. But in the Arcade they have all the advantages of concentration, and all the attractions of palatial architecture and all the pecuniary economy derived from scientific construction.[2]

It has been pointed out that the Arcade is a cross between the light court and a commercial passage or shopping street.[3] The building is actually a complex of three structures, two nine-story office buildings facing Euclid and Superior Avenues, connected by the five-story iron and glass enclosed arcade. The Euclid and Superior fronts are monumental facades of sandstone and brick in a variant of the Romanesque style. The great Richardsonian arched entrance on the Superior Avenue front is original, but the Euclid Avenue front was remodeled in 1939.

The inherent drama created by moving from the solid masonry facades to the open, light interior is enhanced by two factors. First, the level of the Superior entrance is some twelve feet lower than the Euclid one, so that in effect there are two main floors, which are connected by staircases at either end. Second, Euclid and Superior are not parallel, a fact which is compensated for by a passage leading at a 23 degree angle from the Euclid entrance to a rotunda at the south end of the arcade. The arcade itself is a 300 foot long covered light court ringed by four levels of balconies which step back above the Euclid Avenue level. The effect of the vertical lines of the columns rising approximately 100 feet to the glass roof creates what is surely the most breathtaking interior in the city. The visual appearance of the ceiling is a "Gothic" arch because the lower sides of the roof trusses are curved, but the skylight itself is a gable roof which supports a light monitor along the ridge.

Coming when it did, the Arcade reflects the time's rapid changes in building technology and contains a mixture of techniques and materials. With regard to the relationship between wall and support, three distinct methods were used. First, the central entrance towers on both facades had load-bearing walls (before the alteration of the Euclid Avenue front, when steel beams had to be inserted to support the wall above the entrance). The side walls not visible from the streets are also load-bearing. Second, the masonry facades above the ground story on either side of the towers are carried on I-beams which rest on brackets attached to iron columns. Thus the facades utilize the skeletal principle which had been used in Chicago a few years earlier and which made the "skyscraper" possible. Third, the

The Arcade, Euclid Avenue facade.

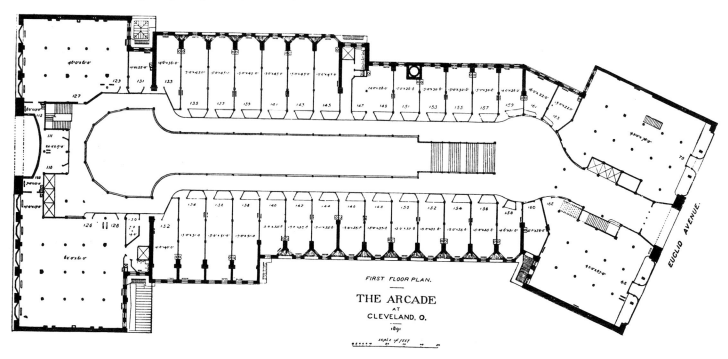

FIRST FLOOR PLAN.

### THE ARCADE
AT
CLEVELAND, O.
1891

floors and roofs of the buildings and the arcade itself are supported on a skeleton of iron columns and oak, wrought iron, and steel beams. The arcade roof trusses were of a new type, being hinged in three places, at the bases and the apex. The roof monitor was also hinged at the top. It is said that no Cleveland builder would bid on the unconventional construction of the roof, and the work was done by the Detroit Bridge Company.

The only major alteration of the interior has been the change in the stairs at the Superior entrance. The early stairs rose from the entrance and branched to the two balconies. They were replaced in 1930 by the present reversed stair which blocks an immediate view of the interior space from the Superior entrance. At the same time the original Art Nouveau light fixtures were removed and replaced with the present modernistic design.

The architects of the Arcade were George H. Smith and John Eisenmann. Smith (1849–1924) had designed Brush's home, and had also planned the Hickox Building, erected in 1890 at the northwest corner of Euclid and East 9th, at that time the limit of the business district. The composition of the Hickox Building facades was very similar to those of the Arcade, even to the grouping of the first six stories in

The Arcade, facade, showing the iron and masonry construction.

The Arcade, East West Section. (*Historic American Buildings Survey*)

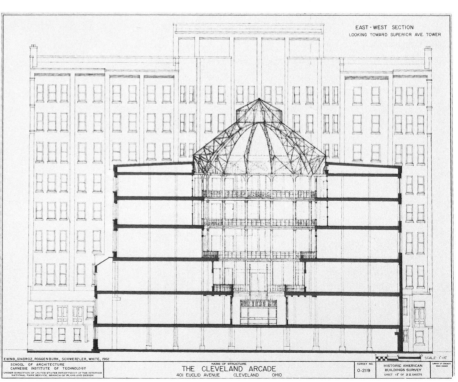

36

arched ranks, the heavy cornice between the seventh and eighth stories, and the slight projection of the piers above the roof line. In the next two decades Smith designed several other notable Cleveland office buildings, including the Rose Building (1900) and the Colonial Arcade (1898), a two-story shopping passage inspired by the success of the Arcade and connecting Euclid Avenue with the Colonial Hotel on Prospect. John Eisenmann (1851–1924) was trained primarily as an engineer at the University of Michigan, and studied architecture at the Polytechnics of Munich and Stuttgart. As we have seen, he was Professor of Civil Engineering at Case School and architect of the Case building. The respective contributions of Smith and Eisenmann are not known, but it is reasonable to assume that the facades and the office buildings were designed by Smith, while Eisenmann was responsible for the structural design of the arcade.[4]

The Colonial Arcade, 1898, George H. Smith, architect.

Hickox Building, Euclid Avenue and East 9th Street, 1890 (demolished), George H. Smith, architect.

Society for Savings Building (Society National Bank), Public Square, 1889, John Wellborn Root, architect.

# 1890–1903

## Skyscraper, Marketplace and Factory

The "Gay Nineties" and the last decade of Victoria's reign evoke the image of an age of confidence and optimism. To the extent that this was truly justified, Cleveland shared in it. With a population of over 260,000 in 1890, it had become the tenth city in the nation. Of this number, foreign-born peoples made up 37 percent. Cleveland was the largest shipbuilding port in the United States and the greatest iron ore market in the world. During the 1890s the city increased its size by annexing portions of Newburgh, Brooklyn, West Cleveland, and Glenville.

Several events loomed in the consciousness of Clevelanders. The reform of municipal government was an important issue, and in 1891 the executive and city council form of government based on the federal plan was adopted in Cleveland, testifying to its progressive tendencies. It was the heyday of Marcus A. Hanna the "kingmaker," and of the gubernatorial and presidential campaigns of William McKinley. The centennial of Moses Cleaveland's landing in 1796 was anticipated and celebrated with great enthusiasm. During the decade two major commemorative monuments were dedicated, the Garfield Monument and the Soldiers and Sailors Monument. The Columbian Exposition in Chicago was a great attraction for people all over the country. Its significance for Cleveland would last well into the twentieth century, since it inspired the city's unique grouping of public buildings in the Group Plan of 1903. As the decade opened, there was a continuing building boom to accommodate the forces of industrial expansion, and a number of significant office buildings were erected.

The evolution of the tall office building has usually been presented as if there were two kinds of builders: geniuses who let the inner steel structure express itself, and poor compromisers who cloaked the structure with fakery. Actual contemporary writing indicates that some of the latter understood the problem and knew exactly what they were doing:

> This state of things [practical but inartistic building] is purely transitional, and when the architects hold the chief points of steel and iron beam construction in the hollow of their hands a style will be evolved from it which will be full of artistic merit. In the meantime leading architects manage to conciliate the new materials with some ancient forms whenever they are permitted to build artistically, and in this manner the country has obtained some structures that are truly ornamental.[5]

This passage refers to the Society for Savings Bank building designed by John Wellborn Root of Burnham and Root and erected in 1889–1890. Built to replace the bank's 1867 building by Joseph Ireland on the same block, the structure was conceived by Root as representing a medieval donjon or fortified tower. The owners believed that "this building is the one that will keep his memory green. In many of his Chicago structures there are traces of weariness and dissatisfaction with his theme; but he loved the Red Tower of the Society for Savings, of Cleveland."

The president of the Society for Savings was Samuel H. Mather, and other officers included Samuel Andrews and Myron T. Herrick. Their aim indeed seemed to be a special attempt to bring together the industrial and decorative arts. The exterior design combines elements of the Gothic, Romanesque and Renaissance styles, of which the most prominent are the short granite pillars of the ground story Gothic arcade, the arches of different styles at the second, fifth and ninth stories, and the massive corners with their turrets reaching 152 feet. Structurally the building was transitional, like the others of its time. According to Root's biographer, "The outer walls of the building were as thick as 5 feet: as a deliberately monumental expression of a financial citadel, they were plainly self-sustaining. In contrast, the interior structure was advanced—the odd-numbered floors diagonally windbraced and the columns built-up from Z-bars, a technic pioneered only in 1886. . . ."[6]

On the interior, the main banking room is a startling and splendid space. The ceiling, twenty-six feet in height, is supported by twelve columns faced with marble, and the center portion is a stained glass skylight. The colorful "Gothic" decorative scheme was planned by Chicago decorator William Pretyman, and the murals were executed by Walter Crane, the English painter and illustrator who was

Western Reserve Building, West 9th Street and Superior Avenue, 1891, Burnham and Root, architects. 1895 view.

the leader of the romantic movement in decorative art and an associate of William Morris. Above the first floor, one of the most important features of the building was a nine-story light court surrounded with balconies which provided access to the offices. This has been covered over at certain floors, so that the stained glass skylight is now illuminated artificially. The contractors of this substantial and craftsmanlike structure, McAllister and Dall, had also erected the homes of Samuel Andrews, Charles Brush, Charles Bingham, and Sylvester Everett.

Two other office buildings by Burnham & Root and D. H. Burnham & Company were erected in the next three years. The Western Reserve Building at the corner of Superior and West 9th Street is in some respects the most interesting of the three. It stands on an irregular site and required an unusual design because of the triangular shape and the descending grade of old Superior Avenue. Furthermore, much of its design seems related to Root's great Monadnock Building erected in Chicago at the same time (1891–1892). The treatment of the oriel bays, the simple wall surfaces, and especially the flared cornice are similar. The Western Reserve was built by Samuel Mather (not the banker Samuel H. Mather), an industrialist in iron ore, coal mining, and shipping, primarily to house the offices of Pickands, Mather & Company. Like the Society for Savings, it has external stone and brick load-bearing walls, with interior iron columns and tile arch and cement floors.[7]

The Cuyahoga Building, completed in 1893, had the first complete steel frame in Cleveland. It is faced with sandstone, brick, and terra cotta. Erected facing Public Square by Myron T. Herrick and James Parmalee, it housed the offices of Herrick, secretary of the Society for Savings, advisor to McKinley, and later Governor of Ohio and ambassador to France.[8] The rhythms of the window ranks and bays are pleasing, and the design is the most stable and classically resolved of these Chicago Style buildings by Burnham and Root. For this reason the Cuyahoga Building is perhaps the most sedate of the three.

Advertising pieces, promotional literature, and view books of the nineties presented an established pantheon of important new office buildings.[9] Two adjacent ones always included were the Garfield Building and the New England Building, now combined and occupied by the National City Bank. Harry A. and James R. Garfield, sons of the late President James A. Garfield, erected the building bearing their name at Euclid and East 6th Street in

Cuyahoga Building, Superior Avenue at Public Square, 1893, D. H. Burnham & Company, architects.

1894. The ten-story structure was called the first steel-framed commercial office building on Euclid.[10] The facades of the Garfield Building, which follows the angle of East 6th Street, displayed the most direct expression of the steel frame so far seen in Cleveland. The building was designed by Henry Ives Cobb, one of Chicago's more innovative architects and the designer of the Fisheries Building at the Columbian Exposition, a structure which has always been considered one of the few truly original buildings at the Fair, being outside the prescribed classical mold.

It is an interesting fact that nearly every Cleveland building of ten stories or more was commissioned from an out-of-town architect. The next-door New England Building, completed in 1896, was designed by Shepley, Rutan & Coolidge of Boston. The senior partner, George F. Shepley, was a member of Henry H. Richardson's office, and the firm is considered his successor firm. The biography of Charles A. Coolidge includes the New England Building among the firm's "most important buildings," and certainly the fifteen-story sandstone-faced structure was an elegant example designed with restrained Renaissance detail. The facade had a single arched

center entrance on Euclid Avenue which was more appropriate to the overall design than the colossal colonnade added after it became the Guardian Building in 1914. Among the tenants of the New England Building were professional men and architects, including Schweinfurth, Coburn & Barnum, F. C. Bate and Steffens & Searles.[11]

Two exceptions to the rule of out-of-town architects were the thirteen-story Mohawk Building (1895) on the northwest side of Public Square, designed by Schweinfurth, and the fourteen-story Schofield Building (1902) on the site of the Scofield family residence at Euclid and East 9th Street, planned by Levi T. Scofield. The Mohawk became the American Trust Building and later the Public Square Building.[12] Both of these have been so completely altered by new facing in the mid-twentieth century that they no longer bear any resemblance to their original appearances.

The use of an out-of-town architect did not guarantee superior or even uniform architectural quality. The tallest building of the period was the eighteen-story Williamson Building, erected in 1900. Next to the Cuyahoga Building on Public Square, with which it was later connected, it was designed by

Garfield Building, Euclid Avenue at East 6th Street, 1893, Henry Ives Cobb, architect.

New England Building, 623 Euclid Avenue, 1896, Shepley, Rutan & Coolidge, architects.

George B. Post & Sons. Post was a member of the classical contingent at the Columbian Exposition, having designed the vast Manufactures and Liberal Arts Building, and the Williamson Building is clear evidence of the triumph of that classical ideal by the turn of the century. However, the vertical design is marred by the stacking of two-story sections, the unusually heavy cornice at the twelfth story, and the Roman colonnade embracing three stories above that. The building confirms the consensus of critics that Post's strength was chiefly structural and that there is little artistic unity in his buildings.[13] The most successful aspect of the building's design is its function as a frame for the southeast corner of Public Square and as a monumental entrance to Euclid Avenue.

Commerce and industry made the tall office building possible. The commercial and industrial structures themselves are seldom remarkable for

their architectural interest, but in every age a certain few rise above the commonplace. That one of the most humble yet essential commercial enterprises should have produced one of the most evocative interiors in the city is intriguing. The market house known as the Sheriff Street Market was erected by a stock company formed in 1890 and completed in 1891. In the typical "boosterism" of the local press, the opening announcement claimed that Cleveland "possesses the finest and most complete exclusively market building on this continent."[14] The five main aisles contained 312 stands, each of which could be connected with cold air conduits beneath the floor. The market had its own electric power plant, and fresh supplies of meat and produce were brought in daily. The second-floor gallery contained spaces for commission brokers' offices and restaurants. The architects of the structure were Lehman and Schmitt, a Cleveland partnership established in 1885 and lasting until the 1930s as the Lehman-Schmitt Company.

The Sheriff Street Market was a quintessential nineteenth century building—all space and light and exposed structure on the interior, and all "style" on the exterior. Old photographs of the interior bring to mind the cliche "cathedral of commerce." The wide-span central aisle was bridged by slender iron trusses, with light from a clerestory, roof skylights, and a great domed skylight at the center of the "nave." Actually the curved forms of the roof, the windows, and the seven arched entrances on Sheriff Street were more probably derived from the Roman basilica, which was originally a market place. On the exterior the 400-foot long structure was symmetrical, with two six-story buildings framing the ends and the great glass-domed pavilion in the center. Enclosing the ground story front was a wide veranda sheltering the produce stalls. This facade, together with the open, functional interior space, anticipates to a considerable degree the ideal of the World's Fair buildings three years later, though without the plethora of classical detail. In 1930 the bulk of the market structure was destroyed by fire, and only the building at the south end remains at the corner of East 4th and Bolivar, shorn of its two ornamental domes.

The new building of the Brown Hoisting Machinery Company, erected in 1901-1902 after the original plant was destroyed by fire, was another landmark building in both structure and architecture. It was the first building erected employing a new fireproof structural method invented by the owner. It is also an unusually expressive example of industrial architecture. The architect was J. Milton Dyer.

Alexander E. Brown was one of the men who conceived a more efficient method of unloading the great ore ships on Lake Erie. He developed a mechanical unloader consisting of two movable towers with cantilever arms supporting a cableway with an unloading bucket. This invention eventually revolutionized the handling of ore ships on the Great Lakes. The Brown Hoisting and Machinery Company was organized in 1880 to manufacture and distribute the unloader and various other kinds of cranes and plant equipment.[15]

After the fire of 1900, Brown set out to invent a cheap and light fireproof building material. The resulting process was called Ferroinclave and consisted of corrugated steel sheets formed by alternating Z-angles into dovetails, covered on both

Williamson Building, Euclid Avenue at Public Square, 1900, George B. Post & Sons, architects.

sides with cement. This idea was also the origin of the steel-formed stairs with cement treads which are a part of standard building practice seventy-five years later.

The main building of the Brown Hoisting Company is an imposing structure measuring 312 by 500 feet. The central arched span is 90 feet in height. As stated in *The Ohio Architect and Builder*, "it greatly resembles Machinery Hall at the World's Fair, and seems more like a grand exhibit than a practical plant."[16] From the architectural point of view, the external design of the structure clearly expresses its functions of enclosing and spanning the interior space. On the Hamilton Avenue facade, the central shed is framed by a giant flattened pointed arch, faced with the Ferroinclave cement. The walls at the base of the structure are made of brick; they form a simple visual podium, but apparently were used simply because there were bricks left over from the earlier buildings.

The Brown Hoisting building was one of the first commissions of J. Milton Dyer (1870–1957), who opened his Cleveland office in 1900. Dyer had studied

Sheriff Street Market, East 4th Street at Bolivar, 1891, Lehman and Schmitt, architects.

Sheriff Street Market, interior. (*Cleveland Public Library Picture Collection*)

44

Brown Hoisting Machinery Company, Hamilton Avenue at East 45th Street, 1902, J. Milton Dyer, architect.

Cleveland, Terminal & Valley (Baltimore & Ohio) Passenger Depot, Canal Road, 1898, Dutton & Heide, architects.

at the Ecole des Beaux-Arts in Paris for five and a half years, twice as long as the average American architect. He was one of the most versatile and original architects in Cleveland, equally adept in the conception of a public building or a purely functional one as a work of art. The excellence of the Brown Hoisting building lends further support to the renewed realization that the Beaux-Arts trained architect was usually a thoroughgoing realist in the planning behind his facades.

Among the other buildings from this era of industrial expansion, two of the most notable were produced for a railroad and for the new electrical industry. In 1897 Sylvester Everett's Cleveland, Terminal & Valley Railroad began construction on a new passenger depot on Canal Road in the Flats.[17] Within a few years it was acquired by the Baltimore & Ohio, which continued to operate the railroad as a part of its system. Planned by architects Dutton and Heide, the depot was a handsome three-story building of stone and brick in the Richardsonian Romanesque style, which had now become assimilated to the point of being a commonplace idiom. The main story of rusticated stone rises from

45

an exposed basement on the track side which accentuates its resemblance to a fortress with corner turrets. The building was used as a passenger depot until 1934, when the Baltimore & Ohio joined two other railroads in the new Union Terminal. In spite of the loss of its hipped roof, the depot remains an impressive relic of the importance of railroad passenger traffic at the turn of the century.

Myron T. Herrick and James Parmalee, builders of the Cuyahoga Building, were partners of Washington Lawrence in the formation of the National Carbon Company, which later became a unit of Union Carbide. Lawrence had been associated with Charles F. Brush as superintendent of the Brush Electric Company. The growth of the electrical industry in which Cleveland played a pioneer role promoted the manufacture of carbons for the arc lights used in street and industrial lighting. After purchasing the carbon department of the Brush Company, Lawrence organized the National Carbon Company in 1886. In a dozen years National Carbon, manufacturers of a diverse line of

electrical products as well as carbons, had acquired and consolidated over twenty carbon and battery companies.[18]

Between 1893 and 1896 a new plant and office building were constructed on Madison Avenue at West 117th Street in Lakewood. The plant included twelve factory buildings of brick and wooden beam mill construction, with roof monitor windows. However, it is the office building at the corner of West 117th which holds architectural interest. It was designed by the Cleveland firm of Knox and Elliot, which had just been formed in 1894. A three-story brick and stone structure with hipped roofs, it boasts a facade with two polygonal towers and a round-arched vestibule entrance.Large gabled dormers add further interest to each facade, and there is a wooden dentilled cornice above the second story. Taken together, these elements give the building a character more institutional than industrial. Still, it would not be of exceptional interest, were it not for the relationship of its design to that of Washington Lawrence's own house west of Cleveland.

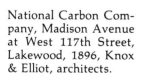

National Carbon Company, Madison Avenue at West 117th Street, Lakewood, 1896, Knox & Elliot, architects.

## Homes For Clients And Architects

While new houses continued to be built by wealthy clients on the older streets such as Euclid and Franklin Avenues, the nineties saw the beginning of the movement to the suburbs. Lakewood, Glenville, and the Heights all began to attract residents, but few went as far west as Dover Bay Park (Bay Village), where in 1898 Washington Lawrence built his home near an older summer residence. Its design is so similar to the National Carbon office bulding (the polygonal bays, round-arched entrance, hipped roofs, and dormers) that one is almost forced to infer that Lawrence specified a similar kind of architecture. If so, this would provide an interesting case of an industrialist truly taking his work home with him.

The Lawrence house is not only a rather spectacular example of eclectic domestic architecture, but also illustrates the experimental bent of architects with an unlimited budget. It was designed by Coburn and Barnum, but Forrest A. Coburn died in 1897. Frank S. Barnum had become public school architect in 1895, and by 1900 he had developed a modern school plan in which efficiency and fireproof construction were essential considerations. The Lawrence house is constructed entirely of steel and concrete sheathed with masonry. The residential application of these materials at the turn of the century is notable, although this building is by no

means unique. The very large house included ten bedrooms, several sitting rooms, a ballroom, servants' quarters, and other facilities.[19] Although Romanesque arches and bright red tile roofs give it a distinct charm, its external appearance is in other respects somewhat institutional. For this reason the mansion was easily adapted for the purposes of the Bay View Osteopathic Hospital, which acquired it in 1948.

During the nineties Charles F. Schweinfurth designed fifteen residences for Clevelanders, ten of them on Euclid Avenue. Seventy-five years later two remained, the Samuel Mather residence "Shoreby" in Bratenahl, and Schweinfurth's own home on East 75th Street. One of those gone is the house built for Marcus A. Hanna when he moved from Franklin Avenue to Lake Avenue in West Cleveland in 1890. Founder of M. A. Hanna & Company, Hanna was not only a leading coal and iron executive, but also "banker, builder of a steamship line, owner of the city's opera house, newspaper publisher, streetrailway magnate, and a constructive force in numerous organizations."[20] It was in 1896 that Hanna mounted McKinley's presidential campaign against Bryan and mobilized the wealth of the country's biggest corporations for campaign funds. Among others, Standard Oil, J. P. Morgan, and the Chicago meat packers gave amounts from $250,000 to $400,000, making a total conservatively estimated at $2,500,000. Following his election as a result

Washington H. Lawrence house (Bay View Hospital), Lake Road, Bay Village, 1898, Coburn and Barnum, architects.

Marcus A. Hanna House, Lake Avenue, 1890 (demolished), drawing by Charles F. Schweinfurth, architect.

Samuel Mather house "Shoreby", Lakeshore Boulevard, Bratenahl, 1890, Charles F. Schweinfurth, architect.

of Hanna's skillful propaganda machine, McKinley used his influence to have Hanna appointed Senator in 1897.[21]

Hanna's Lake Avenue house was practically a textbook example of the Shingle Style which had become popular in the East in the 1880s. A basement story of random ashlar supported a rambling, three-story, many-gabled structure with shingled siding which emphasized the surface sheathing rather than the structural elements. A round tower with bell-shaped roof indicated the style's relationship to the Queen Anne. Schweinfurth's drawing of the south

elevation shows an elaborately half-timbered frontispiece, which represented a fairly unusual grafting of Elizabethan-inspired detail onto a Shingle Style house.

The Bratenahl house designed for Samuel Mather in the same year is likewise a suburban home, and a particularly significant one because it represents a stage in the development of Schweinfurth's increasingly personal style. Samuel Mather (who was about to build Root's Western Reserve Building) will keep reappearing in the story of Cleveland's architecture. Reputed to be Ohio's richest citizen, he

48

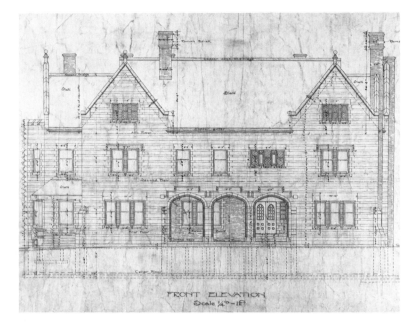

Cox-Prentiss House, Euclid Avenue, 1898 (demolished), drawing by Charles F. Schweinfurth, architect.

made millions of dollars in steel and shipping and gave away millions to philanthropic causes.[22] The style of "Shoreby" might be catalogued as Romanesque with some Tudor details. The latter are confined to a band of half-timbering above the arcaded entrance loggia and a small porch at the east end. Overall, the facade shows a subtle play between symmetry and asymmetry. It is basically symmetrical, framed by a tall gabled mass at each end. The window arrangement, however, is unsymmetrical, articulating the surface of the front in a calculated abstract pattern.

In another house built toward the end of the decade, the simplification and the subtle play of the wall surface were carried even further. The Cox-Prentiss house had a curiously specialized plan, even for those extravagant days. It was a double house, with a flat facade and a U-shaped court at the rear. The eastern two-thirds of the house was the home of Jacob D. Cox, Jr., son of the Ohio Governor and partner of Francis F. Prentiss in the Cleveland Twist Drill Company. The western third was occupied by Lucretia J. Prentiss, the sister of Francis and a cousin of Cox's wife Ellen, and two other ladies. The two parts were separate and complete residences divided by a party wall, each one including its own servants' quarters. However, the facade gave the appearance of a single house. A further simplification of the Mather house theme, it consisted of two gabled masses framing the center section with an arcaded loggia. The stonework was coursed ashlar instead of random, giving a much more regular texture to the

walls. The symmetry was subtly altered by a three-part window above the eastern arch of the loggia.[23]

These tendencies toward utter simplification and a play between regularity and irregularity reached a climax in the house that Schweinfurth built for himself in 1894. The house is doubly interesting because Schweinfurth apparently built it to a design originally conceived for a client; the plans carry the notation "Residence of W. K. Vanderbilt." Vanderbilt was chairman of the Lake Shore & Michigan Southern Railroad, and his Fifth Avenue chateau by Richard Morris Hunt introduced the most ambitious kind of revivalism heretofore known. The lot for the proposed Cleveland residence was owned by Henry Rouse, president of the Missouri, Kansas & Texas Railroad. Whether the house was planned as a Cleveland base for a railroad executive or for some other reason is not documented. In any case, when Rouse moved to New York in 1894, Schweinfurth purchased the lot and built the house himself.

The facade is a perfect rectangle with no projections. Stylistic elements remain in the slightly pointed arch of the entrance portal, the battlemented parapet, and the window frame detail. The stonework is not yet coursed, but random. In spite of these details, the basic effect is "cubistic" to an unprecedented degree for 1894. Schweinfurth's biographer states that his house was "entirely original with no peers in America or Europe at that time," and furthermore suggests that it anticipated the modernist principles of the Bauhaus group of the 1920s.[24] While this may be an exaggerated claim, the

Charles F. Schweinfurth house, 1951 East 75th Street, 1894, C. F. Schweinfurth, architect.

Preliminary design by Charles F. Schweinfurth for the Albert L. Withington house, Euclid Avenue near East 71st Street (demolished), ca. 1894.

Levi T. Scofield House, 2438 Mapleside, 1898, Levi T. Scofield, architect. (*Beautiful Homes of Cleveland*)

tendency of Schweinfurth's thinking in these houses seems clear.

Levi T. Scofield was another architect who built a residence for himself at this time. Scofield's house is somewhat eccentric, and one would be hard pressed to show that it is characteristic of developments in his other work. The location itself is highly romantic. The house stands on the brink of the Heights, which were just beginning to be developed in 1898. Overlooking Baldwin Road, the Fairmount Reservoir and the whole of the city, it seems from below to be perched on a precipice. Its basic form and plan are not unconventional, but its corner tower is. The house is constructed of stone, and the round two-story tower has a crenellated parapet following the roof line of the rest of the building. Above this point, with no transition from the round tower, the attic story is suddenly square, with great windows making a belvedere. This in turn is topped by a circular convex conical roof, again with no transition. The circular forms were repeated by a wide circular veranda which has since been removed.[25]

All of these houses, whether for client or architect, were clearly "made-to-order." Important as they are, both artistically and socially, they only represent one side of the times in which they were built. During the nineties another side came to the fore.

## Toward a New Community

For better or worse, the monuments of industry and commerce, and especially the great homes of the wealthy class, were the embodiment of the philosophy of social Darwinism and laissez faire. The enormous concentrations of wealth were justified by applying Darwin's "survival of the fittest" in biological life directly to social and economic life as well. This philosophy was already being questioned in the eighties. At the same time there was a new awareness of the problems of urban life caused by the great movement of peoples into the cities in the years following the Civil War. Cleveland, like other cities, already had its slums and sections of squalor, some just a few blocks from Euclid Avenue. The questioning of these conditions and inequities made the nineties an "age of reform."[26]

Some reformers saw the problem in religious rather than political terms. Ministers preached the "social gospel," with the message that Christianity should be less concerned with the hereafter and more with making this life endurable. The "institutional" church came into being, devoting its energies to charity, social work and providing classes, athletics, social halls and hospitals. Related to this religious work was the development of settlement houses which attempted to improve the conditions of slum dwellers. They provided clubs, kindergartens and day nurseries, as well as rudimentary efforts in public health; eventually settlement workers entered the political arena and fought against child labor and sweatshops. From all of this emerged a new role for women, and some of the Cleveland women working in these areas were among the most notable citizens of the period.

It has been said that the new immigrant populations were largely an obstacle to political reform, having come from the Eastern European countries which were under absolutist rule and being unfamiliar with their potential civic role in democratic self-government. However, the more established groups (Germans and Bohemians in Cleveland) had institutions in their communities which served the same social purposes as those of the reformers, building gymnastic and social halls, hospitals, orphanages, and old people's homes.

When visitors returned from Chicago's Columbian Exposition in 1893, they had seen a vision of a model city, conceived and built in a short time, with all the necessary services intelligently planned and provided. Some observers believe that America's "civic awakening" dates from the Fair; certainly its effects for Cleveland would be far-reaching in the next three decades. One result of the awareness of the need for city planning was the development of public parks. The idea of connecting existing or proposed parks by a chain of boulevards first appeared in the nineties, and Cleveland profited by the establishment of Gordon and Rockefeller Parks.[27]

Not only were the nineties an age of reform; they were also a time of new consciousness in education and culture. This was the period of John Dewey's philosophy of closing the gap between school education and the social world to make education socially productive by developing the student's manual facility, powers of observation, and personality as well as his mind. It was also a period of new emphasis on higher education for women. Finally, the nineties saw the first civic art museums and large public libraries. In order to house the new activities produced by these movements, some of Cleveland's most interesting architecture was erected.

The Pilgrim Congregational Church was one of the first institutional churches specifically designed for social and community work. While the exterior design is an excellent example of the Romanesque style and the auditorium proper is a superior achievement in architectural space and decoration, two-thirds of the original structure was devoted to educational, social, and community work. At the time it was called "an epoch-making church building." The church's origins were in a Sunday school in University Heights, as the West Side area around Lincoln Park was known in 1854. As the University Heights Congregational Church, its first building was erected in 1865–1869. The earliest institutional work began in 1873 with the establishment of recreational rooms for the young men in the vicinity to keep them out of the saloons. The present building was erected in 1893–1894. The Church Institute was organized at that time and maintained Fine Arts, History and Travel Clubs, a Literary Society, a Boys' Brigade, a Sewing School, a Gymnasium for all ages and both sexes, and classes in various practical subjects. The structure contained forty-three separate rooms to house these activities. In 1899 complete photographic views and models of the building were sent to the Paris Exposition, where it was praised as the "finest example of an institutional church."[28]

The auditorium is a lofty, square space framed by

Pilgrim Congregational Church, West 14th Street and Starkweather, 1894, Sidney R. Badgley, architect. Institutional wing in the foreground.

Pilgrim Congregational Church. (*Cuyahoga County Archives photo by David Thum*)

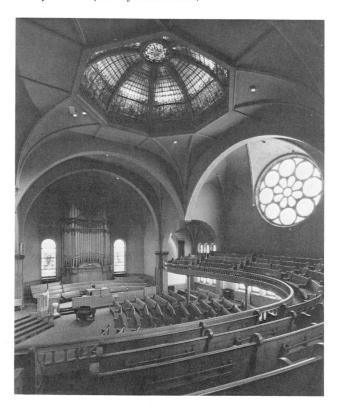

four great semi-circular arches and culminating in a leaded glass dome twenty-four feet in diameter. The auditorium and the large Sunday school room could be thrown into one space by the lifting of giant sliding doors, although the partition has not been operated for years. This widely adopted idea was claimed to have been originated "in its typical and successful application" by the architect Sidney R. Badgley. Active in Cleveland from 1887 to 1916, Badgley specialized in church and college architecture. He enjoyed a national reputation, having designed buildings all over Ohio and in many other states. A native of Canada, he was the architect of a number of Canadian buildings and also of the Methodist Church in Foochow, China.[29]

Another innovation of Badgley's was the use of steel domes unsupported by columns. The most notable example was considered to be the Epworth Memorial Methodist Episcopal Church, whose central dome was the largest of the kind known. Unfortunately, the church is no longer standing, and it must be appreciated from photographs. Stylistically the design was called "modernized Byzantine"; actually it was a mixture of Romanesque and Renaissance elements assembled with little regard for purist consistency. The auditorium and connecting Sunday school were similar in plan to those of Pilgrim Church, with the addition of the monumental exterior dome. The church was built in 1891–1893 on the site of Central Methodist Church, which became Epworth Memorial Church in 1891. The new church was a memorial to the organization of the Epworth League on that site in 1889. One of the most influential religious youth groups in the world, this organization of young people grew from twenty-eight members to 2,000,000 in a dozen years.[30]

In a *Centennial History of Cleveland*, Clara A. Urann remarked that Willson Avenue (East 55th Street) "presents as fine an illustration of the typical enlarging of the city and of public opinion as any one distinctive feature . . . the Baptists, Methodists, Hebrews and Roman Catholics have each erected elegant buildings in close proximity, the sects being kindly disposed one toward the other. . . ."[31] She was referring to Epworth Memorial Church at the corner of Prospect Street, Tifereth Israel Temple at Central Avenue, and Ursuline College at Scovill Avenue.

The Ursuline College and Convent was another Schweinfurth building which is no longer standing. The college for women had been established by Ursuline Sisters from France at the request of Bishop Rappe and had been housed since 1852 in the enlarged home of Judge Cowles on Euclid Avenue. According to Orth, "the alumnae of this institution . . . are to be found among the most influential Catholic and Protestant families in Cleveland."[32] The new building to which the

Epworth Memorial Methodist Church, East 55th Street, 1893 (demolished), Sidney R. Badgley, architect.

Ursulines moved in 1893 was a brick and stone edifice which was called "English Gothic" in style. Housing classrooms, convent, and chapel, it was naturally more complex in form than the Schweinfurth residences, yet it displayed the same restraint in Gothic detail and the same emphasis on the planar character of the facade. This was true in spite of the projecting vestibule and entrance stair unit; the chief feature which relieved the basic simplicity was the central fleche. Such a building indicates that the architect was a far more complex and versatile designer than has been realized.

Ursuline Convent, East 55th Street, 1893 (demolished), Charles F. Schweinfurth, architect.

Temple Tifereth Israel (Friendship Baptist Church), East 55th Street and Central, 1894, Lehman and Schmitt, architects.

The temple of the Tifereth Israel Congregation, unlike the Ursuline Convent and the Epworth Church, was still standing more than eighty years later. First organized in 1850, the congregation had resolved to build a new temple when Rabbi Moses Gries came to Cleveland in 1892. The new building was dedicated in 1894. The Temple, as the congregation and the new house of worship were called, was another historic institutional society. It was the first "Open Temple" in the world, where all interested in religious, cultural and educational activities were welcome regardless of affiliation. The Temple was a Reform congregation; it worshipped on Sunday and many of the participants were non-Jews. Practically all use of Hebrew was abolished from the service and the Sabbath School. The activities, directed toward liberal education, included lectures, extension courses and a free public library.[33]

The nineties were not a period during which a specific architectural style was identified with a particular faith. Esthetically, the Tifereth Israel building (now housing the Friendship Baptist Church) is indistinguishable from any other sanctuary. It is a huge square stone structure in the Romanesque idiom. The west facade has an arcaded porch flanked by two round towers which indicate that the designer was not unfamiliar with Richardson. The elevation on Central Avenue is a massive, towering fortress-like wall, and dominating the entire composition is a great square lantern with a domical roof. The basic effect, when compared with contemporary Christian churches, exhibits fewer differences than similarities, perhaps suggesting the fundamental common social aims and supporting Mrs. Urann's statement. The architects were Israel Lehman and Theodore Schmitt, planners of the Sheriff Street Market and many other important Cleveland buildings, including the Central Armory, the Euclid Avenue Temple (Anshe Chesed, another Reform congregation), and—most notable of all—the Cuyahoga County Courthouse.

Several important social settlements were initiated in Cleveland which, according to contemporary observers, set a pattern in social work for the nation. The first was Hiram House, established by George A. Bellamy of Hiram College in 1896 to carry out social service work with the poor immigrant groups in the Orange Street neighborhood. Among the sponsors were Mr. and Mrs. Samuel Mather, F. F. Prentiss and William G. Mather. Through the generosity of Mrs. Samuel Mather the first public bathhouse was erected on Orange Street, and Hiram House built its own home in 1900. Mrs. Mather also initiated the Goodrich House settlement, planned to supplement the parish work of the Old Stone Church. Goodrich House immediately erected a building in 1897 at St. Clair and East 6th Street, designed by Coburn, Barnum, Benes & Hubbell. The Goodrich House building gained a national reputation as a model facility for social settlement work. Legal aid services were provided and later a program for rehabilitating juvenile offenders. The settlement moved further east in 1914, and neither the Hiram House nor Goodrich House is still standing.[34]

Another settlement building, Alta House, was still standing on its seventy-fifth anniversary. Architecturally it is more interesting than other institutional buildings in that it has the appearance of a large residence. It was also one of the charities in which John D. Rockefeller took a direct interest. Alta House stands on Mayfield Road, a connecting link between Euclid Avenue and the Heights, where the new suburban development was beginning. This area had been settled by Italian immigrants who found employment in the marble works near Lakeview Cemetery and is still known as "Little Italy." Because of an accident of topography, it is the one area which has a suggestion of national character, if one stretches the imagination to picture an Italian hill town. However, the only thing Italian about the architecture is the eclectic Baroque Holy Rosary Church (1909).

The settlement started in 1895 with the organization of a day nursery and kindergarten by Joseph Carabelli and others. Rockefeller agreed to provide support, and the nursery was named after his daughter Alta, who observed, supported and participated in the settlement work.[35] The house was designed by Charles Hopkinson, a Cleveland architect who later planned many public schools. It is a large, substantial red brick structure whose picturesque character, deriving from the steep bracketed roof and many dormers, is enhanced by the change of elevation on Mayfield Road. This requires a steep single flight of stairs to an arcaded porch at the main entrance, while the side portico on Fairview stands on a high arched basement with a turning stair. All in all, Alta House still presents a most effective image on the ascent to the Heights.

Of the special homes erected in these years for the care of dependent groups, two may be taken as examples. The Jones Home for Friendless Children was founded by Carlos L. Jones of Brooklyn Village and his wife on their forty-acre farm as a home for the "care, support and education of destitute children." The home was chartered in 1886, and among the trustees were Rutherford B. Hayes and Lewis Miller, Akron industrialist and founder of the

Alta House, Mayfield Road and East 125th Street, 1901, Charles Hopkinson, architect.

55

Jones Home for Children, 3518 West 25th Street, 1903, Sidney R. Badgley, architect.

Altenheim Home for the Aged, Detroit Avenue at West 77th Street, 1891, Andrew Mitermiler, architect.

Chautauqua movement. When the inadequacy of the old homestead became evident, it was decided to erect a new building. Completed in 1903, it housed seventy-five children, whereas the older home could accommodate only forty or fifty. The architect was Sidney R. Badgley, and the building was one of the earliest institutional structures in Cleveland built in the Colonial Revival style.[36] The pedimented center piece has a Palladian window in the gable and a one-story entrance porch, and the roof cupola was a standard recognizable Colonial feature.

The Altenheim Association was organized in 1875 by the West Side Deutscher Frauen Verein (German Association of Women), and the cornerstone of the Association's Home for the Aged was laid on September 19, 1891. Despite the differences in age and style, the Altenheim building and the Jones Home are essentially alike in their basic organization, being placed lengthwise to the street and having roof dormers, a gabled center piece, and a one-story entrance porch. However, the solid curved balustrade and the steep roofs of the Altenheim somehow suggest its German origins. The architect was Andrew Mitermiler, the designer of breweries, business blocks, and social halls for Germans and Bohemians.[37]

Mitermiler was also involved in the planning of one of the most significant social and cultural centers of the time—the Bohemian National Hall located in the Czech neighborhood on Broadway. Already the home of one of the largest Slavic groups in the United States, Cleveland was well on its way to having the fourth largest Czech population in the world, exceeded only by Prague, Vienna, and Chicago. The hall became a genuine social center for Czechs of liberal thought, and its auditorium was used for speakers, plays, concerts, and operas for years. The building later housed a Czech free-thinkers language school.

A group of forty Czech societies began plans for the hall in 1887, the property was purchased in 1889, and fund-raising efforts continued until 1896. Initial plans were prepared by Mitermiler and John W. Hradek, another Bohemian-born architect. In 1895, however, because their plan was estimated to cost around $60,000, "it was decided to wait," and in 1896 Andrew Mitermiler died. In October, 1896, new plans were prepared by architects Steffens, Searles and Hirsh for the existing building at an estimated cost of $40,000. The cornerstone was laid in December, 1896, and the building was dedicated in 1897.[38]

The style of the hall contains elements of both the Romanesque and the Renaissance styles, the latter being represented by the Tuscan columns at the entrance and the balcony on console brackets above. The interior plan is complex and well-designed for the simultaneous handling of many large groups for meetings, public events, athletics, and refreshment. The auditorium occupies the two middle floors of the four-story structure. The arched auditorium windows on the facade and the west side are unusually large for the period, and an interesting detail is the blind arch on the side wall at the auditorium stage house. The large proscenium stage on the interior is flanked by two levels of boxes, and there is a

Bohemian National Hall auditorium, 1897, Steffens, Searles and Hirsh, architects.

profusion of ornament in the Renaissance style. A number of sets of scenery for various stage and operatic productions are still intact, and the main curtain is painted with a view of Prague.

If it is true that the concentration of private wealth in the hands of a few was responsible for social inequities, it is also true that it was responsible for many of the most vital reform programs. The sponsors of institutional churches, settlement houses, and homes for orphans and the elderly become familiar names that appear over and over again. These philanthropists were the same people who built their own commercial and personal monuments. Nowhere is their public interest more evident than in the lands donated for public parks.

In 1893 the estate of William J. Gordon turned over 122 acres of parkland on the lakefront to the city. Gordon, a wholesale grocer, had been purchasing tracts on the lake bordering Doan Brook since 1865. In 1894 an adjoining thirty acres were purchased from the Gordons, and in 1901 the first large bathhouse and pavilion were erected in the park. The city purchased land in the Doan Brook valley connecting Gordon Park with Wade Park in 1893. During the Centennial celebrations in 1896, John D. Rockefeller gave $300,000 to reimburse the cost of that land and donated an additional 270 acres along Doan Brook valued at $270,000. In 1894 the city was given twenty-five acres between Cedar

Avenue and Ambler Heights by Mrs. Martha Ambler, and the next year fifty acres were purchased to complete Ambler Parkway, a deep ravine which connected Rockefeller and Wade Parks with the Heights. The land along Doan Brook on the Heights had been the site of the Shaker settlement from 1823 to 1889. The 278-acre stretch, including two man-made lakes, was donated by Rockefeller to the city in 1896, thus completing the seven miles of continuous parkway from the source to the mouth of Doan Brook.[39]

The four bridges designed by Schweinfurth to span the Rockefeller Parkway superbly fulfill Vitruvius' conditions for architecture: commodity, firmness, and delight. They are ample enough to accommodate undreamed-of traffic seventy-five years later; they stand in virtually perfect condition; and they are among the most pleasing ornaments in Cleveland's landscape. John D. Rockefeller donated $100,000 toward the construction of the Superior Avenue bridge, on condition that an additional $20,000 be raised by Cleveland citizens. The condition was met, and the city erected all four bridges during the next few years. They are constructed of brick, stone and concrete. The arched vaults spanning the roadway are made of brick and support a concrete core, while the stone voussoirs and ashlar work act as facing and as retaining walls.[40]

Each of the four bridges has a different architectural character. The one carrying the Lake Shore & Michigan Southern (now the Penn-Central) at the north entrance to the parkway is designed as a monumental gateway. The semi-elliptical arch is framed by two polygonal turrets, the whole forming a massive central bay in the entire length of the bridge. The St. Clair Avenue bridge has small pedestrian arches on either side of the semicircular roadway arch. The supporting vault, however, spans all three arches. The Superior Avenue bridge has a single wide arch over the roadway and a smaller pointed arch over the bed of Doan Brook. Two lookouts project from the sides of the bridge. The Wade Park Avenue bridge has two unique features. The stonework is not carried up to form a parapet; instead the upper roadway berm slopes down to meet the tapered upper edge of the masonry. Also unique is the serpentine stair descending from Wade Park Avenue to Liberty Boulevard at the southeast end of the bridge. Because of these features, plus the fact that the roadway arch springs from the grade level rather than from piers, the Wade Park Avenue bridge has been the most generally admired of the group.

The Doan Brook parkway skirted the recently established campuses of Western Reserve University and Case School. At the University a sustained controversy over coeducation had been going on for several years. In 1888 the College for Women was authorized, and it met in the old Ford homestead on

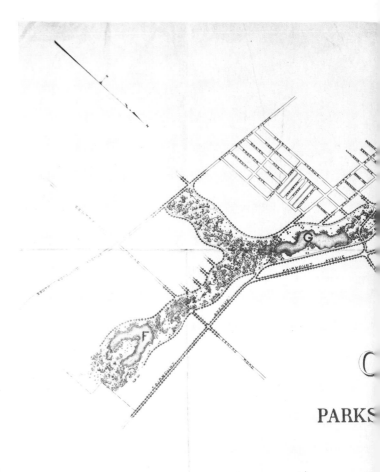

PARKS

Euclid Avenue for four years. While there had long been a number of coeducational colleges and separate women's colleges, Western Reserve's was the first undergraduate women's college that was part of a university.

In 1891 the college acquired land across Euclid Avenue donated by Jeptha Wade, grandson of the donor of Wade Park, and Mrs. James F. Clark provided funds for the construction and maintenance of a classroom building. Clark Hall was designed by Richard Morris Hunt of New York, but the reason for the selection of this architect of national reputation is unknown. Samuel Mather, as a member of the building committee and having the Western Reserve Building under way at that moment, was appointed to confer with Burnham and Root as to their terms for furnishing plans, specifications, and supervision of the building. The outcome of this conference is not known, but Hunt received the commission. Guilford Cottage, the dormitory built at the same time, was designed by Cleveland architects Coburn and Barnum. It was given by Flora Stone Mather, daughter of Amasa Stone and wife of Samuel Mather.[41]

Superior Avenue Bridge, Rockefeller Park, 1897, Charles Schweinfurth, architect.

58

BOARD OF PARK COMMISSIONERS
CHARLES H BULKLEY PRES.
AMOS TOWNSEND   JOHN F PANKHURST   ROBERT BLEE, CHAS A DAVIDSON
F C RANGS, SEC Y

VELAND, OHIO.
CONDENSED PLAN OF
PARKWAYS ON THE EAST SIDE
DECEMBER 31, 1894.

CHARLES W. PRATT JR
CHIEF ENGINEER

F   UPPER SHAKER POND
G   LOWER    --   --
H   OLD QUARRIES
I   AMBLER PARKWAY
J   WADE PARK
K   DOAN BROOKWAY
L   GORDON PARK

Nº 49.

Plan of the Doan Brook parkways from Gordon Park to the Shaker Lakes, 1894, Charles W. Pratt, chief engineer, and Ernest W. Bowditch, landscape gardener.

Wade Park Avenue Bridge, Rockefeller Park, 1899, Charles Schweinfurth, architect.

Mrs. Mather (1852–1909) was probably the most memorable Cleveland woman of her era. She supported nearly every philanthropic cause and was personally active in the work of the Old Stone Church, Goodrich Social Settlement, the College for Women, and many other institutions. On her death, tributes were received from three dozen institutions, in addition to newspaper editorials and personal memorials. The Cleveland *Leader* editorialized, in an ultimate accolade for 1909, "Mrs. Mather achieved a career of which any man might well be proud."[42] Mrs. Mather had already endowed a professorship at Adelbert College, and in addition to Guilford Cottage, named after her own teacher, she donated funds for the erection of the second women's classroom building, Haydn Hall, in 1901. The chapel built at the same time was a memorial to Florence Harkness, the daughter of Stephen Harkness, who had died shortly after her marriage to Louis H. Severance. The large classroom building erected in 1911–1913 was named for Flora Stone Mather after her death, although she always refused any such designation while she was alive.

The first four buildings were built in two pairs,

59

Clark Hall, Bellflower Road, 1891–1892. Richard Morris Hunt, architect. (*Case Western Reserve University Archives*)

Clark Hall and Guilford Cottage in 1891–1892, and Harkness Memorial Chapel and Haydn Hall in 1901–1902. They provide a most instructive contrast in the attitudes of the beginning and the end of the decade. Clark and Guilford still contain a relatively free combination of stylistic elements and in this sense are still late Victorian buildings. Harkness and Haydn, on the other hand, represent a much more "correct" application of the English Gothic style. Clark Hall has not been fully appreciated in recent years. It is a three-story building of sandstone and buff brick which is irregular in mass and has a number of gable projections. The interior, as with many early colleges, was designed to contain classrooms, a chapel, library, gymnasium, and offices. It is an ingenious arrangement of many rooms of different sizes, shapes, and heights. The pointed oaken arches and large traceried window of the second floor lecture hall make it a particularly impressive room. It is not easy to relate Clark Hall to the contemporary work of Hunt, who was planning the great Renaissance palaces at Newport for the Vanderbilts at this time, as well as the Administration Building for the Columbian Exposition. Clark Hall looks backward to the 1880s. Guilford Cottage, while more unassuming, partakes of the character of the early Colonial Revival, but without its strict symmetry. It makes a most effective screen to the west end of the green.

Harkness Memorial Chapel and Haydn Hall rely more directly on the sixteenth century Tudor style which had become the primary source for the popular idiom of the collegiate Gothic. Haydn's entrance, based on an Oxford or Cambridge gatehouse, is a modest example. Harkness, particularly its interior with elegant hammerbeam arches, is a more ambitious one. When the Flora Stone Mather building on the corner was added by Schweinfurth a decade later, the great Tudor gatehouse was rendered in stone and almost overshadowed the whole block.

In the same years three more Schweinfurth buildings were added to the Western Reserve campus. The two science buildings near Adelbert College were recognizably "Schweinfurthian." The physics building (1894–1895) was constructed of brick and the biology building (1899) of stone. The battlemented parapet and unsymmetrically placed Gothic doorway on the physics building recalled the architect's own residence of the same year. The roof observatory with its telescope, given by Warner and Swasey, was added in 1899. The biology building consists of two rectangular blocks, the north one with a gabled end toward the street and the south one with a battlemented roof line. The functional specifications for the building were drawn up by Francis H. Herrick, Professor of Biology. Both of these buildings displayed an irregular arrangement

An early view of the campus of the College for Women. Left to right: Harkness Chapel, Clark, Haydn, and Guilford Halls. (*Case Western Reserve University Archives*)

of windows according to the interior needs, where a lesser architect might have forced them into a symmetrical format.[43]

A more distinguished structure, and one less typical of Schweinfurth, was the building erected for the law school in 1896. Established in 1892, the law school first occupied the Ford home just vacated by the women's college. It soon developed a reputation for high standards, and in the early twentieth century was one of the three law schools in the country to require a college degree for admission. A bequest offered by the widow of Franklin Thomas

Backus gave the school its name, although the funds were not forthcoming until after her death in 1907, and the university had to borrow money for the 1896 building.[44] The rectangular structure has a hipped copper roof and is constructed of buff Ohio sandstone. Two pink marble Ionic columns stand in the recessed porch, which is lined with yellow Roman brick. The classical detail only points up the exact symmetry of the facade, although the design is hardly pure Renaissance. No doubt the classical style was seen as appropriate to the Roman origins of the law. An inscription on the frieze reads: "The Law is

Florence Harkness Chapel, Bellflower Road, 1902, Charles Schweinfurth, architect. (*Case Western Reserve University Archives*)

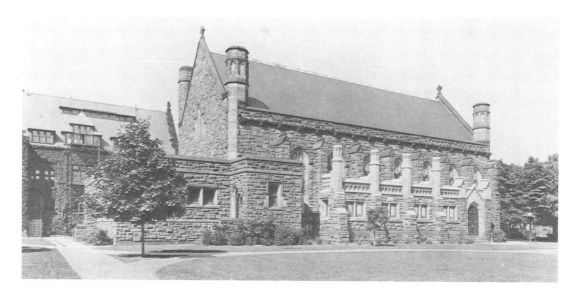

the Last Result of Human Wisdom Acting Upon Human Experience for the Benefit of the Public."

The most classical of the institutional buildings of the period was erected for the Western Reserve Historical Society in 1898. The Society moved from the old Society for Savings building on Public Square, which it had occupied since 1867, to Euclid Avenue and Fairmount (East 107th Street) at University Circle. The new building provided a stately fireproof home for the valuable manuscripts, relics, specimens and books collected over the years. It contained a museum, a library, an auditorium, rooms for special collections, and a basement storage vault. Crowned with a red tile roof and faced with brick and terra cotta, the building was an elegant essay in the Renaissance idiom. It was designed by Coburn, Barnum, Benes and Hubbell. The firm was only in existence under that name for one year (they also designed the Goodrich Social Settlement), after which Hubbell and Benes began a separate career.[45]

It is important to emphasize that the classicism of the nineties was still the servant of the architect rather than his master. While its six arches alternating with medallions may recall Alberti's San Francesco at Rimini, the Historical Society building was not a slavish Italian imitation. The entire treatment, both in overall conception and in detail, including the sculptured portral, the windowed frieze, and the ornamented cornice, was a highly original design.

*top left*: Physics Building, 1895 (demolished), and Biology Building, 1899, Western Reserve University, Charles Schweinfurth, architect. (*Case Western Reserve University Archives*)

*center*: Backus Law School, Western Reserve University, 1896, Charles Schweinfurth, architect. (*Case Western Reserve University Archives*)

*bottom*: Western Reserve Historical Society, East 107th Street at University Circle, 1898 (demolished), Coburn, Barnum, Benes & Hubbell, architects.

## The Monumental Consciousness

Regardless of whether it sheltered offices, marketing, industry, living, service, or education, and regardless of whether it took on the forms of the Romanesque, Gothic, Renaissance, or pure engineering, late nineteenth century architecture is incomprehensible unless an attempt is made to understand the value that was placed on symbolism. This dimension is found in its purest form in commemorative and monumental structures, and these flourished between the Civil War and the end of the century as they did in no other period in American history.

Almost immediately after the assassination of President Garfield in 1881, a movement began in Cleveland to erect a monument to his memory. The committee appointed for the purpose included J. H. Wade, H. B. Payne, and Joseph Perkins. Fund-raising continued into 1882 and $150,000 was realized. In 1883 architects were invited to submit competitive designs, and two nationally known architects were selected as judges, Henry Van Brunt and Calvert Vaux. The design adopted was by George W. Keller of Hartford, Connecticut, in whose biography the Garfield Memorial is mentioned as his most noted monument. Keller made a trip to Europe in 1884 to study monuments there and perfect his design. Construction began in 1885, and the Memorial was dedicated in Lakeview Cemetery with great ceremony on Memorial Day, 1890 (the same day as the Arcade).[46]

The design of the Garfield Memorial is thoroughly characteristic of the date of its conception. Constructed of native sandstone, the tower, which stands on a broad terrace approached by a wide flight of steps, is fifty feet in diameter and rises 165 feet to the summit of the conical roof. Its design draws freely on Romanesque, Gothic, and Byzantine architecture and was greatly admired and commended upon completion. Above the memorial room which contains the statue of Garfield there are two spacious chambers which have been unseen by the public for many years. The first level contains a three-foot thick circular wall supporting the vaulted floor above, and the perimeter aisle is spanned by arched buttresses. The uppermost level consists of one great circular room with a vast beehive dome beneath the conical masonry roof. The outward thrust of the roof is counteracted by an iron tension ring whose spokes are embedded in the stonework of the dome. Thus the Memorial is a massive engineer-

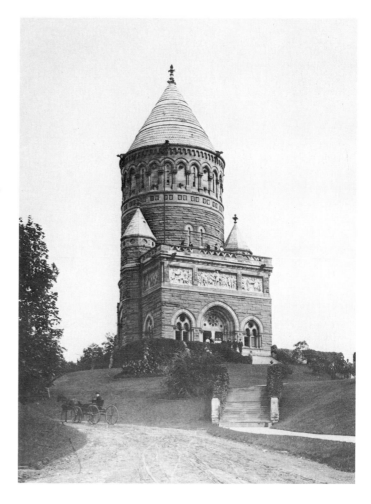

Garfield Memorial, Lakeview Cemetery, 1890, George W. Keller, architect.

ing work whose powerful effect rivals that of the Superior Viaduct.

It was considered important that the Memorial was called the first true mausoleum in America, a structure combining the tomb and memorial functions; that it was called the fourth such structure in the world, after those of Mausolus at Halicarnassus and Metellus and Hadrian in Rome; that the five sculptured relief panels of the frieze epitomized general conditions of mankind in the specific events of Garfield's life, namely education, bravery, democracy, government, and death; that the decoration of the interior was carried out through the revival of lost ancient and medieval arts, the gold mosaic of Venice and the marble mosaic of Rome; and that the "soul" and the "central thought" of the Memorial was the statue of Garfield in white

63

Cuyahoga County Soldiers and Sailors Monument,
Public Square, 1894, Levi T. Scofield, architect.

that Scofield consulted men from every branch of
the armed services and incorporated their ideas. The
actual modeling and construction was apparently
done by teams of local artisans. The bronze
sculptures were cast in the New York studio of John
Quincy Adams Ward, the noted American sculptor.
Scofield received no remuneration, and the cost of
the Monument was $280,000.[47]

The Monument consists of a square stone building
standing on a sandstone esplanade 100 feet square,
reached by four flights of curving steps and
surmounted by a 125-foot granite shaft with a
fifteen-foot statue of Liberty on top. Bronze
sculptures on each of the four sides represent the
Infantry, Artillery, Cavalry, and Naval branches of
service. A bronze eagle stands over the north and
south entrances. The memorial room, which is
entered through large bronze doors, contains relief
panels depicting several wartime events and marble
slabs inscribed with 6,000 names of Cuyahoga
County veterans. Upon its completion in 1894, the
building was lighted and heated with electricity.

To a large degree the design reveals its "planning
by committee," but it is strikingly original in
conception. Contemporary descriptions insist that
the Monument does not reflect any historic style.
Instead, all of the ornamental forms are derived from
military symbols, for which years of research were
required. For example, the volutes on the capital of
the great shaft are based on the wheels of an artillery
piece. Other ornamental details include miniature
cannons, a rammer, a piece of rope and a capstan, a
saber, a pistol, and a musket. Originally even the
gardens surrounding the Monument were symbolic;
the flower beds depicted the badges of the various
army organizations.

While the monuments had only a commemorative
function, the two armories erected in 1893, one for
the Cleveland Grays and the other for the Central
Armory, combined associative symbolism with
practical use. Both were designed essentially to look
like military fortresses.

The Cleveland Grays was a private company
formed in 1837 to provide trained men for military
service and to serve at state, civic, and official
occasions. The cornerstone of the Grays Armory at
Bolivar and Prospect, which was still in use over
eighty years later, was laid on Memorial Day, 1893.
The drill hall served as a public auditorium
throughout the years. At the beginning it was used
for events of the 1896 Centennial celebrations and
later for early Cleveland Orchestra concerts. The

Carrara marble standing in the center of the
mortuary chapel. While such considerations are light
years rather than decades from the late twentieth
century, similar ones infused the thinking that
produced most buildings of the eighties and nineties.

If possible, the Cuyahoga County Soldiers and
Sailors Monument is an even more graphic example
of the late Victorian artistic principle of ac-
cumulating realistic detail to symbolize abstract
ideals. The Monument was first proposed in 1879,
authorized in 1885, and planned and executed
between 1888 and 1894. There was considerable
controversy over its location and design before it
was finally placed on the southeast quadrant of
Public Square. The architect-sculptor was Levi T.
Scofield. As contemporary accounts are more
politically than artistically oriented, the design
process is not completely clear, although it is known

Grays Armory was designed by Cleveland architect Fenimore C. Bate. The rusticated basement and Romanesque portal are Richardsonian in character, and the upper walls are brick. The five-story tower with its progressively smaller openings suggesting the defensive function is easily imagined as part of a medieval fortress.[48]

The Central Armory on Lakeside Avenue at East 6th Street was erected by the county to house units of the National Guard, but it was also quickly put to use for public events. In the celebrations of 1896 it housed mass meetings, a concert and historical spectacle, gymnastic exhibitions by German, Bohemian, and Swiss groups, and a floral exposition. The Central Armory was designed by Lehman and Schmitt, and like their Sheriff Street Market was essentially a large covered hall. The 122-foot width of the hall was spanned by six arched plate girders hinged at the apex. The balcony was suspended from the girders by iron rods. On the interior the structural engineering was dramatically exposed, but the exterior was sheathed in a castellated Gothic envelope. The northwest tower was reminiscent of a Florentine or Sienese thirteenth century municipal fortress tower, and the walls of the long, rambling structure were punctured with Gothic windows. The fanciful late Victorian treatment, the rough-hewn surfaces, and the round turrets of varying sizes at the corners and entrances of the building gave a picturesque effect which today suggests the castles of Disneyland. This is not a derogatory

Grays Armory, Bolivar Street at Prospect Avenue, 1893, Fenimore C. Bate, architect.

Central Armory, Lakeside Avenue at East 6th Street, 1893 (demolished), Lehman and Schmitt, architects. Measured drawing of the north facade.

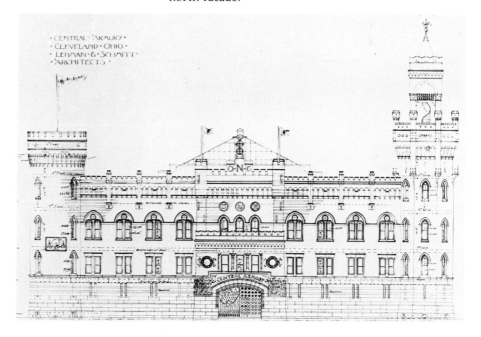

Centennial Arch, Superior Avenue at Public Square, 1896, W. Dominick Benes, architect.

Wade Memorial Chapel, Lake View Cemetery, 1900, Hubbell and Benes, architects. *right*, Tiffany window representing the Consummation of the Divine Promise.

comparison; it simply points up one of the essential elements of eclecticism, that of make-believe.[49]

As we have seen, the classical revivals began to supplement the medieval style in popularity some time around the mid-nineties. It was perceived that they would also be appropriate for certain kinds of commemorative and monumental structures. This was due in no small degree to the vision of the "Great White City" that had been seen at the Columbian Exposition in Chicago, although the tendency had been growing since the late eighties. The Centennial celebration of Cleveland's founding in 1796, with the temporary character of an exposition, provided a perfect opportunity to display the new classicism. A large temporary structure in the form of a Roman triumphal arch was erected over Superior Street directly north of the Soldiers and Sailors Monument. The Centennial Arch was 79 feet high, 106 feet wide, and 20 feet thick. It was constructed of a wooden framework covered with lath and staff, a temporary building material whose base is plaster of Paris. The arch was ornamented with six plaster-cast groups on pedestals, a band of relief decoration around the arch itself, and a sculptured frieze. At night it was illuminated with 900 electric lamps. The architect of the Centennial Arch was W. Dominick Benes.[50]

Another memorial structure designed by the firm of Hubbell and Benes was the funeral chapel erected to the memory of Jeptha H. Wade by his grandson in 1900. It has been widely considered the most

important structure in Lakeview Cemetery after the Garfield Memorial. The portico of four fluted Ionic columns is not merely an imitation of a Greek or Roman temple, nor is it a frontispiece from a Palladian villa or an American Greek Revival house. Rather, it forms a carriage driveway similar to those in contemporary domestic practice. The spacing of the half-round columns on the sides of the building is determined by the driveway width, and there are half as many as one would expect on an ancient temple. Due to the sloping site, the entrance to the chapel is at grade level, but the rear is raised on a rock-faced sandstone platform, which contains the crypt. In other words, the classical style was not rigidly copied; instead, various elements and proportions were adapted to the requirements of a modern building.

However, the most significant point about the design of the chapel was the collaboration between architects and decorative artists. The interior was designed by Louis C. Tiffany and executed by the Tiffany Studios. The walls and ceiling are made of marble with two murals of glass mosaic, each eight feet high and thirty-two feet long, designed by Frederick Wilson and symbolizing the "Voyage of Life." One represents the Prophecy and Law of the Old Testament and the other the Fulfillment and Light of the New Testament. At the end of the chapel, the center window by Tiffany represents the consummation of the Divine promise.[51] Thus the Wade Memorial Chapel combines the late nineteenth century desire for symbolic representation, a free adaptation of classical architectural style, and the important principle of collaboration between architects and artists which would continue in force until the 1930s.

The final important classical building of the century was the one erected on Public Square by the Chamber of Commerce. Located on the former site of the Western Reserve Historical Society, the Chamber of Commerce Building was designed by competition. The supervising architect to the building committee was William R. Ware, partner of Van Brunt and founder of the first American architectural school at Massachusetts Institute of Technology. The unanimous choice of the committee was Peabody & Stearns of Boston. Later the Chamber of Commerce was forced to defend itself against criticism for not selecting a Cleveland architect. There was also controversy over the material to be used; a considerable sentiment existed for sandstone instead of the brick and terra cotta

Chamber of Commerce Building, Public Square, 1898 (demolished), Peabody & Stearns, architects.

finally chosen. A competition design by Cleveland architect William R. Watterson was quite similar to the five-bay facade, ranks of arched windows, and classical cornice of the selected design. This suggests that the basic proportions of the building were pretty well determined by the building committee, and that it was clearly planned to be a gracious neighbor to the Society for Savings building next door.[52]

The completed building was an excellent example of the Beaux-Arts interpretation of the classical idiom current by 1897–1898. Discussions of grouping several new public buildings in an architecturally unified scheme were already under way, and the Chamber of Commerce Building was seen as "an object lesson" in the development of that plan. Externally, the building's most important functions were to provide a link between the Society for Savings and the planned Federal Building, to serve as a symbol of civic pride, and to make a dignified screen for the northeast corner of Public Square. Its replacement by a parking lot has been most unfortunate.

John Hartness Brown Building, Euclid Avenue, 1901, Warren, Wetmore & Morgan, architects.

## Entering the Twentieth Century

Nothing in Cleveland, and few examples in nineteenth century architecture, could have prepared Euclid Avenue for the building which John Hartness Brown began in 1901. Brown was a real estate promoter who is credited with the conception of the Circle at Euclid and East 107th, and also with the idea of developing the Euclid Heights residential area.[53] In 1901 Brown made plans for an immense (150 feet by 207 feet) six-story commercial and office building to occupy the Euclid Avenue frontage just east of the present Union Commerce Building. At that time a street known as Lennox Lane passed to the east of the old Lennox Building. Thus the Brown Building had two facades, one on Euclid and one on

Lennox Lane. The building was planned to cost $275,000.

For his architects Brown engaged Warren, Wetmore & Morgan, a youthful New York firm which would become known principally as the architects of Grand Central Terminal (begun in 1903). Whitney Warren (1864–1943) had spent ten years in Europe while studying at the Ecole des Beaux-Arts before returning to New York in 1896 and forming a partnership with Charles Wetmore.[54]

The design of the John Hartness Brown Building was unique. The Lennox Lane facade was a concave curve of metal and glass which joined the Euclid Avenue facade by a curved glass bay. The major bays on Euclid Avenue were fifty feet wide and were filled with an unprecedented amount of glass supported by slender exposed steel members. The major piers were faced with terra cotta and granite. Cornices at the upper three floors displayed ornament in varying degrees of departure from classical examples, with some suggestion of the Art Nouveau idiom. One precedent for a structure of this kind was the glass and iron architecture of Victor Horta (1861–1947) in Brussels. His masterpiece, the Maison du Peuple (1896–1899), had a curving facade of iron, glass, and brick very similar to the Brown Building, and was considered the culmination of the metal and glass aesthetic of the Art Nouveau period.[55]

The innovative design of the John Hartness Brown Building has been all but forgotten. The building was never occupied. Around 1908 Brown's real estate transactions became overextended, and he lost control of the building as well as his own home in Cleveland Heights. Later he left Cleveland for London, England. In 1913 Cleveland architects Walker and Weeks remodeled a portion of the unfinished building for the Loomis Company, and in 1916 the firm of George B. Post & Sons, who had designed the Statler Hotel just to the east, was engaged to design a new front for another portion of the building. In subsequent years the facades were further remodeled by a succession of owners.[56] However, the rear elevation of the original structure was still visible seventy-five years later in the alley leading from East 12th Street.

An equally startling building for Euclid Avenue opened in 1903 two blocks west of the Brown Building. It was built for the J. L. Hudson Company, which occupied the store only until 1912, and later housed the W. B. Davis clothing store. The six-story facade was apparently Cleveland's only other major Art Nouveau design. A contemporary description stated that the architects "have given a new business type to this, the whole front being treated as a great arch, outlining the inner scheme of large window exposure artistically, and being emphasized by being traced in electric lights. They have sought to embody the large ideas typical in church architecture to modern business problems, and have in this a Renaissance type of boldness and freedom."[57] The great curving concave arch was executed in terra cotta and embraced three ranks of clearly articulated square bay windows with large expanses of glass. Each uppermost bay was arched, and the scheme was clearly intended to complement the arched ranks of the Arcade facade immediately to the east. Filling in the spandrels was the interlacing organic ornament so characteristic of the Art Nouveau idiom.

The designers were Godfrey Fugman and Emile

J. L. Hudson store, Euclid Avenue at East 4th Street, 1903, Fugman and Uhlrich, architects.

Uhlrich, who were primarily ecclesiastical architects. Uhlrich was born and educated in France, and had begun work in the United States at Cincinnati in 1894. Fugman and Uhlrich were partners from 1899 to 1904, after which Uhlrich planned a great many churches, schools, and business blocks in various styles. There are no records to show how the sophisticated and original store front came to appear in Cleveland, but Uhlrich's French connections are suggestive. This design may also be linked with Victor Horta, whose famous Brussels department store "l'Innovation" (1901) displayed a glassy facade embraced by a large flattened arch. It is ironic that the contemporary description referred to the J. L. Hudson store in terms of Renaissance church architecture, with no apparent recognition of its modern European counterparts, nor of the fact that the design, like that of the Brown Building, was not in the mainstream of the Cleveland architectural scene in the early twentieth century.

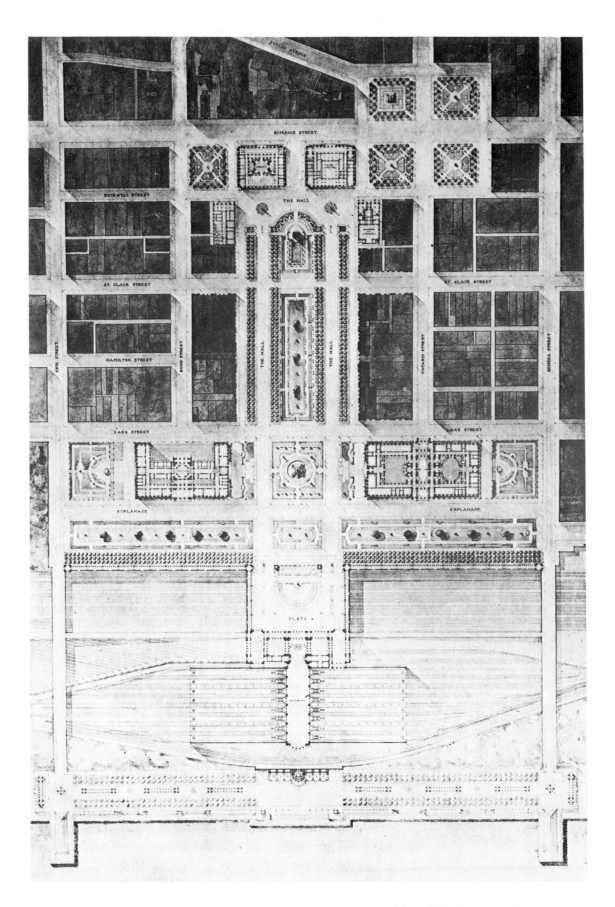

The Group Plan, 1903, Daniel Burnham, John M. Carrere, and Arnold W. Brunner, Group Plan Commission members.

# 1903: The Group Plan

"Sirs:—The opportunity of grouping the principal buildings of a city the size of Cleveland and providing them with proper setting in the way of approaches and other accessories, has never before come to any city. . . ."[1] Thus began the Report of the Group Plan Commission to the Mayor of Cleveland in 1903. Except for the McMillan Plan of 1902 for Washington, D.C., which was essentially a restatement of L'Enfant's plan of 1791, Cleveland was the first of a number of cities to make a comprehensive plan for grouping its major public buildings. More important, Cleveland's Group Plan was the only one which was actually carried out with any degree of completeness.

At the turn of the century the federal, county and municipal governments were all planning to build large new structures, and the concept of grouping these public buildings occurred to many people. The inspiration of the monumental grouping at the Chicago Columbian Exposition of 1893 gave added impetus to the idea, and as early as 1895 the Cleveland Architectural Club arranged a competition to produce a "grouping" plan. There were no immediate results, and in 1898 the Architectural Club held another competition. The prime mover of the group plan idea seems to have been one of the judges, Professor Charles F. Olney, who introduced a resolution to the Chamber of Commerce in January, 1899, providing for the appointment of a Grouping Plan Committee. The report prepared by this committee and adopted by the Chamber of Commerce in 1900 showed five major buildings grouped on the north side of Lake Street (Lakeside Avenue) between West 3rd and East 9th Streets. A park was shown sloping down to the lakefront with the existing railroad tracks either bridged or completely covered. Wood Street (East 3rd Street) appeared as a north-south axis leading to the site of the planned Federal Building. In 1902 the local chapter of the American Institute of Architects and the Cleveland Chamber of Commerce presented a bill to the Ohio legislature authorizing the creation of a Group Plan Commission. The bill was passed, and Governor Nash appointed three members recommended by Mayor Tom L. Johnson. All architects of national stature, they were Daniel Burnham, director of public works for the Chicago Exposition, John M. Carrere, and Arnold W. Brunner, who was already designated as the architect of the new Federal Building.[2]

According to Daniel Burnham's biographer, Thomas Hines, "the first urban reformer to exploit Burnham's talents was Cleveland's controversial mayor, Tom L. Johnson."[3] Mayor from 1901 to 1909, Tom Johnson was primarily known as an advocate of home rule and municipal ownership of the street railways. His liberal Democratic programs were anathema to conservatives like Mark Hanna, but he left Cleveland at the end of his career, according to Lincoln Steffens, "the best governed city in America." Johnson was one of the best known representatives of the Progressive Movement which had resulted from the reform spirit of the nineties. In this atmosphere arose the "City Beautiful" movement, of which the Cleveland Group Plan was a preeminent example. Among other things, it helped to fulfill such Progressive goals as the elimination of the notorious slums in the designated area, the revitalization of the lakefront, and the creation of a civic center. It is doubtful that the plan could have

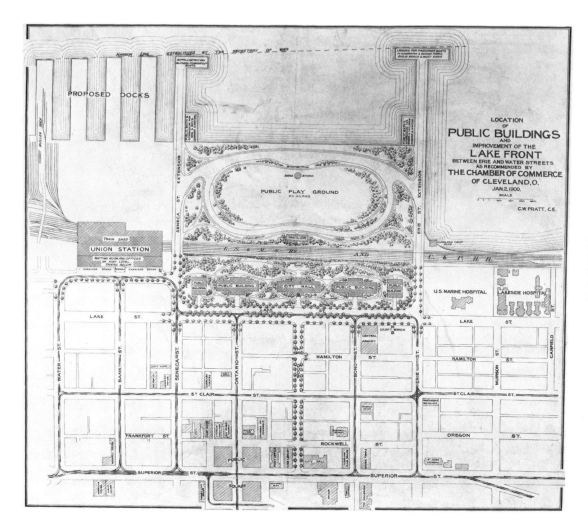

Plan of the grouping of public buildings as recommended by the Chamber of Commerce, 1900.

come to fruition without Johnson's support and influence.

The recommendations of the Group Plan Commission were presented to the mayor on August 17, 1903.[4] Most of the elements near the Mall that are recognized by Clevelanders today were established in the visionary plan. The main feature was a broad mall or Court of Honor along East 3rd Street, intersecting with a second major axis on Lakeside Avenue. The locations of the County Courthouse and the City Hall on Lakeside were indicated, as well as the two symmetrical structures for the Federal Building and the library at the foot of the mall. The report pointed out the fact that the Courthouse and City Hall would terminate long vistas on Ontario and East 6th Street respectively. The space to the east of the library was designated as a park to balance the Public Square to the west of the Federal Building. The report recognized that a library large enough to

balance the Federal Building might never be economically feasible, and alternatives were suggested.

The Commission also pointed out that a maximum effect could be achieved with minimum expense. European precedents were illustrated, especially the Palais Royal and the Place de la Concorde in Paris. The necessity for uniformity of style and building height were stated as the lessons of the Court of Honor at the Columbian Exposition of 1893. Order and uniformity were seen to be essential qualities of the plan. These were to be achieved in the architecture through a distinguishing character, and the Roman style was recommended, which meant of course the Beaux-Arts interpretation of antiquity.

One major element in the plan was never realized. The north end of the mall was closed by a monumental railroad station over the lakeside tracks. This placement was finally arrived at to solve

72

the problem of the unsightly tracks, to satisfy practical requirements of grade and approach, and to provide an architectural focus for the composition. In addition, the symbolism of the depot as a "vestibule" to the most magnificent portion of the city was used to justify its location. However, initial studies had shown the station located either to the east or to the west of the mall. Moreover, during the discussions in 1918 on whether to locate the terminal on Public Square, Burnham's chief designer, Pierce Anderson, was to point out that the location of the station in the Group Plan was "imposed upon them by the necessities of the situation, and was not a matter of first choice."[5]

There were other predetermining factors in the Plan. The location of the Federal Building had already been selected, the existing Chamber of Commerce Building had to be considered, and the plan adopted by the Chamber of Commerce in 1900 was strongly influential. Thus it seems that Daniel Burnham's chief contributions were the concept of a Court of Honor approximately 500 feet wide and the general recommendations concerning the character of the architecture.

The Plan was favorably received by the Mayor, city officials, the press and the public. The significance of the conception was immediately recognized across the country, and articles appeared in local and national journals. The comments in *Harpers Weekly* in 1904 are characteristic of the general appreciation of the Group Plan:

> Probably no city in the country, outside of the capital, has undertaken the systematic development of public architecture and parkage on so splendid a scale as has the city of Cleveland. . . . [The creation of the Group Plan Commission is] the most significant forward step in the matter of municipal art taken in America. It is comparable to the designs of Napoleon III, who remade Paris, with the aid of Baron Hausmann, or to the prescience of Jefferson, who called to the aid of the new government a distinguished architect in the laying out of the national capital on its present scale. . . . Here is a city among the most radical in its democratic tendencies of any in the country courageously authorizing the expenditure of from ten to fifteen million dollars in the development of an idea. It suggests a new conception of the municipality.[6]

However, approval was not unanimous. The most vociferous opponent was Frank E. Cudell, who had retired by 1903. He wrote letters and broadsides, and only two weeks after the presentation of the Plan he published a large brochure stating his objections. The principal ones were that the mall was far too wide to be comprehensible to the pedestrian, and

that the main buildings were too far apart. Cudell's alternative was a court 300 feet wide with the principal buildings placed along its sides. Still later, in 1916, when the Courthouse and City Hall were an accomplished fact, he published a leaflet stating that the two buildings could not be properly seen unless there were open plazas in front of them. Cudell appeared to be disinterested, but in fact he felt that his own ideas had been ignored. In September, 1903, he had stated: "Last March it was reported to me by unquestionable authority [Brunner] that the supervising architects had adopted my plan."[7] He felt that "despotic" citizens from the Chamber of Commerce had influenced the architects and the Mayor to abandon his concept. These allegations are impossi-

The Group Plan scheme submitted by Frank Cudell, 1903.

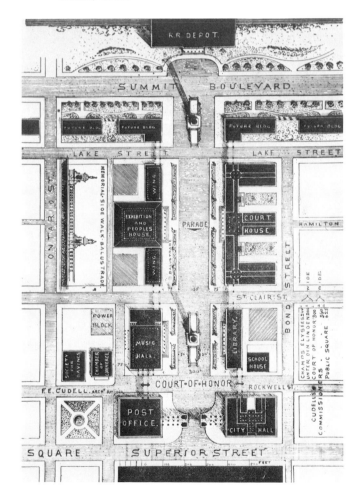

73

United States Post Office, Custom House and Court House, Superior Avenue at Public Square, 1910, Arnold W. Brunner, architect.

THE NEW CITY HALL

Renderings of the Cleveland City Hall and Cuyahoga County Court House, from the *Report on the Group Plan*, 1907 edition.

THE NEW CUYAHOGA COUNTY COURT HOUSE

ble to corroborate from the perspective of seventy years, but they provide some additional insight into the political nature of the evolution of the Group Plan.

Although the overall concept of the Group Plan is more significant than the architecture of the individual buildings, they are not undistinguished. The Federal Building was the first one completed. One entire bay of Brunner's design was erected at full scale in temporary materials, in order to judge the final effect.[8] The building was reported as being "nearly complete" in the second edition of the Group Plan Report in 1907, but it was not occupied until 1910. The five-story granite structure displays the rusticated basement, colossal Corinthian colonnades, and massive entablatures of Beaux-Arts classicism. It is not surprising that the collaborating decorative artists, including Daniel Chester French, Kenyon Cox and Edwin H. Blashfield, had all participated in the 1893 Exposition.

The Federal Building's twin, the Public Library, which was constructed of marble and designed by the important Cleveland firm of Walker & Weeks, was not completed until 1925. The Cuyahoga County Courthouse was completed in 1912 in the same Beaux-Arts idiom. The architects were Lehman and Schmitt, and evidence indicates that their principal designer was Charles Morris, an alumnus of the Ecole des Beaux-Arts and the office of Carrere & Hastings. Charles Schweinfurth was partly responsible for the design of the interiors.[9] The Cleveland City Hall was designed before 1907 by J. Milton Dyer but was not completed until 1916. Since all of the commissions after the first building were given to Cleveland architects, it is apparent that the criticism of the Chamber of Commerce for using an out-of-town architect was keenly felt.

The Courthouse and the City Hall were designed with very similar facades. It is interesting that both buildings were shown in early sketches as having

Cleveland City Hall, 1916, J. Milton Dyer, architect.

Cuyahoga County Courthouse, Lehman & Schmitt, architects. (*Cuyahoga County Archives photo by David Thum*)

been longer by two additional bays on each end. As built, each has the same arcaded ground story, two-story colonnades, and balustraded roof line as the two buildings at the opposite end of the mall. Each has a central pavilion with three entrance bays. Each was planned to have a series of standing sculptures above the cornice of the entrance pavilion, but these were completed only on the Courthouse. However, in all of these major buildings the interior vaulted spaces and the functional plans are far more impressive than the exterior facades, where the consistency of the standardized formula robs the buildings of much individuality or drama.

The three other major buildings occupying the area originally laid out for the Group Plan were erected in the 1920s. The Public Auditorium was completed in 1922 and the attached Music Hall in 1929. The first portion of the Plain Dealer building, located on the park east of the Public Library and now housing its annex, was designed by George H. Smith, architect of the Arcade, and built in 1909–1911. It was enlarged from plans by Hubbell & Benes in 1920–1922. The Board of Education building which completes the east side of the Mall was finished in 1930. All three of these submitted to the uniform height and generally classical formula established by Burnham.[10]

The use of classical forms in buildings like those of the Group Plan is still frequently described as reactionary, in the same way that half a century of criticism has been leveled at the 1893 Exposition itself. The fact is that the academic classicism of 1890–1925 was the authentic style of the period.

While it was the Progressive Movement which helped to make these buildings possible, America was also at the height of its imperialistic "destiny." The Beaux-Arts Roman style was built by and for men convinced of an American Renaissance and an important place in the world. In this sense it was the appropriate style for the times, for it accorded with Americans' ideals and self-image. Furthermore, the fact that such buildings have functioned well for three-quarters of a century shows that they were conceived and built as modern buildings, not as dry exercises in archaeology.

The idioms usually suggested as a possible alternative to classicism are those of the Chicago School of Root and Sullivan or the Prairie Style of Wright. These were commercial and residential styles, and it was impossible in 1903, let alone 1893, to conceive of their appropriateness for a monumental civic architecture, although a festival architecture might have been a possibility. It was only with the hindsight of the active advocates of "functionalism," beginning with Sullivan and Wright themselves, that we much later came to recognize the seminal character of those styles.

The last remaining older structure within the mall area was demolished in 1935, and the Mall was used for the Great Lakes Exposition of 1936. The fact that the Mall was finally realized a third of a century after the conception of the Group Plan is an affirmation of Burnham's famous assertion that "a noble, logical diagram once recorded will never die, but long after we are gone will be a living thing asserting itself with ever-growing insistency."[11]

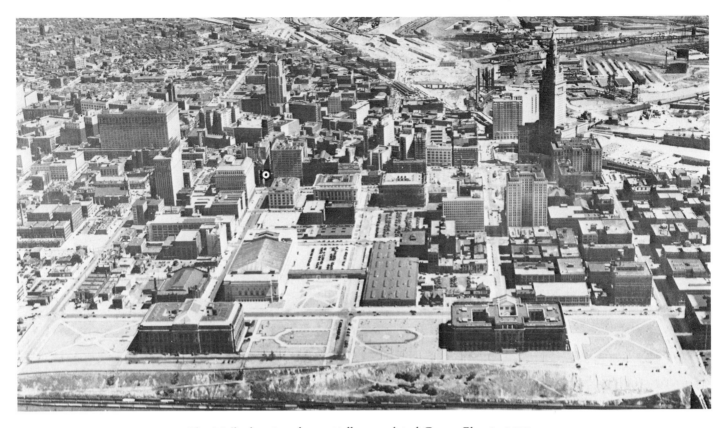

The Mall, showing the partially completed Group Plan in 1930.

Trinity Cathedral, Euclid Avenue at East 22nd Street, under construction, completed 1907, Charles F. Schweinfurth, architect.

## Architects in Transition — I

The existence of progressive and eclectic tendencies side by side in the architecture of this period is sometimes regarded as kind of schizophrenia. In actuality, the evidence suggests that architects found no discomfort in working with various styles simultaneously. It was an age when the harmonizing, or at least coexistence, of such transitional and apparently contradictory forms was commonplace. Ragtime music, for example, is based on strictly classical forms, but its syncopated rhythms were startling and appealing. A trained and responsive architect could prepare plans in any of the historical styles, and it is nearly impossible to speak of an architect's personal style during this period. Furthermore, if a modern work was recognized as having estimable values, they could easily become part of the classical architect's repertory. This situation can perhaps be best understood by examining the work of a particular architect such as J. Milton Dyer.

Dyer's career was unusual in that his most productive period encompassed only one decade (1900–1911). By 1906, however, he was so well established that *The Architectural Record* devoted a nineteen-page article to his work. It concluded by saying that "He has shown in his work flexibility, a sense of propriety, the utmost technical competence, executive ability, and the determination to remain true to his standards."[12] We have already seen the extremes of Dyer's work in the Beaux-Arts classicism of the City Hall and the expressive functionalism of the Brown Hoisting building. During the same decade he planned several other equally varied buildings. In 1904 the Brooklyn Savings & Loan Association erected a building on the corner of West 25th Street and Archwood, formerly in the village of Brooklyn before its annexation to Cleveland in 1894.[13] The bank building is a robust combination of diverse architectural elements. The general effect of symmetry and regularity is classical, but there is a deliberate crudity to the cornice brackets and entablature which can best be visualized by recalling the individual stamp of Philadelphia's Frank Furness. The deep-set segmental arches over each bay are also more of a late Victorian detail. Altogether it is a highly individual building.

Two buildings erected in 1904–1905 appeared to be more traditional, but only at first glance. The Tavern Club on East 36th Street and Prospect was an essay in the Northern Renaissance style. Originally organized in 1892 as a "rendezvous" for

Brooklyn Savings & Loan Association, West 25th Street and Archwood, 1904, J. Milton Dyer, architect.

Cleveland sportsmen and socialites, among them Harry K. Devereux, son of the Civil War general, and Charles A. Otis, Jr., stock broker and publisher, the downtown club was one of three built in this decade. The private club, both downtown and in the country, was beginning to influence the form of the upper-class residence in these years by moving formal entertaining out of the home, which could then become smaller and more livable. The new home of the Tavern Club opened on January 1, 1905.[14] Its most salient feature is a great hipped roof containing two stories of the four-story building. By combining this with giant gables on both facades and horizontal groups of small pane windows, a definitely Old World look is achieved. Nevertheless, the sophisticated composition of horizontal and vertical elements also owes something to contemporary developments, and the interior of the club is a functional, if somewhat sombre, social gathering place away from home.

Three months later, on March 26, 1905, the First Methodist Episcopal Church occupied its new $250,000 structure of Indiana limestone on Euclid at East 30th Street. When one remembers that the Methodist Church is an episcopal church with a succession of bishops, and that it had only recently started to develop from an evangelistic sect into a

Tavern Club, East 36th Street and Prospect Avenue, 1905, J. Milton Dyer, architect.

First Methodist Church, Euclid Avenue and East 30th Street, 1905, J. Milton Dyer, architect.

solid middle-class church, it is difficult to avoid the suspicion that the new church was designed specifically to rival the Trinity Episcopal Cathedral which was rising just two blocks away. It is more than coincidence that the external profile of Dyer's church is almost a duplicate of Schweinfurth's cathedral, although the interior was planned as a preaching auditorium instead of a Eucharistic sanctuary. The common exterior features are too obvious to ignore: the great square crossing tower with three lancets and corner pinnacles, the gabled facade with pinnacles, a traceried window, and a vestibule with three entrances, the transepts repeating the facade composition. On the interior, however, the aisled nave and altar are replaced with a sloping floor and curved auditorium seating extending into the transepts. The tower is fifty feet square on the interior and rises 100 feet above the floor. However, the typical "Akron plan," with the Sunday school opening into the sanctuary, was abandoned for this church. Thus the features of English Gothic architecture were ingeniously adapted for twentieth century Protestant worship.[15]

Between 1906 and 1909, Dyer designed two business buildings which are generally believed to show his acquaintance with Frank Lloyd Wright's Larkin Company office building in Buffalo (1904). The Peerless Motor Car Company plant was begun in 1906. Cleveland was eventually to rank with any other automobile manufacturing center, and the Peerless was one of the finest luxury class automobiles of the day. It was made until 1931, after which the plant was converted to a brewery and occupied by the Carling Brewing Company and more recently by C. Schmidt & Sons.[16] The facade of the plant administration building on Quincy Avenue at East 93rd Street is marked by two large brick piers topped with stone spheres, a direct reference to the Larkin building (demolished in 1950). The rectangular ornament of the attic facade is also Wrightian. A large curved entrance canopy attached to the piers shows the influence of Art Nouveau ornament. The basic character of the building is that of a well-planned industrial structure with brick piers and recessed spandrels providing the design. On the interior, the main lobby staircase is wrought iron with curvilinear Art Nouveau railings, and the rectangular stained glass patterns in some of the meeting rooms is of Wrightian or Arts and Crafts inspiration. It was not uncommon for Beaux-Arts trained architects to experiment with the Art Nouveau (as Whitney Warren did), and Dyer's

Peerless Motor Car Company (C. Schmidt & Sons), Quincy Avenue at East 93rd Street, 1906, J. Milton Dyer, architect.

decision to combine this experimentation with references to the recent work of Wright indicates a special power of assimilation.

The Sterling and Welch Company moved into its new store on Euclid Avenue east of 12th Street in 1909. Succeeding the earlier Beckwith, Sterling Company in 1889, it was a fine home furnishings store selling carpets, furniture, draperies, and wallpaper, with a large commercial gallery of decorative art. The new building contained a central light court surrounded by five stories of balconies. Simple flat piers rose through all five floors. The flat skylight had a small grid pattern with a decorative border.[17] While light courts were common, as we have seen, these features also describe the Larkin

Sterling and Welch Company light court, 1909,
J. Milton Dyer, architect.

building interior, and the similarities could not be
accidental. The proportions and spatial effect were
identical, although the Sterling and Welch interior
was more ornamental. The strict rectangularity of
Wright's interior was softened, as each bay was
spanned by a flattened arch, and decorative brackets,
medallions, and light fixtures adorned the balconies.
These variations reflect the difference between a fine
commercial interior and an office building. The
similarities suggest that Dyer's admiration for the
Wright building was not exhausted by his adaptation
of its facade on the Peerless plant.

In 1909 the Chamber of Commerce held a
Cleveland Industrial Exposition. It was planned by
manufacturers who "wanted Clevelanders to understand the message of stack, and hammer, and
wheel, and to realize the extent and variety and
quality of Cleveland-made products." F. F. Prentiss
was Chairman of the Exposition Committee and
Charles F. Brush was President of the Chamber of

Commerce. When it was found that existing public
halls would not hold the prospective exhibitors, a
temporary exhibition building was planned on the
site of the proposed city hall at the foot of East 6th
Street. The Central Armory, located just across the
street, provided additional exhibition space.[18]

The Exposition Building covered 72,030 square
feet of exhibit area. It was more than twice as large as
the arena floor of Stanford White's Madison Square
Garden (demolished in 1925) and larger than any
existing exposition structure in the United States.
To cover this area Milton Dyer devised a tent. The
outer walls were of wood covered with staff, and the
fireproofed canvas roof was supported on three steel
masts with radiating struts, rather like an umbrella,
supporting a network of steel cables which held the
roof. There was an exotic ornamental gateway at the
6th Street entrance, with plaster ornament
representing wheels, gears, and hammers. The
street approaches were elaborately decorated, and
the Exposition lighting was supplied by twenty
thousand electric lamps. Dyer also designed two
statues representing the "Spirit of Progress" which
stood at the approach beginning at Superior Avenue
and East 6th Street. The Exposition Building was
erected in forty-seven working days; unfortunately
the temporary nature of Milton Dyer's marvelous
tent has caused it to be all but forgotten.

A second private men's club was planned by Dyer's
firm and built in 1910–1911. The Cleveland Athletic
Club had been organized only two years earlier, but
its fast growing popularity made it possible to plan a
costly building with complete facilities. The structure was unique in that it was built upon an already
existing building which was under construction on
the southwest corner of Euclid and East 12th Street.
The framework had been completed to the fifth story
when the club decided to lease the sixth floor with
the right to build eleven stories on top of the
building. This arrangement had unique legal
features which attracted wide attention. The cost of
the new club was nearly half a million dollars.[19]

The building was designed to separate the social
and athletic functions. From the Euclid Avenue
entrance elevators run to all floors of the club. The
main lobby, reception, and service areas are on the
sixth and seventh floors, while the eighth, ninth, and
tenth floors contain private rooms, eighty sleeping
rooms, and baths. On the eleventh through the
fourteenth floors are the gymnasium and other
athletic rooms, including a spacious swimming pool.
The differentiation of these functions is clearly

Cleveland Industrial Exposition of 1909, entrance gateway and tent, J. Milton Dyer, architect.

Beaux-Arts civic monument, his dabbling in Art Nouveau and Wrightian idioms, and his adaptation of Tudor and English Gothic forms, it indicates that the architect's brief output was significant and original. At the same time, it was also characteristic of a period of flux and transition, of high standards and experimentation, and of the clash of old and new.

The first modern comprehensive building code was another product of this age of ferment, experimentation, and faith in legislative solutions to social problems. It was created by city ordinance on

Cleveland Athletic Club, Euclid Avenue near East 12th Street, 1911, J. Milton Dyer, architect.

expressed in the exterior architecture of the building, which is faced in white terra cotta. The first seven floors have a single window to each bay, the next four floors have two, and the upper athletic floors have three-part windows which make a traceried frieze around the top of the building.

The development of large and complex structures meant that architectural firms also became larger and more complicated, and often it is very difficult to determine who was the actual designer of a particular building. In the case of the Cleveland Athletic Club, two of Dyer's assistants, Frank R. Walker and Harry E. Weeks, were the principal designer and the job supervisor. During these years, according to acquaintances of Dyer, his social habits became more and more erratic, sometimes keeping him away from the office for days and even weeks at a time. In 1911 and 1912 many of the younger men left him, and Walker and Weeks formed their own partnership, which was to become one of the most successful in Cleveland's architectural scene.[20]

The Cleveland Athletic Club was considered to be years ahead of its time. Taken together with Dyer's mastery of industrial and exhibition space, his major

June 20, 1904, after more than a year's work by John Eisenmann, engineer of the Arcade. Other cities had had building laws of various kinds; Cleveland's first was passed in 1888. Eisenmann studied many of these, but finally rejected the idea of using any one as a model for Cleveland. He found that they were confused and patched together, many having been created specifically as a response to a particular disaster. Eisenmann therefore began with the fundamental premises of safety, public benefit, and the current state of building knowledge, and from these evolved the first "scientific" comprehensive code.

The Building Code of 1904 contained five major sections. The first was administrative. It created a department of building, specified the duties of inspectors in six areas according to structure, listed the regulations on permits and drawings, and provided for the process of appeal. The second section, by far the longest, specified the rules applying to the erection of buildings and structures. These were written in minute detail, but arranged with impeccable logic and good sense. The third section dealt with the relation of the building to its site, both the permanent situation and the occupation of public right of way during construction. The next section was entirely on fire protection, and the last a separate section on elevators.[21]

Writing about the code in 1906, Eisenmann observed that while they had begun with the idea of making a code for Cleveland, the commission "to its surprise had evolved a model for the National Building Code in the country . . . . Twenty-nine cities have already used it as a model in formulating their building codes, with several more to hear from."[22] There were also inquiries from foreign countries. Some critics found that the code was excessive in length (it ran over 200 pages), and that many items were too specifically prescribed, leaving no discretion to the builder. Eisenmann pointed out that this was a positive virtue, as it meant that no one could be favored because of position or influence, and all would be treated alike. He stated that no one was happier than the officials who had to administer the code, precisely because they were relieved of requests for interpretation and "discretion." From these observations one can perceive another manifestation of the "radical democracy" of the city, and another confirmation of the fact that Cleveland was leading the rest of the country in its idea of municipality.

## The Downtown Grows Out

J. Milton Dyer was not the only one to be aware of recent work of the Chicago architects. The Cleveland firm of Knox and Elliot paid homage to Louis Sullivan when they designed the Rockefeller Building, a seventeen-story office building erected by John D. Rockefeller in 1903–1905. Previously standing on the site at the corner of Superior and West 6th Street was the historic Weddell House hotel (1847), where President-elect Lincoln had addressed Cleveland citizens en route to his inaugural in Washington in 1861. Upon its completion in 1905, the Rockefeller Building housed offices of iron, coal, and lake shipping concerns. The original structure consisted of the seven bays at the West 6th Street corner of the Superior facade. In 1910 an additional four bays in the same design were added to the west. The name was changed to the Kirby Building in 1920 when Josiah Kirby became the owner. Rockefeller, angered by the change, bought the building back and restored his name in 1923.[23]

Wilm Knox and John H. Elliot practiced together from 1894 to 1915, although the firm name continued for another dozen years under Elliot alone. Knox was a native of Scotland and had practiced in Edinburgh before coming to the United States in 1886. He went to Chicago, where he worked in the office of Burnham and Root and was later the office manager for Henry Ives Cobb. This explains his interest in the Chicago School upon coming to Cleveland in 1893.

When designing the Rockefeller Building, Knox and Elliot must also have looked at Louis Sullivan's Guaranty (Prudential) Building in Buffalo (1895), although their adaptation of Sullivan's esthetic was belated in the architectural world of 1905. The functional or "Sullivanesque" treatment of vertical mullions and slightly recessed spandrels which express the steel cage construction is apparent. Moreover, the scheme and the ornamentation of the lower stories and the entrance is very similar to the Buffalo building. However, there is a difference in the use of the interlacing organic-geometric ornament. Sullivan's ornament was placed in such a way as to complement and heighten the awareness of the underlying structure, whereas the ornament on the Rockefeller Building is drawn over the surfaces of the lower stories like a textured tapestry. On the upper stories the surfaces are perfectly plain, and the structure is even more frankly expressed than in the Sullivan building.

The Caxton Building, completed in 1900, could also be called Sullivanesque. Planned by Frank Barnum for Ambrose Swasey, it housed the commercial printing and graphic arts trades. Named for William Caxton, the first British printer in the fifteenth century, it was occupied in 1905 by the business which subsequently became the World Publishing Company. Some of the floors in the rear part of the building were constructed to bear unusually heavy loads in order to accommodate printing presses. Although only eight stories tall, in its upper stories the Caxton Building is one of the finest examples of the clear expression of the skeletal frame. A large Romanesque portal on Huron Road is adorned with a kind of foliated ornament which does not really derive from either Richardson or Sullivan, but which marks a transition from Barnum's Historical Society building.[24]

The Caxton Building is more than twice as far from Public Square as the Rockefeller Building. The fact that large commercial structures were going up as far out as East 9th and East 12th Streets was already considered in 1900 to be a threat to the residential character of Euclid Avenue. The Rose Building was erected on the corner of East 9th and Prospect in 1900 and the Schofield Building on the southwest corner of Euclid and East 9th in 1902.

When the First Methodist Church moved all the way out Euclid to East 30th Street, they sold their former site on the opposite corner of East 9th Street to the Cleveland Trust Company. The granite temple built by the Cleveland Trust in 1905–1908 demonstrates, as Dyer and others were doing, that eclectic architects were inventive and not merely imitative. George B. Post & Sons developed a plan within the Beaux-Arts tradition that achieved an ingenious solution to several problems. The site was an irregular trapezium; the space was too small to permit a free-standing portico or colossal orders; and the activities of modern banking required a complex plan. These problems were specified in the instructions to the competing architects. Post's solution was the construction of a rotunda with an uneven number of bays (thirteen), thus providing a bay on the axis of each entrance, as well as a bay on the axis of the corner, which formed the entrance to the officers' quarters. The bank is essentially an irregular three-story office building wrapped around the rotunda. The central space is sixty-one feet in

Rockefeller Building, Superior Avenue at West 6th Street, 1905, Knox and Elliot, architects.

Caxton Building, 812 Huron Road, 1900, Frank S. Barnum, architect.

Cleveland Trust Company, Euclid and East 9th Street, 1908, George B. Post & Sons, architects.

Floor plans, Statler Hotel, Euclid Avenue at East 12th Street, 1912, George B. Post & Sons, architects. (*Architectural Review*)

Typical Floor Plan

First Mezzanine Floor Plan

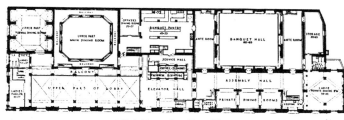

First Floor Plan

diameter and eighty-five feet in height and is covered by a luminous dome of stained glass. The exterior style is based on the Italian Renaissance, and the pediments contain sculpture by Viennese-born Karl Bitter depicting an allegory of the sources of wealth. The temple porticoes are suggested but are engaged to the walls, in a treatment similar to the one Post had used on the New York Stock Exchange (1904). There is no sense of distortion in the way the classical forms adjust to the acute corner, and the effect must have been even more imposing before the bank was overshadowed by the taller structures of the growing downtown.[25]

In a letter written to Ambassador Myron T. Herrick in Paris in June, 1912, Mrs. Edward A. Merritt pasted a number of snapshots showing views up and down Euclid Avenue. They are especially revealing of the rapidly changing scene beyond East 9th Street. Mrs. Merritt commented on John H. Brown's "famous empty building" just east of 9th Street.[26] Sterling and Welch had moved into their new building east of 12th Street in 1909, while the Cleveland Athletic Club on the corner of 12th Street was occupied in 1911. The Halle Brothers Company, a women's ready-to-wear and fur store founded in 1891, moved into its new store east of

12th Street in 1910. A forthright skeletal structure with elegant terra cotta ornamentation, the Halle building was designed by Henry Bacon and completed just the year before he received the commission for the Lincoln Memorial in Washington, D.C. The addition doubling its size, in the location between the original section and the Athletic Club, was constructed in 1914.[27]

On the northwest corner of East 12th Street the first portion of the Hotel Statler was opened in 1912. The 1,000-room hotel was designed by George B. Post & Sons, with Charles Schneider, who would later make his own reputation as a residential architect, as supervisor. According to his biographer, Post was "one of those responsible for the development of the typical modern hotel plan, with its hundreds of rooms, each with bath, and a monumental suite of public rooms below—all arranged to give the maximum income through the leasing of shops and concessions. . . . In the Statler Hotel, Cleveland (1911–1912), the type found its first complete expression."[28] Following Post's death in 1913, his sons designed a number of other Statler hotels in other cities.

On the northeast corner of Euclid and East 12th Street stood the other large private men's club of the period, the Union Club designed by Charles Schweinfurth. One of the most influential gathering places in the history of Cleveland, the club had been organized in 1872 and united "men of influence and ambition as a social and intellectual force in the community." Members at various times included Marcus A. Hanna, James A. Garfield, Myron T. Herrick, Charles F. Brush, Ambrose Swasey, Liberty Holden, Samuel Mather, and William G. Mather. The 12th Street property was acquired in 1901 and the club opened in December, 1905. The entrance lobby leads to a great stairhall, and the principal main floor lounge, paneled in dark walnut with a twenty-two foot ceiling, occupies the Euclid Avenue end of the building. There are a main dining room-ballroom, also paneled in walnut with tall Corinthian pilasters, billiard and recreation rooms, a library, various other facilities, and member's sleeping rooms and baths. The exterior appearance gives no hint of all these functions; it is a sandstone Renaissance palace. The entrance porch and third floor balcony, the clearly marked stories, and the heavy overhanging cornice convincingly recall a sixteenth century Roman facade. Such a design was

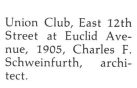

Union Club, East 12th Street at Euclid Avenue, 1905, Charles F. Schweinfurth, architect.

Samuel Mather house, 2605 Euclid Avenue, 1910, Charles F. Schweinfurth, architect.

unusual for Schweinfurth, who was more at home in the medieval modes. It was undoubtedly inspired by the University Club in New York (1899) by McKim, Mead & White, and by the general impetus which that firm gave to the numerous variations on Renaissance styles. One club member, in fact, dissenting from the Schweinfurth plans, asked Stanford White to draw alternate plans on a speculative basis. Nevertheless, Schweinfurth's club is a solid, handsome, and satisfying Renaissance Revival design.[29]

Still farther out, at East 22nd Street, was the site selected by Trinity Church for its new buildings. Trinity had become the cathedral of the Episcopal bishop in 1890, and the building of a cathedral church still had a great symbolic significance. It was built as a center of worship for the metropolis; it was intended to embody the idea of the permanence of the church; and it was meant to stand as "a benediction . . . to charity and to humanity." Charles F. Schweinfurth had been chosen as architect for Trinity Parish in 1890, and the Parish House was completed in 1895. At the same time, Schweinfurth was preparing plans for the main church. His original concept was Romanesque, and the idea evolved through several plans into the Gothic structure that finally was erected, apparently as a result of the consensus of the building committee. The final plan was accepted by the vestry in January, 1895. Construction did not begin until 1901, however, and the completed building was consecrated on September 24, 1907.[30]

Trinity Cathedral is one of the very earliest examples of the late Gothic Revival, as distinguished from the early nineteenth century Gothic revivals. The first joint work of the theorists and leaders of the movement, Ralph Adams Cram and Bertram Goodhue (All Saints Church in Ashmont, Massachusetts), had only been built in 1894. The chief source of the late Gothic Revival was the English Perpendicular style, and in Trinity every attempt was made to create the plan and effect of an English Gothic cathedral.[31] The plan is cruciform, with the choir being nearly as long as the nave, which is divided into three aisles by arcades. The spaces of the nave, choir, and transepts are clearly articulated into separate compartments. The chancel wall is flat rather than apsidal as in the French Gothic. The ceiling consists of wooden barrel vaulting supported by heavily molded ribs. The narthex projects beyond the facade wall, forming an entrance screen, and is entered through three recessed portals. The Cathedral is built of solid masonry construction, the exterior walls being of Indiana limestone. The bell-tower over the crossing is forty feet square, and its corner pinnacles reach to 125 feet, considerably topping those of the First Methodist Church at East 30th Street. All of the interior furnishings were executed in conformity with the design of the building. The altar and reredos, choir stalls, pulpit and lectern, executed in marble and oak, create a unity which gives a genuinely exalted character to the church, considered by many to be Schweinfurth's masterpiece.

Leonard C. Hanna house, Euclid Avenue, 1904 (demolished), Stanford White, architect.

There is an apocryphal but often repeated story to the effect that when the "magnificent" plans were shown to the building committee, it was learned that the cost would exceed the funds available by a million dollars. After the meeting adjourned, Samuel Mather is said to have pondered the matter and then announced, "I'll give the million dollars." However, in a complete description of the Cathedral written for the dedication, Schweinfurth wrote, "Five years have been consumed in the structural work, and the total cost has been approximately $650,000. To the value of about $100,000 has already been contributed in memorial furnishings for the Cathedral." It is true that the central tower, which might otherwise not have been built, was made possible by a gift of Samuel Mather.[32]

It was still fashionable in the 1900s to build a mansion on Euclid Avenue beyond East 22nd Street. Samuel Mather and Schweinfurth were brought together once again for the building of Mather's town house at 2605 Euclid. On the other hand, Leonard C. Hanna, brother of Mark Hanna, went to New York for his architect and commissioned Cleveland's only building from America's most famous architect of the period, Stanford White. The two houses, side by side, epitomized two extremes of the academic eclecticism of the decade, Tudor and Neo-Classic. The Mather house was built between 1907 and 1910. It will be remembered that Schweinfurth's Flora Stone Mather building at the university

was begun in 1910, and there are striking similarities in the bay windows of the college and the house, as well as in the brick and stone trim, apparent on the wings of the college building. Otherwise, the house has the fundamentally cubic look developed in Schweinfurth's own house, and the crenellated roof line was replaced by a classical parapet.

The Hanna house, built in 1904, was basically a Georgian Revival mansion of yellow brick with quoins, a steep hip roof, and a roof balustrade. The porch of four giant fluted Corinthian columns was a Neo-Classic feature. In plan, both houses were arranged around a great central hallway with an imposing staircase and a major entrance from a side driveway. Both were enriched with carved paneling of mahogany and oak. Both had a long servants' wing extending to the rear, making them deeper on the lot than the facade they presented to the street. In these and other features both mansions were still essentially late nineteenth century houses, and the last of that breed to be built on "Millionaire's Row." Mrs. Mather died in 1909 before the house was completed. After Mather's death in 1931, it was occupied by the Cleveland Institute of Music until 1940, then by the headquarters of the Cleveland Automobile Club until 1967, and more recently by Cleveland State University. The Hanna house was the home of the Cleveland Museum of Natural History from 1921 until 1957, when it was demolished to make way for the Innerbelt expressway.[33]

## Neighborhood Buildings — II

For another class of residents, the years at the turn of the century saw a veritable explosion in the building of apartments, flats, and "terraces" or row houses. In 1900 there were only a handful of apartment houses listed in the city business directory; in 1910 there were over 750, plus nearly 200 terraces. The Cleveland Architectural Club observed, "Within the past four or five years many modern flats and apartment houses have been built in Cleveland, of varying degrees of design and construction. The pure investment idea, of a quick and large return upon a small invested capital, has too largely dominated and a consequent cheap construction has resulted in many cases."[34] A brief glance at a few examples of the entire range of apartment building shows the same indiscriminate mingling of stylistic treatments and rational planning which characterized the development of the downtown architecture.

One of the first "high-rise" apartment houses must have been the Jennings Apartments on Jennings Avenue (West 14th Street), not far from Pelton Park, which had been renamed Lincoln Square in 1896. Jennings Avenue was a fine residential street when the apartment was built in 1898. The Jennings was only six stories tall, but it boasted an elevator. Its yellow brick walls are impressively simple and, together with the corbelled parapet and two ranks of bay windows, are related to some of the best Commercial Style buildings. The apartment house was designed by John N. Richardson, whose partnership with Cudell had dissolved in 1891.[35]

*top right*: Jennings Apartment (The Argonne), 2711 West 14th Street, 1898, John N. Richardson, architect.

*above*: Alhambra Apartments, Wade Park Avenue at East 86th Street, 1902, Searles & Hirsh, architects.

*left*: Colonial Apartments, Euclid Avenue at East 70th Street, 1901, Edward E. Smith, architect.

Oppmann Terrace,
West 102nd Place, 1905,
Andrew W. Oppmann,
builder.

The walls of the Colonial Apartments on Euclid Avenue are even more highly articulated by the ranks of projecting bays marching along the elevation on East 70th Street. The front is further enlivened by recessed balconies framed with semicircular arches. The elliptical fanlights over the entrances evidently inspired the "Colonial" name. The architect was Edward E. Smith, who designed many other multi-dwelling units including the Emrose Terrace, an interesting U-shaped group just two blocks away on Cedar Avenue.

If a Spanish medieval flavor was fancied, architects Searles and Hirsh provided it in The Alhambra (1902). Five square towers were projected above the roof of the four-story building, supported on machicolations to give the effect of a fortress, and topped off with pyramidal roofs. This provided a suitably monumental yellow brick facade for the upper middle-class inhabitants of the middle East Side. The same design was repeated on the West Side at Franklin Avenue and West 57th Street and called the Franklin Apartments.[36]

The "pure investment idea" and an enlightened approach to an irregular piece of property were combined in a unique development at West 101st Street between Detroit and Madison Avenues. The investor-contractor of the block erected in 1905 was Andrew W. Oppmann, retired president of the Oppmann Brewing Company. His architect or builder is not known.[37] Oppmann Terrace is a continuous row of sixty-eight two-story dwelling units with a single facade approximately 1,100 feet long. The land slopes almost imperceptibly upward from Detroit to Madison, and each unit of four apartments is slightly stepped up, making a pleasing variation in the front elevation. The architectural style is very plain. Segmental-arched windows and corbelled cornices reflect the commonest builders' commercial vernacular of the day. Each pair of entrances has a front porch with spindle posts. The matching block at the south end across a sixty foot wide court (formerly West 102nd Place) is only about one-fourth as long, seeming to be part of another incomplete row. The overall effect is unusually agreeable for an obviously economical income-producing structure, but one that was laid out with a rare regard for the possibilities of land use.

The various types of commercial building could also be found anywhere in Cleveland in 1910, when the city extended from West 117th Street to East 172nd Street. South Brooklyn Village and Glenville City had been annexed in 1905 and the Village of Collinwood in 1910. As these localities were incorporated into the city, activity continued to revolve around their older commercial centers, and in the first decade of the century such business centers and neighborhoods began to assume the definitive shape that they would have for the next forty years. The same process of consolidation was also taking place in older centers. Just east of the

intersection of Euclid Avenue and East 55th Street, an area long established as a commercial and industrial section by the location of the railroad station there, a number of new commercial buildings were erected. The Victorian Italianate blocks on the southwest corner of 55th Street have survived to the hundred-year mark. Between the railroad and East 57th Street there were also some fine examples of the commercial building of the eighties, with its polychromatic brick and stone, and the nineties, with its vertical ranks of bay windows. A six-story office building on the northeast corner of 57th Street built by the Equity Savings & Loan Company in 1905 was designed by Hubbell and Benes in the current commercial classic idiom.[38]

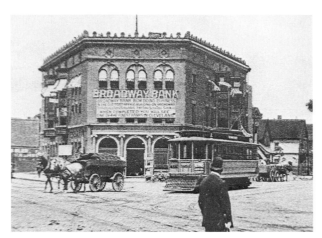

Many of the older commercial intersections became the centers of immigrant neighborhoods. The height of the European immigration came in this decade, and 80 percent of Cleveland's population were either foreign-born or had foreign parents, with peoples from Germany, Great Britain, Russia, Italy, and Austro-Hungary making up the largest new groups. However, their neighborhoods still exhibited no national architectural character. For example, Broadway and East 55th Street was the crossroad of the Bohemian community, where various family stores and offices, frequently with a second-story residence, were located. On three corners of the five-way intersection stand a moving picture theater and apartment building (1912), an older savings and loan company (1891), and the Broadway Bank. All display a generalized commercial vernacular with standard classical ornament. The local public library donated by Andrew Carnegie was built on the northwest corner behind the bank in

*top*: Euclid Avenue at East 57th Street, 1885-1905.

*center*: Corner of Broadway and East 55th Street, ca. 1901.

*bottom*: Hruby Conservatory (1917), Steffens & Steffens, architects, and Broadway Free Library (1905), Charles Morris, architect, Broadway near East 55th Street.

Our Lady of Lourdes Roman Catholic School (1907), Emile Uhlrich, architect, and Church (1891), East 54th Street near Broadway.

Cleveland Worsted Mills, Broadway at East 59th Street, 1909, George S. Rider Company, engineers.

1905. A decagon with a domed central lobby surrounded by reading rooms, it has a brick and stone exterior detailed in such a way that the classical Carnegie library look is unmistakable. It was designed by Charles Morris, the Beaux-Arts trained architect and associate of Lehman and Schmitt who worked on the County Courthouse plans.

One block west of the intersection was the parish church, Our Lady of Lourdes. Built in 1891, this Victorian Gothic church became the focus of the Bohemian population. An unusual feature of the next-door parish school, built in 1907 in the Renaissance Revival style, is the open recessed porch in the base of its Italian tower. A few years later (1917), the Hruby brothers, a noted Cleveland musical family, built their music conservatory one block northwest on Broadway. The charming brick and terra cotta building, in a rather more

thoroughgoing early Renaissance style, has a store front on Broadway and the school entrance from a side areaway.[39]

Three blocks to the southeast on Broadway sprawled the Cleveland Worsted Mills. Nothing could be a clearer illustration of the fact that residential, commercial, and industrial uses were indiscriminately mixed in the circumstances of unprecedented urban growth with its characteristic lack of zoning and planned land use. Few industrial structures attained the status of architecture, but the Cleveland Worsted Mills was a modest exception. The company had grown out of a small mill established by Joseph Turner & Sons in 1878, and would become one of the largest manufacturers of woolen goods in the field.[40] Built in three stages, the factory was given a brick facing that enhances the expressed supporting structure. The segmental arches of the lower two-story bays relate to the scale of the street. The most attractive detail is the rounded corners of the banded brick piers, which give a molded look to the structure.

Other immigrant neighborhoods were characterized by the same building types and architectural styles, and usually the church was the chief structure with any claim to architectural distinction. Centered around East 79th Street and Holton Avenue was the Hungarian community, which built the modest stone First Hungarian Reformed Church in 1904 and the two-story brick First Hungarian Lutheran Bible School on Rawlings Avenue in 1907. On Scranton Avenue near Clark, the German congregation of St. Michael's built a new parochial school in 1906. Its sculptured, ornamented mass and open lantern tower make it one of the most lavish and European-looking of the eclectic Gothic buildings in Cleveland. The school

St. Michael's Roman Catholic School, Scranton Road, 1906, Emile Uhlrich, architect.

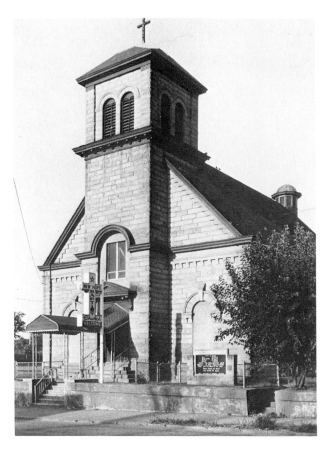

First Hungarian Reformed Church (Second New Hope Baptist Church), East 79th Street, 1904, Paul Matzinger, architect.

was planned by Emile Uhlrich, designer of the Art Nouveau J. L. Hudson store, and illustrates the versatility of the eclectic architect.[41]

Eastern European Jews continued to settle near Scovill Avenue between East 22nd and East 55th Streets, and three historic synagogues were built within a two-year period (1904–1906) and survived into the 1970s. The Anshe Emeth synagogue on East 37th Street and Longwood, and the Oheb Zedek synagogue at East 38th Street and Scovill (renamed Community College Avenue), were both erected by Orthodox congregations opposed to the more liberal Reform and Conservative movements. Both temples are medieval in style. While one has pointed arches and the other round ones, there are striking similarities in the disposition of their building elements, the most obvious being the twin facade towers with corner turrets. The Conservative B'nai Jeshurun Congregation moved from its Eagle Street Synagogue to a new temple on East 55th Street and

Scovill in 1906.[42] Its building, however, is Neo-Classic, with a portico of six Corinthian columns and a golden saucer cupola and lantern on a windowed drum. Because of the centralized emphasis, B'nai Jeshurun is more related in spatial concept to the Temple built a dozen years earlier by Tifereth Israel, a Reform congregation. Furthermore, the classical style used in religious structures was taken to symbolize rationalism and enlightenment. For these reasons, it is interesting to speculate whether the more "modern" idiom was purposely chosen by the non-Orthodox synagogue as being more appropriate to its beliefs.

In the newly annexed Collinwood Village section, the mixture of residential, commercial, and industrial uses was again dramatically demonstrated. The main axis of the old village was East 152nd Street (old Collamer Street), and the commercial area was centered between Pepper and Aspinwall Avenues. The location, size, and type of commercial and community buildings were very similar to those in the older Cleveland areas, and a non-native would be hard pressed to discern significant differences. To the north, however, the extensive yards of the Lake Shore and Michigan Southern Railway cut a vast swath through the residential area of north Collinwood. They included a roundhouse, locomotive machine shops, passenger and freight car shops, coaling tower, various other shops, mills, and storehouses, and a new administration building on East 152nd Street. The yards were intensively developed and expanded in the early 1900s and eventually included over 120 miles of track.[43]

North of the yards (later separated from south Collinwood by the shoreway) was the Collinwood Memorial School, built in 1909–1910 and planned by Frank S. Barnum. It was erected following the disastrous North Collinwood School fire of 1908 in which 172 children were lost and epitomizes the modern type of school developed by Barnum after he was appointed school architect in 1895. The school featured fireproof construction and more functional planning, but the most visible external characteristic was the flat roof. It also belonged to the first generation of school buildings in which all classrooms were lighted from one side only, necessitating some blank exterior walls. The Memorial School made a virtue of this necessity by displaying ornamental brick patterns set in the end walls.[44]

The kind of neighborhood housing that came to form the matrix for school, church, store, and

*top*: Anshe Emeth Synagogue (Zion Hill Baptist Church), East 37th Street and Longwood, 1904, Albert F. Janowitz, architect.

*bottom*: B'nai Jeshurun Temple (Shiloh Baptist Church), East 55th Street and Scovill Avenue, 1906, Harry Cone, architect.

95

factory was already being criticized by the Cleveland Architectural Club in 1900:

> The contractor still designs (?). Since 1885 a *building*, not *architectural*, feature has developed, which . . . is not indigenous, nor confined to Cleveland, i.e., the real estate, "buy-a-home-on-monthly-payment" house. The idea is all right, but why is it necessary to line street after street with ill designed, poorly constructed, gaudily decorated, duplicate houses, for which the unsuspecting investor pays a comparatively big price? [45]

The pace of this type of building was accelerated enormously in the early 1900s. Cleveland's population in 1900 was 381,768. By 1910 it was 560,663, making Cleveland the sixth largest city in the nation. In order to accommodate nearly 179,000 people (a 47 percent increase), the speculative developer flourished. By the end of the decade, for all practical purposes, the city was built up to the existing city limits. The pattern of platted subdivisions (usually no more than a few streets in one direction and three or four blocks in the other) is familiar. Duplicate or nearly identical houses were erected on speculation and sold on a mortgage. They march up and down the streets, row upon row, literally by the thousands. Neighborhoods have a similar appearance whether on the East Side or the West Side, and whether inhabited by Russians, Italians, Jews, Poles, or Czechs, these houses fulfilled a portion of the "American Dream" of equality.

Almost without exception the developers' houses were wooden. The typical house was two-and-a-half stories tall with its gable end toward the street and a front porch of one or two stories. Sometimes variety was introduced by an overhanging attic gable, a bay window, classical porch columns, or occasional contractor's ornament derived from the "Queen Anne" idiom. Later on more individuality was attempted by the application of imitation brick asphalt shingle or aluminum siding, an enclosed porch, metal awnings, or varied color schemes. Lewis Mumford, speaking of the speculative development, has observed that "capitalist enterprise, hypnotized by its own preoccupation with gain, over-reached itself, for an overcrowded plan does not necessarily bring maximum return immediately, nor is it likely to remain sound and attractive enough to ensure profitable exploitation during a long period of years." [46] Nevertheless, these

*top*: Collinwood Memorial School, East 152nd Street, 1910, Frank S. Barnum, architect.

*left*: Typical developer's houses, 1895, East 86th Street.

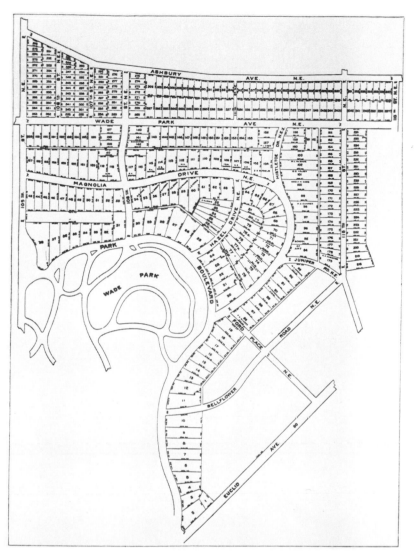

Plan of the Wade Park Allotment, 1918.

houses made homes for three generations of urban dwellers and three-quarters of a century later remained stable and livable in many areas because of devoted maintenance.

There were subdivisions for the well-to-do as well. The Wade Park Allotment near the emerging East Side cultural center saw the building of many excellent early twentieth century residences. The property was developed by Jeptha Wade III and extended from East 105th to East 115th Street, and from East Boulevard to Ashbury Avenue north of Wade Park Avenue. The streets, of which Magnolia Drive was the main stem, were laid out before 1892, but the residences were largely built between 1905 and 1915. Going from south to north, the order of the streets indicated the status of the residents. The very wealthy lived on East Boulevard, the well-to-do on Magnolia Drive, and the upper middle-class on

Wade Park Avenue. Typical residents included Amasa S. Mather and Samuel Livingston Mather, Edmund S. Burke, governor of the Federal Reserve Bank, Francis K. Glidden, an officer of the Glidden Varnish Company, Gordon Morrill, a physician, and Justin Sholes, an executive of Ohio Chemical and Manufacturing.[47]

The architecture of the Wade Park homes was different from that of the earlier mansions on Euclid Avenue. The houses were designed for a different scale of entertaining and living, and many of them partook of the character of an indigenous suburban type that was developing in the first decade of the century, having a basically horizontal look, with the long facade facing the street. Others displayed details from various eclectic sources, such as Georgian Revival, Tudor, and even French Renaissance. More to the point, however, is the fact

Gordon Morrill house, 1025
Magnolia Drive, 1915,
Charles F. Schweinfurth,
architect.

Edmund S. Burke
house, 11125 Magnolia
Drive, 1910, J. Milton
Dyer, architect.

Mrs. John Hay residence,
10915 East Boulevard, 1910,
Abram Garfield, architect.

that these houses were architect-designed. Charles Schweinfurth, for example, produced an untypical design for Dr. Morrill's house (1915). Stylistically, it is in the Neo-Adamesque mode of the Georgian Revival, resembling very closely the Boston and Salem houses of Charles Bulfinch and Samuel McIntire. One of J. Milton Dyer's few residential commissions was Edmund Burke's forty-two room mansion built in 1910 and acquired by the Cleveland Music School Settlement in 1937. It was planned to fit the angle at the intersection of Magnolia Drive and Mistletoe Drive and represents a very free adaptation of an English manor house. Meade and Hamilton, a Cleveland firm whose Cleveland Heights residences provide a case study in the development of the suburban house of the period, designed the home of Justin Sholes, son-in-law of Sylvester T. Everett.[48]

An architect who designed several of the best homes was Abram Garfield (1872–1958). The son of President Garfield, he was educated in New England and attended the Massachusetts Institute of Technology, then travelled abroad and settled in Cleveland in 1897. From 1898 to 1905 he was the partner of Frank B. Meade, after which he opened his own office. Garfield was also a member of the Group Plan committee charged with directing that undertaking. The Wade Park homes were among his early residential work. The most important was the house built for Mrs. John Hay, widow of the author, statesman, and Secretary of State under Presidents McKinley and Theodore Roosevelt. Hay had died in 1905, and his widow, who was also the daughter of Amasa Stone and the sister of Flora Stone Mather, never actually lived in the house. However, the mark of her consultation with the architect is evident. Portions of the woodwork from the old Hay house (1876) on Euclid Avenue were incorporated into the new house, including the long walnut hall staircase by Bavarian woodcarver John Herkommer. On the original plans, elevations of the rooms contain several marginal notes by Mrs. Hay directing Garfield to eliminate much of the suggested ornament. The interiors, although generous, are more domestic in scale than those of earlier mansions. The exterior design is a chaste Renaissance palace with a symmetrical facade and seven arched openings on the ground floor. The house was much larger than it appeared from the street, having a U-shaped plan enclosing a rear garden in the Italian style. The building represents a collaboration between an excellent architect and a woman of discriminating

Amasa Stone Chapel, Western Reserve University, 1911, Henry Vaughan, architect. (*Case Western Reserve University Archives*)

and highly refined taste. Although begun in 1908, it was not occupied until it became the residence of Price McKinney, president of the McKinney Steel Company, in 1918. It was acquired for the museum of the Western Reserve Historical Society in 1938.[49]

Clara Stone Hay and Flora Stone Mather donated the Amasa Stone Chapel of Western Reserve University in memory of their father in 1911. Located on Euclid Avenue across from Wade Park, it was designed by Henry Vaughan of Boston and built of Indiana limestone at a cost of $168,000. A keystone bearing the carved head of Amasa Stone, taken from the old Union Depot on the lakefront which Stone had built in 1866, was placed over the rear entrance. The chapel was designed in the late Gothic Revival style in a more scholarly approach to the fourteenth-century Gothic. It is instructive to note that the Mathers' library contained many books on European and especially medieval architecture, including one by Ralph Adams Cram.[50]

Church of the Covenant (Euclid Avenue Presbyterian Church), 11205 Euclid Avenue, 1909-1911, Cram, Goodhue & Ferguson, architects.

In fact, there are two churches in Cleveland by Cram, Goodhue & Ferguson, although Emmanuel Episcopal Church on Euclid at East 87th Street was not completely finished according to their plans. In the Euclid Avenue Presbyterian Church (later Church of the Covenant) a number of the social, economic, and architectural forces of the decade were joined. The rapid expansion of the business districts was swallowing up parishes, with the result that churches either had to follow their membership or become "downtown" institutional churches. In 1905 there were eleven Presbyterian churches between Public Square and East 107th Street; within twenty-five years these were reduced to five by union or removal. In 1906 the Euclid Avenue Church and Beckwith Memorial Church merged, and it was decided to move eastward to the site near Wade Park and the Women's College campus. The sale of the old Euclid Avenue site at East 14th Street brought $300,000, making it possible to erect the magnificent Gothic structure by Ralph Adams Cram in 1909–1911. In 1920, after another merger with the Second Presbyterian Church, the name was changed to Church of the Covenant.[51]

As the philosopher of the late Gothic Revival, Cram endeavored to "express the nature of the Presbyterian Church in beautiful and historical forms." The style was the "early and simple Gothic of England and Scotland." The Euclid Avenue front is a great arch enclosing a rose window and a portal below, flanked by octagonal turrets. The 140-foot tower stands at the intersection of the north end of the sanctuary with the parish house. Cram described the sixty-six foot tall nave as "broad, unbroken by columns, covered . . . by an open timber roof. . . . The severity of an otherwise rectangular interior" was relieved by transepts with deep galleries. The exterior was constructed of Indiana limestone and the interior finished with stone, tile, marble, wrought iron, Philippine mahogany, and white oak. Cram's local associate architect was John W. C. Corbusier, a national authority on church architecture and the designer of many notable churches throughout the Midwest. In 1930–1931 the chancel was redesigned by Cram & Ferguson and rebuilt with a new organ and handsome reredos. Cleveland architect Alexander C. Robinson was vice-chairman of the building committee and the local supervising architect.[52]

## To the Suburbs

University Circle, which now refers to the entire cultural center, was originally the name of an actual traffic circle. Located just east of 107th Street, the circle was one of the features in the widening and relocation of Euclid Avenue in order to provide easier access to the Heights. It was the joint conception of Patrick Calhoun and John Hartness Brown, builder of the ill-fated Brown Building.

Calhoun was the grandson of statesman John C. Calhoun and an attorney and developer of real estate and public utilities. According to various accounts, it was Brown who showed Calhoun the land on the Heights above Edgehill Road, and together they conceived the access from University Circle through Cedar Glen. It seemed obvious to both men that the farmland on the Heights was the ideal location for a new suburban "village" development. The land consisted of about 300 acres extending from the base of the bluff east to Coventry Road, and from Mayfield Road on the north to Cedar Road on the south. Ernest W. Bowditch, noted Boston landscape architect, was employed to make the plans for platting the land. At the same time Bowditch was working on the comprehensive Cleveland park plan which he had made for the development of Gordon Park, Wade Park, and Rockefeller Park.

The Euclid Heights development (now a part of Cleveland Heights) was conceived as a rural village "with straight streets to carry the traffic, curving boulevards that followed the natural terrain, and large residences set in spacious lawns." The English names of the streets—Kenilworth, Derbyshire, Berkshire, Coventry—speak volumes about the ideals of both residential planning and domestic architecture in the period. In 1896 Calhoun obtained a street railway franchise and a railway was built from Euclid Avenue up Cedar Hill and out Euclid Heights Boulevard to a point just beyond Edgehill. The first residences were built in Euclid Heights in 1895–1896.[53]

At about the same time, the land between Cedar Hill and the Doan Brook parkway was platted on the property of Dr. Nathan Ambler and became known as Ambler Heights. It was the locale of some of the most progressive architecture in Cleveland in the early years of the century. To the east, another development was laid out on the lands which formerly belonged to the North Union Shaker community. The area paralleled Doan Brook and the Shaker lakes, and was the nucleus of Shaker

University Circle, laid out in 1895. In the background, Adelbert College and Case Main.

Heights. Fairmount Boulevard, part of which had been an existing Shaker road at least since 1858, was the main artery. Although planned shortly after the dissolution of the Shaker society in 1889, the area was not really developed until after 1906. The western end of Fairmount Boulevard, between Cedar and Coventry, was located on property owned by John D. Rockefeller, Sr. He leased the land to the Euclid Golf Association from 1900 to 1912, after which it was purchased and developed by Burton and Grant Deming. Along this broad boulevard with its divided strip for street cars, large houses on generous lots were built.[54]

Along Lake Erie on the West Side, in what is now Lakewood, another suburban residential area grew up in the 1900s. Clifton Park had received its name as early as 1868, when the Clifton Park Association was formed by a number of Clevelanders to promote a summer resort. Among them were Daniel P. Rhodes and other residents and developers of the area around Franklin Circle and Lorain Avenue. The Rocky River Railroad was built in 1868 to bring tourists to the lake resort. The lake shore was improved, and the park became a popular amusement locality during the 1870s and 1880s. The winding streets along the lake and east of the Rocky River were laid out in 1894 by E. W. Bowditch, at the same time as Rockefeller Park and Euclid Heights. The houses on the north edge of the lakeshore development range in a stately procession along the

Plan of Clifton Park in 1918.

cliff above Lake Erie, the lots averaging some 300 feet in depth and 100 feet in width on Lake Road. The most important lakefront residences were built between 1900 and 1915. Among the typical residents were John G. Jennings, an officer of Lamson & Sessions Company, Walter C. Baker, founder of the Baker Motor Vehicle Company, architects Herman J. Albrecht and W. Dominick Benes, and Francis H. Glidden, founder of the Glidden Varnish Company. In the early years the nucleus of the community was formed by summer residents, and some of the houses of 1899–1903 convey that spaciousness, calm, and generally rustic quality of summer living.[55]

On the lakefront to the east, between Gordon Park and East 140th Street, the residents north of the railroad elected to remain independent when Glenville was annexed to Cleveland in 1905, and Bratenahl became an independent village in 1906. The Lake Shore Boulevard curved along the lakefront at a distance from Lake Erie ranging from 500 to over 1200 feet, creating deep private lots on which large and expensive houses could be built. There were already some earlier homes, including

those of the original nineteenth century land-owners, such as Daniel Coit, and notably Samuel Mather's Shoreby. During Bratenahl's early years some of Cleveland's most famous houses were built, including William G. Mather's "Gwinn" and Howard M. Hanna's home designed by McKim, Mead & White. In all of these suburban areas building continued through the 1930s, and there was some new construction even after World War II. Nevertheless, these suburban enclaves retained much of their early twentieth century atmosphere three-quarters of a century later.

In the suburban homes as in other types of buildings, the early 1900s were a period of transition and experiment, of tradition and progressivism. There were remnants of the Shingle Style of the eighties and nineties. Some houses reflected a mixture of styles, combining the sheathing of the Shingle Style with Jacobethan half-timbering and even Gothic windows, the basic form being broken up by numerous gables. The dominant mode was eclecticism. The classical domestic styles, Neo-Classic and Georgian Revival, produced many

102

homes, as did the Tudor or Jacobethan Revival. Homes might be either formal or informal in fundamental effect, and the choice would determine the style; the classical, Italian, or American Colonial lent themselves to formality, while the Tudor, English contemporary or Japanese produced an informal effect. The Italian Renaissance was adopted for several of the more palatial homes, although they were in the minority. Basically the forms of this period were those of the late nineteenth century, while the internal plan was undergoing experiment and modification.

The homes of John Hartness Brown and Patrick Calhoun themselves are late nineteenth century residences. Built in 1895–1896, they were among the earliest houses on the Heights. The Brown house, at the intersection of Overlook and Edgehill Roads, is a large three-story sandstone structure very much in the baronial manner of an architect like Schweinfurth a decade earlier. Calhoun's home on Edgehill Road is a large square wood frame residence with prominent half-timbered gables in a mixture of the Jacobethan and Queen Anne manners. The Brown house was designed by Alfred Hoyt Granger, and the Calhoun house by Granger in partnership with Frank B. Meade. A native of Ohio, Granger had studied at the Massachusetts Institute of Technology and the Ecole des Beaux-Arts. The partnership of Granger and Meade lasted from 1894 to 1897, after which Granger went to Chicago where he was associated with the planning of the North Western and LaSalle Street Stations. Of the eight original houses built on "the Overlook" in 1895–1898, several were designed by Granger and Meade, including the home of Myron T. Herrick. Only one has survived, Granger's own house at 2141 Overlook.[56]

The oldest house surviving into the third quarter of the twentieth century in Clifton Park is the John Jennings home, built in 1899. It too is a thoroughly Victorian house with half-timbered gables, a charming veranda, and corner battlemented towers, all executed in wood. The original distinctions between various structural and wall elements have been somewhat obscured by painting all of the surfaces white. The Colonial Revival was represented in Clifton Park by the home of Frank C. Case, vice-president of the Lamson & Sessions Company. Built in 1905, it is a simple symmetrical block with a hipped roof, a bowed one-story front porch, and an unusual second-story recessed gallery containing a Palladian window. The Case house was designed by George F.

Patrick Calhoun house, 2460 Edgehill Road, Cleveland Heights, 1896, Granger and Meade, architects.

John Hartness Brown house, Overlook and Edgehill Roads, Cleveland Heights, 1896, Alfred Hoyt Granger, architect.

Hammond, a Cleveland architect equally at home in commercial and institutional design. In 1891 he wrote a treatise on hospital and asylum architecture, and in 1911 he planned the original campus for the Ohio State Normal College at Kent (Kent State University). Hammond was also the architect of the handsome Neo-Classic building of the First Church of Christ Scientist in Cleveland, dedicated in 1904.[57]

The homes in Bratenahl still tended toward the palatial, and as such were exceptions to the general trend. William Gwinn Mather, president of the Cleveland-Cliffs Iron Company and half-brother of Samuel Mather, engaged Charles Platt as his

John Jennings
(1899) and
Frank C. Case
(1905) houses,
Lake Avenue,
Lakewood.

architect. Platt was a New York architect who had spent many years studying in Europe with special emphasis on the buildings and gardens of the Italian Renaissance. He has been called the "best country-house designer of the post-1900 period." Platt was the architect of the Freer Art Gallery in Washington, D.C., and of noted country homes in Lake Forest, Illinois, and on Long Island. Among his few commercial buildings the most important was considered to be the Leader-News Building erected in Cleveland in 1912.[58]

"Gwinn" is an Italian palazzo. The exterior design of the mansion, built in 1907–1908, is restrained. Ornamental detail is concentrated in a few spots such as the Tuscan doorway of the west entrance. The most prominent architectural feature is the great semicircular Ionic portico facing Lake Erie. However, "Gwinn" is perhaps more significant for the planning of the five-acre site, with its lake frontage on the north and garden to the south. A ragged water edge was made into a formal setting by the construction of a symmetrical concrete breakwater. A terraced series of stairs descends to the beach from the house twenty-eight feet above the level of the lake. On the terrace landing, there is a fountain with a sculptured grotesque in the Italian Mannerist style. The majesty and size of the lake facade is counterbalanced by the more human scale of the garden, although even this is formal and symmetrical. The entrance drive runs along the western edge of the property, leaving the garden

frontage open to Lake Shore Boulevard. The servants' quarters and stables were located on additional property across the road. The design and layout of this house and grounds, both in ornamental detail and in overall plan, clearly reflect an attempt to approximate the effect of a sixteenth century Italian palace.[59]

Howard M. Hanna, Jr., nephew of Mark and Leonard C. Hanna, also selected an architectural firm of national importance, McKim, Mead & White. Stanford White was assassinated in 1906 and Charles F. McKim retired in 1907, and the firm's actual designer of the Hanna house (1909–1910) is not known. Although the Tudor idiom was not typical of a firm whose favorite style was the Italian Renaissance, the exterior elevations of the Hanna house are very symmetrical and almost classical in effect. The main rectangular block of the house has a steep gabled roof parallel to the lakefront, and the general massing is not unlike some of the West Side summer houses. As in most McKim, Mead & White buildings, the ornamental detail, especially on the interior, is handled with exquisite taste.[60]

Another house in the palatial manner was built on Fairmount Boulevard for Henry A. Tremaine and subsequently owned by Michael Gallagher, general manager of the M. A. Hanna Company. It was designed by Frederic W. Striebinger and erected in 1912–1914. Also an Italian Renaissance palazzo, it is constructed of stucco on masonry with ornamental detail of white terra cotta. The main feature is the

William G. Mather Residence, "Gwinn," Bratenahl, 1908, Charles Platt, architect.

Howard M. Hanna, Jr., residence, Bratenahl, 1910, McKim, Mead and White, architects.

Tremaine-Gallagher House, Fairmount Boulevard, Cleveland Heights, 1912-1914, Frederic W. Striebinger, architect. (*Martin Linsey*)

105

William H. Warner house, East Overlook Road, Cleveland Heights, 1908, Meade & Garfield, architects.

thirty-five foot long loggia with three arches on the facade. The interior is truly eclectic, the decoration being based on seventeenth and eighteenth century English precedent from the Baroque period to the Adamesque, with an Egyptian room on the second floor. To the rear of the house there is a large formal garden, and the entire site is heavily wooded. Striebinger was a successful Cleveland architect, but was not regarded by his colleagues as particularly creative. His other buildings include the Second and Third Churches of Christ Scientist, the Cleveland Gesang Verein Hall (House of Wills), and the Woodward Masonic Temple (Call and Post Building).[61]

The entire range of eclectic sources in this period can be seen on Fairmount Boulevard and on some streets in Lakewood and Shaker Heights, but perhaps no better than along East Overlook Road between Edgehill and Coventry Roads. Many of the houses in this block were designed by Frank Meade in partnership with Abram Garfield, and one of their most charming architectural conceits was the home built for William H. Warner in 1908.[62] The east wing, with its gable end to the street and a suggestion of timbered structure, is fairly standard, although even here the way in which the chimney rises through the stories, first as a projecting bay, then as a blank wall, is sophisticated. The west wing is turned at a slight angle to the rest of the house, and at the angle stands a projecting staircase, modeled after the famous sixteenth century spiral staircase tower on the chateau of Blois. However, underneath the Francis I cocoon the emerging modern house can be seen.

Even the Prairie Style of Frank Lloyd Wright had become an eclectic choice. A residence which shows Wright's influence was built in 1913–1914 by George Canfield, president of the Canfield Oil Company, on Elandon Road in Ambler Heights.[63] The borrowed stylistic elements, which belong to the houses Wright was building ten years earlier in the Chicago suburbs of Oak Park and Highland Park, include the wide projecting eaves, the division of the wall by horizontal bands of wood, the grouping of the windows by vertical strips, the projecting bay, the massive chimneys, and even the cast cement planters on the steps. However, there are significant differences. Instead of the play of plane against space characteristic of Wright's own work, the Canfield house is fundamentally a mass punctured by openings. Nor are the curved brackets supporting the projecting bay characteristic of Wright. Most important, the correspondence between plan, elevation, and mass that is essential to an actual Wright design is not inherent in this house. Clearly the Prairie Style was simply understood as another alternative to be used for a client who was a little more "modern." There are no houses by Frank Lloyd Wright himself in greater Cleveland and none closer

George Canfield house, Elandon Road, Cleveland Heights, 1914, attributed to Bohnard and Parsson, architects.

than Willoughby and Oberlin, despite occasional rumors and "discoveries" to the contrary.

By the end of the century's first decade, many of the contradictions had been resolved and a definite form had emerged for the suburban American home. In spite of the dozen or so historical styles which might be reflected in these homes, a common aim and a subtle likeness could be observed and were clearly expressed by contemporary writers. The relationship between the house and its grounds and garden was considered of great importance. It was also important that the "bones" of the house be suggested rather than hidden, and that there be an honest expression of the interior plan and structure in the external design, which now tended toward a longer horizontal facade with a low hipped roof parallel to the street. Finally, there was a new freedom and craftsmanship in the use of materials, and a new interest in the contrast and variety of textured surfaces.[64]

It should be pointed out that while these principles have been associated in the popular mind with the work of Frank Lloyd Wright, they were actually part of the common coin of the period. The distinction of Wright was that he expressed them in his own peculiarly original style. As we have seen, that style in turn became one of many alternatives for other architects.

The interior plan developed out of a desire for practical modern living, replacing Victorian ostentation with more informality. It attempted to achieve economy both in the use of space and in the operation of the home. An impression of spaciousness was desired and was achieved by large openings between rooms. The Victorian parlor was gone, replaced by a living room planned for the comfortable grouping of people, with a fireplace as the focal point. Beyond the living room was an attached enclosed piazza or sun porch. The entrance hall remained as an important circulation area from which the stairs were a strong visible feature, but it was no longer a main reception room. Across the hall from the living room was the dining room. These were the public rooms; somewhere there was another room—a study, den, or library—serving the need for privacy. The architect's problem was the grouping of these areas, and this was done with an acute regard for their orientation. The living room should face south and the dining room east, while the den, being a night-time room, could face north.

Based on the developments of the first decade, the "golden age" of the suburban home came in the years immediately before and after the First World War, coinciding with the early years of the partnership of Meade and Hamilton. After three years with Alfred Granger and six years with Abram Garfield, Frank B. Meade formed a partnership with James M. Hamilton in 1911 which was to last thirty years.

107

Meade was born in Norwalk, Ohio, the grandson of William Gale Meade, an architect-builder in Huron County during the Greek Revival period. Prior to settling in Cleveland, Meade studied in Boston and worked as a draftsman in the office of William LeBaron Jenney in Chicago. In 1911 Meade succeeded John M. Carrere as a member of the Group Plan Commission. He wrote a number of articles and critical pieces in the late 1920s which clearly show that his philosophy of domestic architecture was representative of his times.[65]

Meade and Hamilton built over eight hundred houses and six country clubs between Buffalo and Dayton during their career, and the house which they designed in 1917 for Joseph O. Eaton, president of Eaton Axle Company, on Devonshire Drive in Ambler Heights, summarizes the developments of the period. It is characterized by the long horizontal profile and the sloping roof with wide eaves, and like many other Meade and Hamilton houses, the plan forms an angle on a curved street corner. The danger of monotony in such a long facade is relieved by the grouping of the entrance, chimney and bay window near the center, and by the appearance of a gentle curve paralleling the street. The chimneys are plain and massive, with no hint of the picturesque outline previously favored. The house has a garden facade which is as important and architecturally developed as the street front. The bay windows of the dining room and living room overlook a stone-paved porch. Representing the best work of Meade and Hamilton, the Eaton house incorporates the ideals of coherence, convenience, and taste, and sums up the fully developed idea of the early twentieth century suburban home.[66]

Happily, the first large-scale move to the suburbs coincided with a number of favorable factors. Foremost was the change in the scale and style of living desired by the upper classes. Ostentation and display gave way to informal, comfortable living, and this was reflected in the planning and orientation of domestic architecture. There was a renewed appreciation of the nineteenth century philosophy and example of building in relation to nature, from Andrew Jackson Downing to Calvert Vaux and Frederick Law Olmsted. This meant that boulevards and parks were laid out in relation to existing topographical features rather than being imposed in a rigid grid plan. Furthermore, the siting of the house itself and the relationship of house to garden were very important.

Reinforcing these ideas was the attention paid by American designers to contemporary English architects. Study of the revival of a country vernacular by Sir Edwin Lutyens, F. Baillie-Scott, and C. F. A. Voysey encouraged a poetic charm and a certain austerity which were a reaction to extreme Victorian pomposity. The first generation of architects trained in an American architectural school was beginning to practice, but at the same time, the lessons of the Ecole des Beaux-Arts were very much alive. They were reflected in the ability to solve complex planning requirements and to understand the desirability of large overall planning schemes. Finally, there was a renewed interest in craftsmanship and the nature of materials, and a high standard of handicraft was still available. All of these factors conspired to create a domestic architecture located in planned residential suburbs which have never been surpassed for livability and good taste. Those in greater Cleveland are among the finest to be found anywhere.

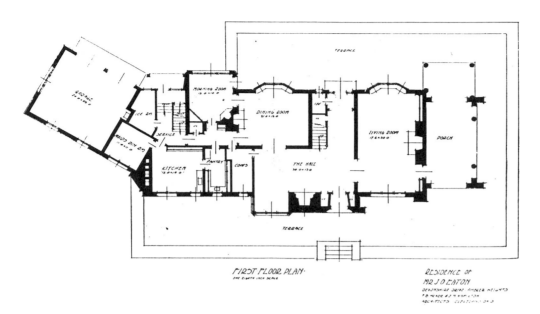

Floor plan, Joseph O. Eaton house, Meade &
Hamilton, architects. (*The Architectural Record*)

Joseph O. Eaton House, Devonshore Drive,
Cleveland Heights, 1917, Meade & Hamilton,
architects.

Nela Park Institute, 1921, showing the statuary group representing the triumph of Light over Darkness.

# 1911: Nela Park

The first decade of the twentieth century was preoccupied with finding ways of coming to terms with the complexities of modern life, of providing for practicality together with some degree of amenity, of embodying a concern for human values, and of developing a new awareness of the larger environment of structures. These aims were to be accomplished through a measure of rational planning, and they were amply demonstrated from the grand scheme of the Group Plan to the layout of residential boulevards, from the formulation of a building code to the development of a practical modern house.

Nowhere were these principles more completely realized than in the conception of Nela Park, which makes a strong claim to being the first planned industrial research park in the nation. When the National Electric Lamp Company outgrew its East 45th Street Plant, company executives Franklin Terry and Burton Tremaine conceived plans for a new suburban plant to be called Nela Park, NELA being an acronym for National Electric Lamp Association. The arguments advanced for the site were extremely forward-looking. Pleasant conditions would make a much more effective working atmosphere. Departments would develop an individuality and morale of their own, thus "creating an atmosphere somewhat parallel to that which exists in an institution of fine arts."[1] And of course construction, operation, and taxes would be relatively cheap compared to their cost in the city.

Already such advanced arguments were not uncommon in the case of individual factory buildings. Robert D. Kohn, architect of the H. Black & Company factory (1907) on Superior Avenue in Cleveland, explained his intentions, if not a coherent philosophy of industrial architectural planning, in an article on the building. It was simply a plea for a commonsense approach to developing an "honest dignified distinctive type of design for factories." Kohn observed that the usual attempts toward "beautification" consisted of adding a false front to a building otherwise "stupid" in mass, arrangement, and fenestration.[2] He intended instead to make the basic utilitarian building—in this case a women's garment factory—practical, economical, and yet "good-looking." He was aware of Wright's Larkin building, but instead of imitating Wright's forms, he attempted to work out his own expression of the same principles. The editor of Kohn's article, like Wright, noted that the attractiveness of the working surroundings in a factory could be regarded by employers as a business facility. Such an observation was exactly consonant with the ideals of the Progressive reformers of the period.

Nevertheless, the courage and imagination which conceived the scale of Nela Park were far in advance of most business thinking at the time. Even after the project was under way, General Electric officials, negotiating to acquire National Electric in 1912, proposed to stop it and abandon the "fanciful display of extravagance." The purchase was concluded only after the Lamp Division was assured of the continuation of the plan.

The site was selected in 1910, a small plateau south of Euclid Avenue and 234 feet above Lake Erie, with some dense woods and a picturesque ravine. Most of the land was acquired in 1911–1913. It was realized from the outset that the entire building program

The quadrangle, Nela Park. Engineering Building and Advertising Building, 1913, Wallis & Goodwillie, architects. (*General Electric Lighting Institute*)

should be entrusted to one architect in order to ensure a consistent scheme, and the company chose the New York firm of Wallis & Goodwillie. It is significant that Frank E. Wallis was a student of English architecture and traveled extensively in America making sketches and measured drawings of colonial houses. At one time he was a member of Richard M. Hunt's office and worked on the plans for George W. Vanderbilt's "Biltmore" in Asheville, North Carolina.[3]

While the land was being surveyed in preparation for rough grading, drainage, roadways, and sidewalks, Wallis made plans based on studies of the requirements of the plant. He spent additional time in England to study examples of Georgian architecture which might be selected as models. The general scheme of grouping the buildings was consciously patterned after the idea of a university with its quadrangle.

The first group of buildings was completed in 1915, and Wallis continued as architect of all the buildings planned before 1921. There followed a hiatus of sixteen years, after which five more buildings were added. The office and laboratory complex finally included some twenty major buildings, plus smaller utility structures and an

employees' camp. All of the buildings have steel frame or concrete structures faced with red brick, and all are two or three stories in height. The exterior trim of the buildings erected before 1915 was an ivory terra-cotta; the trim of some of the later structures is sandstone, artificial stone, or limestone.

The earliest buildings were arranged on two axes around a quadrangle which dominates the architectural scheme of the park. The main axis is almost exactly northwest-southeast, but it is generally referred to as north-south. Four buildings face the quadrangle. The Engineering Building (1913), at the north end of the main axis, stands on the brow of the hill overlooking Nela Avenue and Euclid Avenue. Thus it has two facades, one facing a north entrance lodge and one facing the quadrangle. The Advertising Building (1913) is on the secondary axis at the east side of the quadrangle. Six round, twenty-one foot Tuscan columns of light bluish granite form a portico at the center of the west front. The largest building is the Lamp Laboratory (1914), which consists of three sections with the ends being slightly angled toward the north, making an apparent curve enclosing the south end of the lawn.

The last of the four buildings, and the most elaborately ornamented, is the Institute (1921).

Dominated by a seventy-two foot bell tower, it faces a circular pool on the quadrangle side, with two curved wings embracing the west half of the pool. In 1945–1946 the outside brick wall of these wings was moved eight feet closer to the pool, and a thermopane glass wall was installed, affording a view over the water. The three-story facade features four sets of doubled columns above a rusticated first story, and above the facade is a bronze statuary group symbolizing the triumph of light over darkness. The arrangement of these four buildings around the open yard, with their pedimented frontispieces, red brick, terra-cotta pilasters and late Baroque detail, forcefully suggests the country houses and urban terraces of Georgian England.

Located on a curving drive to the east of the quadrangle are three smaller buildings in the same Georgian idiom—Manufacturing, Administration, and Sales. To the west is a group of attached buildings—(Maintenance, Boiler Room and Operating) connected by a one-story wing facing Noble Road, which was remodeled in 1921 to house a branch of the Cleveland Trust Company. South of Elm Road, the main east-west thoroughfare, are eight large structures for engineering and development (1917–1960). Unlike the earlier buildings, they display only hints of the Georgian style, but they are faced with brick and trimmed with stone to harmonize with them. The entire complex is connected by a system of underground tunnels carrying pipe lines for heating, gas, compressed air, steam, and hot and cold water. Some of the buildings are connected by underground pedestrian subways as well.

The entire park and all the buildings were landscaped according to plans developed from the beginning. The roadways are lined with trees, and there is a great variety in the species of trees and plants represented. Between the buildings and Belvoir Boulevard runs a steep ravine where a walking path with rustic stairs and rails was developed, although its use has been discouraged in later years.

The innovative concept of Nela Park, both industrial and architectural, was immediately noted in the architectural world. In June, 1914, *The Architectural Record* published a thirty-five page illustrated article on Nela Park, in which the author emphasized the executives' recognition of their responsibility for the conditions under which their employees worked. She also pointed out the unusual character of the architectural association, in which the architects became a part of the company organization and were given complete freedom of action without interference. Their development of an overall plan that unified the buildings by style but

Lamp Laboratory, Nela Park, East Cleveland, 1914, Wallis & Goodwillie, architects.
The Nela Park buildings were erected by The Austin Company, pioneers in the concept of one organization integrating the design, engineering, and construction of a project. Austin's work for National Electric Lamp Association led directly to the standardization of construction methods in industrial building. (*General Electric Lighting Institute*)

Engineering Building, Nela Park 1913.

exhibited considerable variety according to their use was considered a great achievement.[4]

The choice of the Georgian style was not purely arbitrary. It was believed to fit the purpose and the environment that was part of the original concept of the park. The prototypes used by Wallis were those of the English Georgian from approximately 1750 to 1775, and the sources were studied in the south of England, around Salisbury and Bath. They certainly included both urban terraces and country houses in which the classical facade is complemented by the English garden in the style of the Adam brothers, John Wood, and some of the early eighteenth century work of Wren. This was also a period of classical brickwork, and in the judgment of Montgomery Schuyler, the brickwork at Nela Park might be called "the best . . . on this side of the water, and without any superior on the other." The distinguished critic, whose assessments of nineteenth century modern architects are a part of the critical canon, also observed:

From the point of view of architecture it is plain how such a scheme, on such a site, with the differentiation of the buildings required by practical or aesthetic considerations, is enough to make any architect's mouth water. It will not be disputed, either, that the actual architects have made a shining success of their work. For such a combination of the institutional and the domestic

as has here been sought and found they have shown that the repertory of British Georgian is adequate.[5]

Both the overall masses and the ornamentation were used to differentiate the buildings, and Wallis' ornamental detail, although classically derived, has endless variations. For example, the Sales Building has a terra cotta frieze with electric lamps inside Adamesque sunbursts.

Schuyler also explained the fitness of a "domestic" style for a commercial enterprise on the basis of the work which was carried on there.

The social element is looked out for at every turn. . . . If 'esprit de corps' is an element of efficiency, and nobody will dispute that it is, how could it be better promoted than by making every one of the thousand or twelve hundred persons who are ultimately to constitute the population of Nela Park feel that he or she is an organic part of the great machine? And how could that conception be better expressed than it is in the architecture of 'this college situated in a purer air'?[6]

The ideals of Nela Park are clearly related to those of contemporary suburban residential developments. The subtle balance between formal planning, natural environment, and good living was the essence of both. The significant point, however, is that Nela Park was not developed for a residential area, nor a government complex, nor an institution, but for "big business."

Advertising Building, Nela Park, 1913. (*General Electric Lighting Institute*)

Terrace Road entrance, Nela Park, East Cleveland.

West Side Market, 1912, under construction, Hubbell & Benes, architects.

# 1911–1920

## Neighborhood Buildings — III

During the decade which was indelibly marked by the First World War, Cleveland, like the rest of the country, was not unaffected. German immigrants who sympathized with their homeland, usually simply out of loyalty to family, were ostracized. Cleveland's Mayor Newton D. Baker was appointed Wilson's Secretary of War, and more than three hundred Great Lakes ships were put into service on the Atlantic. According to one historian, the incident that had the most unfortunate effect on German-American relations originated in Cleveland as an advertisement published by the Cleveland Automatic Machine Company for a machine that manufactured a high-explosive shell. When the advertisement became known in Germany, its gory detail incited the strongest anti-American propaganda.[7]

In the years immediately prior to the outbreak of the European conflict, however, life in an American city continued much as it had in the first decade of the century. By and large, Cleveland's development up to the war years was still characterized by the rapid, unplanned growth that resulted from intensive urbanization. Even the city planning movement, which attempted to cope with disorderly urban growth, could only make small headway. The primacy of commercial, industrial, and transportation interests, plus decades without any form of zoning control, had taken their toll. However, Cleveland was singularly fortunate in that it almost entirely lacked the typical tenement housing of the late nineteenth and early twentieth centuries; the single dwelling remained predominant. While the city had its share of older areas which became decayed through neglect, the worst excesses of urban overcrowding, with its lack of air and light, were avoided.

The provision of public services which had begun under Tom L. Johnson, making Cleveland "the best governed city," continued under the mayoralty of Newton D. Baker, Johnson's former aide. The water supply was good, and the chlorination of city water was introduced in 1911, but large neighborhoods of homes had no bathtubs. Public bathhouses were provided by the city, the first having been built in 1899. By 1921 there were six, and several were still standing and in use as recreation centers in 1976. One of the larger and more elaborate ones was the Woodland Avenue Public Baths at Woodland

Cleveland Automatic Machine Company, Ashland Avenue, 1894, manufacturer of munitions machinery.

Woodland Avenue Public Baths, Woodland Avenue at East 93rd Street, 1915, William S. Lougee, architect.

Avenue and East 93rd Street, erected in 1915. The architect of the building was William S. Lougee. After working for ten years in Eisenmann's office, Lougee had been assistant architect for the Board of Education and the first assistant building inspector under the new building code of 1904. The public bath, containing swimming pool, gymnasium, and club rooms, consisted of two parallel wings with clerestory windows and large arched windows at the gable ends of the wings. The general precedent of the Roman style for a public bath was obvious, as it was in the West Side Market, a prime example of a

civic work for the public benefit. An even more Roman "styled" bathhouse was built in 1921 at Lincoln Park on the West Side.[8]

The public library system also flourished, and by 1919 it had a larger circulation per capita than that of any other major city. One of the most striking branch buildings was the Carnegie West Library. First opened in 1892 on West 25th Street, it had been the first branch in the library system. The West Side library moved to the new Fulton Street building, which was erected with the help of Andrew Carnegie, in 1910. The brick and stone building was triangular in shape, a highly original design in the Beaux Arts manner. Its most prominent features were the columns and pilasters displaying the exaggerated rustication of the Italian Mannerist period. Unlike the Board of Education, the Public Library of the School District of the City of Cleveland, as it was called until 1923, used the services of many different architects. The Carnegie West building was designed by Edward L. Tilton, a New York architect who had begun his career in the office of McKim, Mead and White. Shortly after he opened his own office in 1890, his firm won the competition for the Immigration Station on Ellis Island. A specialist in libraries, Tilton also designed them for Johns Hopkins, Emory University, and Girard College, Philadelphia.[9]

The vast majority of the immigrants in the immediately prewar years came from the old Austro-Hungarian Empire, Russia, and the Balkan states of southeastern Europe. Of the

Carnegie West Library, Fulton Avenue at Lorain, 1910, Edward L. Tilton, architect.

St. Theodosius Russian Orthodox Cathedral,
Starkweather Avenue and St. Tikhon Avenue,
1912, Frederick C. Baird, architect.

Greek Catholic Church of the Holy Ghost,
Kenilworth Avenue at West 14th Street,
1910, M. E. Wells, architect.

neighborhoods in which they settled, the one which has remained the most visually interesting is the area later known as Tremont. Located on the near West Side, it was roughly defined by the bluffs of the Cuyahoga valley to the north and east, Starkweather Avenue on the south, and Jennings (West 14th Street) on the west. The neighborhood was settled by Greeks, Ukrainians, Russians, and older Bohemians and Poles. On opposite sides of the district were two churches which epitomized its national character. In addition, both exemplified the kind of eclecticism then dominant, in which the meaning of the building was specifically represented by the choice of an imitative style.

The Greek Catholic Church of the Holy Ghost was Byzantine. Located on Kenilworth Avenue near West 14th Street, it was built in 1909–1910. Actually, the appropriate Byzantine references are only suggestive; twin facade towers end in onion-shaped domes, with a similar but smaller dome over the sanctuary, but the basic form of the building, with its triple arched entrance and great rose window, could belong to any faith.[10]

St. Theodosius Russian Orthodox Cathedral, erected on Starkweather Avenue in 1911–1912, is one of the best known of the immigrant churches. The impressive external silhouette of its thirteen onion-shaped cupolas has always been a familiar visual landmark on the high land above the Flats. St. Theodosius, the first Orthodox parish in Cleveland, was founded in 1896, the same year that its namesake was canonized. The building is said to have been designed with features adapted from the Church of Our Savior in the Kremlin, Moscow. The design was the result of the collaboration of Father Basil Lisenkovsky and Frederick C. Baird, a

Koreny's Saloon (Lemko Tavern Association), West 11th Street at Literary Road, 1911.

Weizer Block, 8937 Buckeye Road, 1913, Emile Uhlrich, architect.

Cleveland architect. The cathedral was mentioned in an article on Louis Sullivan's Holy Trinity Russian Orthodox Cathedral in Chicago as a most characteristic example of traditional Russian monumental architecture.[11]

The small, concentrated neighborhood also had a number of other nationality churches, including the Polish St. John Cantius Catholic Church, the modest Slovenska Baptist Church, Saints Peter and Paul Ukrainian Catholic Church, and the Hellenic Orthodox Church of the Annunciation.

A good deal of the geographical interest of the Tremont area comes from the fact that the streets were laid out in two intersecting grids. One was parallel to the Public Square grid and to West 3rd Street, which bridges the river in the Flats. The other was the north-south grid of West 14th Street. The street names of Literary, Professor, College, and University were reminders of the ill-fated Cleveland University, located in the center of the eastern grid in 1850. The triangle formed by Tremont and West 10th Streets was the site of the public school. While several older commercial buildings from the 1870s and 1880s stood on West 11th Street, the new shopping thoroughfare was Professor Street. It boasted a Neo-Classic bank and several typical small family stores with the residence on the second floor. The diagonal intersection of the two street grids demanded that some of the buildings be designed as acute-angle, or "flatiron," buildings. Two of the most interesting were Koreny's saloon and hall at the corner of West 11th and Literary Streets, and the Ukrainian-American Building and Loan Association at West 10th and Professor Streets. Koreny's saloon, later occupied by the Lemko Tavern Association, was a brick and stone building with round-arched windows, and a cylindrical corner tower with a pointed dome. The brick savings association building was a more suave and functional design, with large commercial style windows in all three stories. These two triangular buildings spanned the decade in date as well as style, the former having been built in 1911 and the latter in 1920.[12]

In general, the commercial vernacular of the period was uninspired, but occasionally an individual architect-designed building was noteworthy. In 1913 John Weizer erected a business block on Buckeye Road at East 90th Street. Weizer had operated a grocery and then a clothing store at the site since 1893. He began dealing in real estate on the eve of the war, and became wealthy developing the residential area eastward along Buckeye Road. Weizer's Block was designed by Emile Uhlrich, architect of the Art Nouveau J. L. Hudson store. Its lavish facade suggests that the architect was attempting an Eastern European flavor. Rigorously symmetrical, it had two oriel bays which terminated in octagonal cupolas with tile roofs. Alternating brick and stone quoins gave a polychrome effect. The new St. Elizabeth's Hungarian Church designed by the same architect was begun across the street just five years later, and the dual towers of the two were related. Uhlrich's principle of "bringing the large ideas typical in church architecture to modern business problems," enunciated in the J. L. Hudson store, was consistent with the Weizer Block facade.[13]

At the same time, there existed a commercial vernacular type which appears over and over again in the neighborhood shopping streets of the teens. It was typically a two-story block, with ground floor stores and second floor apartments. The distinguishing feature was a tile pent roof overhanging the front. The treatment of the parapets at the roof line had innumerable variations, and frequently there were wrought iron balconies at the second floor. These fronts could be seen in their infinite variety along "upper" Buckeye Road, which became the heart of the Hungarian community during and immediately following the World War.

The Hungarian population had moved steadily eastward from its original settlement at Woodland Avenue and East 79th Street, and in the residential streets off Buckeye Road the typical real estate housing of the decade was built. The form and plan of such houses were predetermined by the small size and narrow shape of the lots, laid out to afford the greatest possible return to the speculative builder. The house architecture which is represented in the Buckeye district was basically similar to that of the previous decade, with an important functional and social difference. The house was a two-family residence, with identical floor plans on each story, enabling the property owner to become an investor and a landlord. The most visible architectural characteristic of these houses was a solid second-story porch railing which flared into a concave parapet roof overhanging the first-story porch. This often rested on stock classic columns without a beam and so stubby in proportion as to be a caricature of the classical orders. This type of income house became enormously popular and could be found endlessly duplicated in every new subdivision of the war years.

Typical store and dwelling, Buckeye and East 120th Street, 1915.

Typical two-family houses, East 126th Street, 1917.

121

## Architects in Transition — II

It is almost a truism that the nineteenth century did not end, culturally speaking, until 1914. It took the upheaval of the First World War to shatter the old value systems which had already begun to erode. The standard history of avant-garde architecture in America is not very helpful in this period. The work of Frank Lloyd Wright, although it had attracted much attention in Europe by 1914, was largely unknown among his countrymen, while the International Style was still over the horizon in the postwar era. The vast bulk of ordinary building was a latter-day continuation of the late nineteenth century spirit. There were some exercises in the more progressive modes, but eclecticism was still the predominant manner. The style of a building was determined less by any discernible architectural philosophy than by its function or symbolism, the wishes of its builders, the type of site or amount of money available, or the dictates of fashion. The most striking work was accomplished in two widely divergent fields, engineering and domestic architecture.

Looking back beyond the turn of the century, we seem to have suggested, without detracting from the work of many remarkably good architects, that certain ones seemed to sum up the character of a decade—Frank Cudell in the eighties, Charles Schweinfurth in the nineties, and J. Milton Dyer in the first decade of the twentieth century. If this is true, probably no architects characterize the second decade of the century better than Hubbell and Benes, and paradoxically, this is precisely because their work exhibits no common style. Their buildings represent the several strands which run consistently through the period, and which come to the surface in varying degrees of intensity.

W. Dominick Benes (1857–1935), the elder of the partners, was born in Prague, Bohemia. His family came to America in 1866. Benes left high school at the age of fifteen and served as an apprentice with Andrew Mitermiler for three years, after which he spent twenty years, from 1876 to 1896, in the office of Coburn and Barnum. Benjamin S. Hubbell (1867–1953), who was born in Kansas and educated at Cornell, also worked in the office of Coburn and Barnum, and Hubbell and Benes formed their own partnership in 1897.[14]

In the prewar years Hubbell and Benes designed several buildings which share certain elements of the progressive architecture of the period, though they differ widely in purpose and external style. The Gymnasium built for the Women's College at Western Reserve (1907), the YMCA building on Prospect Avenue (1913), and the fourteen-story Illuminating Building on Public Square (1915) are very different in size, purpose, and superficial aspect, yet they have some compelling similarities. All are made of very blocky forms, narrow slabs either set on end or resting on the side. Above these are wide, overhanging eaves with flat brackets, recalling Sullivan's skyscraper cornices or the cantilevered eaves of the Prairie Style. The effect of modernity is enhanced on the gymnasium by the horizontal bands of windows. The Illuminating Building was basically conceived as a typical prewar skyscraper, with a clearly defined base, shaft, and attic story. Nevertheless, its segmental arches spanning the ground story and attic bays are unusual, as is the carved stone ornament, which is geometric rather than historically derived. The YMCA is more plainly in a historical style, the Italian Romanesque, but its simple planar treatment and the colored tile frieze at the upper stories are modern.

Hubbell and Benes' design for the West Side Market was also transitional in concept. In 1905 the architects were appointed by the Board of Public Service of the City of Cleveland to make proposals for a group of three public structures at Lorain and West 25th Street—a market house, a flower market and public bath, and an auditorium. A misguided citizen delayed the planning with a suit to halt the project, on the basis that the architects' fees of five percent were excessive. When the matter was settled, the public market alone was begun. It was completed in 1912.[15]

The city-owned market was a vital community center. For recent immigrants its social character had a special significance, as the public market could be traced to medieval times in Europe, and beyond that to classical antiquity. As in the Sheriff Street Market twenty years before, the need for a large covered hall and the associations of the Roman marketplace combined to make the West Side Market essentially an interpretation of the Roman basilica. The structure is 123 feet wide and 245 feet long. As in a basilica, the central hall is lighted by clerestory windows above the two side aisles. The forty-four foot ceiling is vaulted with a series of elliptical transverse steel arches faced with buff glazed brick, and Guastavino tile vaults span the spaces between the arches. A great 137-foot tower

*left*: Women's College Gymnasium, Bellflower Road, 1907, Hubbell & Benes, architects.

*below left*: Illuminating Building, Public Square, 1915, Hubbell & Benes, architects.

*below right*: YMCA Building, Prospect Avenue at East 22nd, 1913, Hubbell & Benes, architects.

West Side Market, West 25th Street and Lorain, 1912, Hubbell & Benes, architects.

principal designer of the Western Reserve Historical Society building. In 1905 Hubbell and Benes designed the University Circle building of the Cleveland School of Art in a distinctly similar style. They had planned the Wade Memorial Chapel in 1900. The towers of the U-shaped front of their Citizens Building (1903) were similar in basic form to the Illuminating Building, but the Euclid Avenue facade had a full Neo-Classic portico, which was later removed after the main floor was no longer occupied by a bank.[16] In the immediately postwar years (1919), Hubbell and Benes planned the western portion of the Plain Dealer Building (Public Library annex) in conformity with the character of the Group Plan, and in 1922 they designed the Pearl Street Bank Building in a sophisticated Florentine Renaissance style with an impressive range of arched windows and a wide corbelled parapet.[17]

Hubbell and Benes' most complete expression of the classical ideal was the Cleveland Museum of Art, erected in 1915–1916. Money had been left for an art museum by three men, John Huntington, Horace Kelley, and Hinman B. Hurlbut, in the 1880s. The site donated by J. H. Wade provided a beautiful setting overlooking the lagoon in Wade Park. Nine years were spent in making adjustments in the land and the design in order to provide for the proper orientation and approach to the building, and for the possibility of future development and expansion. The architects consulted with Henry W. Kent of the Metropolitan Museum of Art and Edmund B. Wheelwright of the Boston Museum of Fine Arts in the planning of the building itself.[18]

The nearly 300-foot long facade of Georgian marble was of striking simplicity, the only architectural treatment being the Ionic portico at the center entrance and the slightly projecting end pavilions. The central pediment was separated from the main entablature by a wide attic frieze in the Beaux-Arts manner, which is not strictly Neo-Classic. As I. T. Frary pointed out, the architectural effect was based on good proportions, good material, and well studied detail, and not on the lavish application of ornament. The original building consisted of two horizontal wings flanking a central entrance rotunda. Each wing contained a sky-lighted court surrounded by galleries. Upon its completion, representatives of museum staffs from all over the country observed that "nowhere had they seen a building more perfectly adapted to its requirements."[19] The arrangement of the public and administrative areas and the access between them were the principal

stands at one corner, attached like the campanile of an early Christian basilica, but functioning as a water tower. A charming ornamental note is the sculptured impost blocks of the aisle arcades, representing various animal and vegetable market products.

The classical references of the Market became much more explicit in other Hubbell and Benes buildings. In fact, the classical strand was probably the dominant one of the decade. Benes' classical credentials were unassailable. The earliest work known to be his design was the Centennial Arch. He became a full partner of Coburn and Barnum in 1895, and evidence suggests that Benes was the

Architects' model, Cleveland Museum of Art, Wade Park, 1916, Hubbell & Benes, architects.

virtues of the plan. The building was thoroughly functional and included atmospheric controls and other technical equipment. One of the notable innovations was the design of light-diffusing chambers between the upper and lower skylights of the top-lighted galleries. Thus the use of the classical style, when handled by a good architect, was consistent with the needs of a practical, modern, and specialized structure.

Earlier it had been proposed that the Art Museum be located in the downtown area being developed after the Group Plan. However, it was decided instead to place it in the cluster of educational and ecclesiastical institutions that was developing at University Circle. While it was recognized that the situation around Wade Park lacked the formality of that in the Group Plan, much consideration was given to the advantages of an ensemble of the cultural buildings. In June, 1916, Hubbell and Benes exhibited a drawing at the National City Planning Conference in Cleveland showing the possibilities of such a grouping. The axis between the Art Museum and the lagoon was developed with formal gardens and terraces, and a pair of symmetrical concert and lecture halls was shown on a cross axis. A small triangular hall was indicated at the eventual location

of the Cleveland Orchestra's home, and other buildings were informally placed along the boulevards.[20]

In 1918 Hubbell interested a group of leading citizens in forming a development company for the purpose of preserving the neighborhood and property values in the Wade Park area. The University Improvement Company was formed in November, 1918. Its president was William G. Mather, and other members were F. F. Prentiss, J. H. Wade, and J. L. Severance. By the early twenties the company controlled most of the property on the east side of East 107th Street from Park Lane to the site of the proposed John Hay High School. Through "friendly" ownership, the influence of the University Improvement Company extended along Euclid Avenue from University Circle to Abington Road. A height limit of four stories was agreed upon. Before the Severance gift for a concert hall, the corner of East Boulevard was allotted for the First Church of Christ Scientist, which was later built on Overlook Road on the Heights. Just to the east was a piece of property purchased by the Catholic Diocese in 1916 as a possible site for a new cathedral.[21]

In 1918–1919, Hubbell and Benes made additional sketches for the area. They showed Euclid Avenue as

125

a grand axis culminating at University Circle in a pretentious administration building for a University of Cleveland, in the event that Western Reserve University and Case School should ever merge. The schemes for the buildings depict grandiose Beaux-Arts edifices with a central pavilion flanked by long symmetrical wings. Thus the axial layout and long vistas of the Beaux-Arts ideal, as exemplified in the Columbian Exposition, the Cleveland Group Plan, and Nela Park, were yet another strand represented in the work of Hubbell and Benes.[22]

Plan for the development of the Wade Park cultural center, ca. 1916, Hubbell & Benes, architects.

Rendering of an Administration Building for a proposed University of Cleveland, Solution No. 7, 1918, Hubbell & Benes, architects.

## The Roman Church

The building of churches was also overtaken by the Neo-Classic revival. Late nineteenth century church building had been dominated by the Victorian Gothic, the Richardsonian Romanesque, and finally a general eclecticism. The new Gothic Revival of Cram began to supplant these styles in the 1900s, but the classical wave also claimed its adherents. It took various forms and was justified in different ways by the several churches.

In the case of the Christian Science church, the use of classicism stood for the rationalism of a new faith which was believed to be based on a scientific system of reason and demonstration. Fine examples of the classical style were built by the church throughout the 1920s, among them the First Church of Christ Scientist of Lakewood (1920–1922), designed by Charles Draper Faulkner of Chicago, the Fifth Church on Lake Avenue (1926), planned by Frank Bail, and of course the First Church in Cleveland Heights (1931), by Walker & Weeks. One of the most Roman of these churches was the Second Church of Christ Scientist, designed by Frederic W. Striebinger and erected in 1916. Its six-column portico, con-tinuous cornice line and balustrades, great elliptical clerestory vaults, and low central dome on a windowed drum made it a worthy successor to the Roman scale and ambition of Burnham. In 1949 the interior was converted into a thrust-stage auditorium for the 77th Street Theater of the Cleveland Play House.[23]

During the tenure of Bishop Farrelly of the Catholic Diocese (1909–1921), a number of elements coincided to produce a great period of Catholic church building and the dominance of a "Roman" style. One reason for the ambitious building program was the large immigrant population. Although the peak of immigration had passed before 1910 and practically ceased with the outbreak of the First World War, the proportion of foreign-born or first generation people in Cleveland's population was larger than it had ever been, and in Catholic communities it was probably even higher. The older nationality groups were well established, and during Bishop Farrelly's episcopate the Poles, Bohemians, Slovaks, Hungarians, Italians, and other groups all built newer and larger churches.

Bishop Farrelly was a native of Memphis, Tennessee, but he studied at the North American College in Rome and was the first Bishop of

Second Church of Christ, Scientist (Cleveland Play House), Euclid at East 77th Street, 1916, Frederic Striebinger, architect.

Cleveland to be consecrated in Rome. He lived and served at the North American College for over twenty years before his appointment to Cleveland. Thus he arrived in 1909 steeped in the architecture of Rome ranging from fourth century late Roman basilicas to the seventeenth century Baroque churches of the Counter-Reformation. While there was a great deal of autonomy among the parish priests in the building of a church, the Bishop's experience could not be ignored.[24]

The most evident pattern in the Roman Catholic churches of the decade was the Baroque facade with two symmetrical towers consisting of open belfries with cupolas. This format was executed in brick in the 1912 building of St. Adalbert, a Bohemian parish formed in 1883 by a partition of the oldest Bohemian parish, St. Wenceslas. A frame church served until 1911, when the new $60,000 building was begun. The buff color and the concave gable, together with the life-size statue of St. Adalbert on the facade and the carved stone ornament surrounding the entrance, lend this church a southern European flavor. St. Adalbert was planned by William P. Ginther, an Akron architect who began as a draughtsman under Frank O. Weary, the architect of several of Ohio's Victorian courthouses. Ginther's career lasted nearly sixty years, from 1875 to 1933.[25]

The same pattern rendered in stone could produce a truly Roman effect. St. Colman's Church, also designed by William Ginther, is such a structure. The parish on West 65th Street was founded in 1880, and a frame church served the congregation for thirty-eight years. Starting as an Irish parish, St. Colman's was to become a cosmopolitan church by the time of the Second World War. The new building, under construction during the war years of 1914–1918, was built of Indiana limestone. It has a monumental two-story facade with doubled Corinthian columns flanking the entrance. Guarding the flight of steps are sculptured winged beasts symbolizing the Four Evangelists. The transepts of St. Colman's are very unusual, being fully developed architectural facades matching the front of the building. On the interior, carved marbles were used lavishly in the altar, the wainscoting, the Stations of the Cross, and the baptismal font. In conception, scale, and detail, St. Colman's Church is among the most Roman of them all.[26]

Almost as impressive is the facade of St. Elizabeth's Magyar Church on Buckeye Road. Built in 1918–1922, it was the second building of the first Hungarian Roman Catholic Church in the United

St. Adalbert Roman Catholic Church, East 83rd Street, 1912, William P. Ginther, architect.

States. The parish was established in 1892 when the first priest of their own nationality was appointed to Cleveland, which for over eighty years has had the largest Hungarian population in the country. From 1893 to 1917 a brick church stood on the same site as the new building. St. Elizabeth's was designed by Emile M. Uhlrich, architect of the Weizer Block across the street. Its facade is unusually wide, a fact which is cleverly disguised by the concentration of the entrances in the center and by the handling of the towers. The interior space has some features of the basilican plan, but it is less an aisled nave than a large square auditorium with a colonnaded center aisle. In essence, the openness and width of the interior have the clarity of a classical space, and the Baroque elements are largely decorative.[27]

However, it is generally agreed that the most important Catholic church of the decade was Saint Agnes. Founded in 1893, Saint Agnes was the first

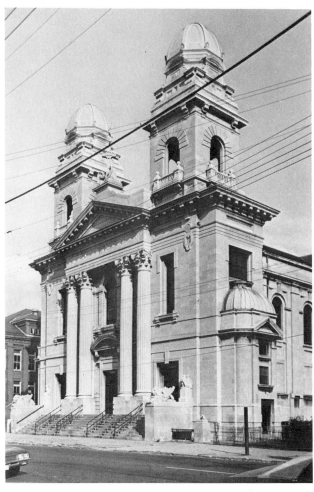

Saint Colman's Roman Catholic Church, West 65th Street near Lorain, 1918, attributed to William Ginther, architect.

St. Elizabeth's Magyar Roman Catholic Church, Buckeye and East 90th Street, 1918-1922, Emile Uhlrich, architect.

Catholic church to "invade" the Euclid Avenue neighborhood that was the choice residential district of the city. The first modest wooden building served from 1893 until 1916, when the new church was completed. Father Gilbert P. Jennings, pastor from the beginning of the parish, was a lover of good architecture who specifically desired a fine building to set a standard for parish churches, not a miniature cathedral. He found a gifted young architect, John T. Comes of Pittsburgh. A specialist in churches, Comes died at the age of forty-nine. It is believed that if he had lived, he might have ranked with Cram, Goodhue, and the few great ecclesiastical architects in America. This judgment is borne out by the brilliant Holy Rosary Cathedral in Toledo and by Saint Agnes.[28]

Father Jennings wished to express the continuity

of the Catholic Church through a modern building reflecting the simplicity and strength of the primitive church. Fundamentally Romanesque, Saint Agnes was conceived in the variant of the style closest to the early Christian basilicas and the churches of southern France, where the Romanesque was still clearly "the child of the Roman" but not yet "the mother of the Gothic." The tower was a campanile, detached from the church. The entrance portals, patterned after the church of St. Trophime at Arles and another at St. Gilles in southern France, opened on a serene interior, with aisle arcades, coffered barrel vaulted ceiling, frescoed half-domed apse, and a domed canopy over the altar. The coloristic treatment was unusual, including mosaics, frescoes and exceptional stained glass.

Contemporary critical interpretations frequently

129

St. Agnes Roman Catholic Church, Euclid Avenue at East 81st Street, 1916 (under demolition, 1975), John T. Comes, architect.

show that Cleveland's architecture, like the Biblical prophet, was not without honor save in its own country. The most positive statement that I. T. Frary of the Cleveland Museum of Art could make was that Saint Agnes "is an interesting example of its type . . . It is a good adaptation and a free rendering of a style that is not generally used." Far more enthusiastic was the appraisal of Anne O'Hare McCormick, a member of the editorial staff of the *New York Times* and a Pulitzer Award winner who wrote three books on Saint Agnes. She stated that "it

was a model of its kind, hailed by competent critics as 'the most perfect parish church in America'." She also quoted the written opinion of Ralph Adams Cram that Saint Agnes was "the most distinguished piece of work I have seen for a long time."[29]

Mrs. McCormick had noted in 1937 that "the story of Saint Agnes' encompasses a social revolution." In January, 1976, continuing social and economic pressures caught up with the parish, which had adapted itself to changing conditions for years, and Saint Agnes was pulled down.

# The Van Sweringen Years — I

Horatio Alger, Jr., died in 1899. In 1913 the Sixteenth Amendment to the Constitution was ratified. Between those two dates began the fabled career of the two Cleveland brothers who fulfilled the formula of the poor but worthy hero who enters life as a bootblack or newsboy, surmounts impossible obstacles, and achieves the heights of success. And as the power of Congress "to lay and collect taxes on incomes" became a tool for the distribution of wealth and a direct attack on the concentration of riches, the end of their era was already announced. The two brothers' magnificent planned garden suburb was at the same time the fruit of the era of progressive reform and among the last of its kind. The development of their transportation empire was characteristic of nineteenth century enterprise, and in spirit the brothers were among the last of the great nineteenth century entrepreneurs.

Oris P. Sweringen was born in 1879, and Mantis J. Sweringen in 1881, and the family settled in Cleveland shortly after 1886. In their youth, the two boys delivered papers on country roads on the Heights. After completing grade school, they worked for the American Agricultural Chemical Company and soon used their savings to buy a lot in the Shaker country, now a part of Cleveland Heights. By buying and selling lots they entered the real estate business, and it was about this time that they assumed the Van Sweringen name of their Dutch ancestors. In 1905 they took options on lots belonging to the Shaker Heights Land Company, a Buffalo syndicate which had been trying to develop the Shaker lakes area since its acquisition in 1889. The Van Sweringen efforts were so successful that they purchased the remaining interest of the syndicate in 1906.[30]

The original venture had failed because of the lack of transportation to the Heights. The Van Sweringens persuaded the Cleveland Railway Company to extend a branch line from the Euclid Heights street railway along Fairmount Boulevard, and Shaker Lakes cars were running out the Fairmount line to Coventry by 1907. The original Shaker Heights subdivision was entirely north of the Shaker lakes, in what is now Cleveland Heights. In 1911 the Village of Shaker Heights was created, extending from the lakes to South Woodland Road and east to Eaton Road. By 1916 the two wide boulevards, Van Aken (originally South Moreland) and Shaker Boulevard, had been laid out and designed to accommodate the rapid transit lines.

The Van Sweringen brothers were men of vision and taste. Very early they conceived the idea that Shaker Heights could be developed into an ideal residential community. The suburban "garden city" idea was not new, nor was the use of architectural restrictions in land sale contracts. However, the development of Shaker Heights was probably the most spectacular of the early twentieth century American suburbs. The subdivision of the Shaker Heights Land Company was laid out by the F. A. Pease Engineering Company. Curving roadways replaced the grid layout of city streets and were determined as much by the topography of the land as by the desire for informality. Natural beauty spots were preserved, and the Shaker dams were rebuilt and the lakes enlarged. The apparently aimless meanderings of the roads were actually calculated to provide access to the main arteries as well as to create the best advantages for beautiful and valuable home sites.[31]

The foresight of the Van Sweringens in planning for a lasting and desirable community has been proven by the stability of the city nearly seventy years later. Probably the most important factor was a stringent set of building restrictions, which gave the Van Sweringen Company control over all building plans and future development. They were written in the form of restrictive covenants in every deed and contained eighteen points covering the plans, location, size, type, cost, and use of structures. They included specific regulations with regard to the proportion of the width to the depth of houses, building lines, additions, driveways, outbuildings, and land use. In 1927 the deeds were rewritten giving the Van Sweringen Company the authority to approve every sale.

Certain locations were reserved for the commercial areas, and certain lots donated for schools and churches. The commercial locations were at Warrensville and Van Aken, Kinsman between Avalon and Lee Road, and later Shaker Square. In 1927 a group of stores which had just been completed on Warrensville Center Road and South Woodland was torn down by the Van Sweringens because they did not conform to the residential plans for the area.

The homes of Shaker Heights could be built for a wide range of prices, depending on the street and the lot. The best architectural examples of the years before 1920 were located on Fairmount Boulevard,

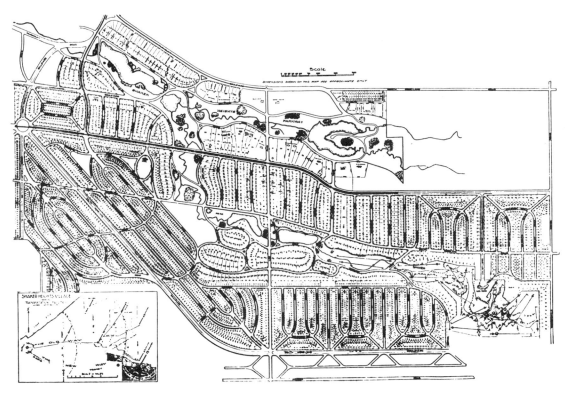

Plan of Shaker Heights, 1918.

O. P. and M. J. Van Sweringen house, South Park Boulevard, Shaker Heights, remodeled 1924, Philip L. Small, architect.

*right*: Union Terminal project, 1919, Graham, Anderson, Probst & White, architects.

*below*: Hotel Cleveland, Public Square, 1918, Graham, Burnham & Company, architects.

South Park Boulevard and South Woodland Road. They were designed by many of Cleveland's finest architects, including Meade and Hamilton, Walker and Weeks, Frederic Striebinger, Willard Hirsh, Charles Schneider, Abram Garfield, and Dercum and Beer. A brochure for "Shaker Village" published in 1923 showed houses of all classes and styles already built—New England Colonial, Dutch Colonial, Tudor, Cotswold, and the low, spreading suburban type. The Van Sweringen brothers' own home on South Park Boulevard had a rather undistinguished aspect as originally designed before 1912, but it was remodeled in 1924 by Philip L. Small into a much more "fashionable" Tudor revival house with a steep all-embracing roof and half-timbered dormers. In keeping with the eclectic predilection of the period, the village high school (now Woodbury Junior High) was built in 1918 with the familiar Independence Hall motif as its entrance tower.[32]

The key to the development of the Heights was always transportation. In 1907 the Van Sweringens approached the Cleveland Railway Company again, with the idea of extending the street railway all the way out Shaker Boulevard (then called Coventry). The company president, however, declared that they would not operate the line even if the Van Sweringens built it themselves. Therefore, the brothers determined to build their own rapid transit line directly into downtown Cleveland. O. P. Van Sweringen had observed the ravine of Kingsbury Run, which led from the city up to the Heights. This property was acquired and the railroad financed. Needing a downtown terminal, the Van Sweringens

also acquired about four acres on the Public Square in 1909. In the course of other land acquisition for the railroad, it was found that part of the right-of-way was owned by the Nickel Plate Railroad. In 1916, after a year of negotiations, the Van Sweringens acquired the Nickel Plate, a 513-mile railroad, in order to control five miles of right-of-way for their rapid transit line. Construction of the Shaker rapid transit began, and after delays caused by the World War, both the Shaker division and the South Moreland (Van Aken) division began operation in 1920, although the section from Warrensville

Center to Green Road was not completed until 1937.

As the plans for the rapid transit depot matured, other railroads indicated an interest in being included or became involved in the land acquisition, and in 1915 the Van Sweringens formed a terminal company to develop this project. However, the beginning of the interurban depot was delayed by the country's involvement in the World War. When the Federal government took over the operation of the railroads in 1917 to increase their efficiency, the regional director of the Railroad Administration found that Cleveland's lakefront route was a bottleneck in the movement of trains from New York to Chicago. In 1918 he asked O. P. Van Sweringen whether his station could be made into a through station accommodating the lakefront railroads. This was the first time that the possibility of a union depot near the Public Square had been thought of, as the proposal for such a depot in the Group Plan location had been renewed in 1915 and endorsed by a public referendum.

In 1918 the Van Sweringens formed the Cleveland Union Terminals Company and prepared a proposed city ordinance under which they would undertake to construct a Union Terminal on Public Square. The ordinance was opposed by some Euclid Avenue merchants and by a minority of a special Chamber of Commerce committee. It was supported by Pierce Anderson, Burnham's successor and the architect for the Cleveland Union Terminals Company. The City's Board of Supervision for Public Buildings and Grounds, now consisting of Arnold W. Brunner, Frederick L. Olmsted, Jr., and Frank B. Meade, took a middle position but generally favored the Group Plan site. The plan was submitted to the voters on January 10, 1919, and passed by a vote of 30,758 to 19,916.[33]

Meanwhile, in 1917–1918, the Van Sweringens built the Hotel Cleveland on their Public Square property. The architects were Graham, Burnham & Company (later Graham, Anderson, Probst and White).[34] When the terminal project became a reality, the brothers decided to incorporate the hotel into the terminal group. Lengthy legal delays in beginning construction were caused by the refusal of the Pennsylvania Railroad to join the New York Central, the Big Four, and the Nickel Plate in entering the Terminal. Moreover, two applications over a year's time were required to obtain the approval of the Interstate Commerce Commission. It was not until September, 1923, that the groundbreaking finally took place for the structures which would become Cleveland's most familiar architectural landmark.

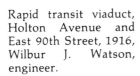

Rapid transit viaduct, Holton Avenue and East 90th Street, 1916, Wilbur J. Watson, engineer.

Detroit-Rocky River Bridge, 1910, Alfred M. Felgate, engineer, and Wilbur J. Watson, consulting engineer.

## Bridges in Concrete

The building of the railroad for the rapid transit through Kingsbury Run to the Heights was itself not a minor construction job. It required making a cut through the shale and sandstone bluffs at Woodhill Road, and the construction of several bridges for two and four-track railroad rights-of-way. All of the Van Sweringen bridges were designed by engineers Wilbur J. Watson & Company. Watson (1871–1939) was one of the most articulate proponents of the collaboration between engineer and architect in the 1920s. Prior to 1900, railroad bridges were generally constructed of stone masonry or metal spans, but by 1915 reinforced concrete had become a standard building material. Although it resembled stone masonry, it had the property of resisting tensile stresses because of the steel reinforcing bars embedded within. Some early efforts imitated the forms of cut stone, but engineers with sensitivity to the expressive power of materials understood that concrete must be treated differently from stone masonry. Watson pointed out that concrete, being plastic and essentially monolithic, should not have any false joints or false architectural details. Instead,

its character could be conveyed by the use of plastic forms. This principle was beautifully demonstrated in two Van Sweringen bridges spanning Holton Avenue and East 90th Street and built in 1916. The larger viaduct has five concrete arches of various widths, hence the spans have arcs of different diameters. There is no ornamentation in the traditional sense. Each arch supports vertical posts which widen into corbels carrying the railway deck. The corbelling gives a massive sculptured appearance to the bridge and transforms an economical utilitarian structure into architecture. The smaller bridge carrying the New York Central over Holton Avenue has a single span, and it was considered a virtue that an artistic result could be achieved at no more cost than steel structures serving the same purpose.[35]

Wilbur Watson was also consulting engineer for the Rocky River Bridge, designed by civil engineer Alfred M. Felgate. After its completion in 1910, this bridge briefly held the record as the longest masonry arch in the United States. More remarkable was the fact that it was not reinforced with steel. The concrete mixture contained an aggregate of sand and stone, some of which was in the form of fairly large boulders. The construction also set a precedent in

135

Detroit-Superior High-Level Bridge, 1918, William A. Stinchcomb, county engineer, Alfred M. Felgate, assistant engineer. (*Cuyahoga County Archives photo by David Thum*)

that steel centering, designed by Watson, was used instead of timber for the concrete forms. The main arch was 280 feet and consisted of two massive ribs. The overall length was 708 feet and the width 60 feet. The central span alone weighed 16,000 tons, and the vertical pressure at the crown was 6,220 tons. Built at a cost of $225,000, the bridge was begun in September, 1908, and dedicated October 12, 1910. One of the officials speaking at the dedication remarked that "no longer did American engineers have to go to Europe for ideas on bridge construction. In fact, Europeans were coming to America." Concerning the architectural design, Watson observed, "The massiveness of the arch rings is in harmony with the span and heavy superstructure, a feature lacking in so many reinforced concrete arch bridges, the designers of which seem to attempt the greatest possible attenuity of the arch rib."[36]

This statement, made in 1927, is clearly a reference to contemporary European bridge design, which culminated in the slender bridges of Robert Maillart in Switzerland. Since concrete is monolithic and plastic in nature, it could assume various shapes and forms as dictated by function, environment, and current aesthetic standards. In his "Specifications for Concrete Structures," written in 1908, Watson also foresaw the possibility of precast bridge beams and slabs, to be made in the factory and assembled at the site.

It was not so much competitive spirit as the exigencies of topography that enabled Cleveland to set another record during 1914–1918. The great width of the Cuyahoga Valley was still an obstacle to a true unification of the east and west sides of the city. The old Superior Viaduct was found to be inadequate by the early years of the century, and it was determined to build a high-level bridge linking the two sides of the valley with a clear span over the river. When the Detroit-Superior High-Level Bridge was completed in 1918, it was the longest double-deck, reinforced concrete bridge in the world.

Planning began before 1908 and continued under three county engineers, Andrew B. Lea (1906–1908), Frank R. Lander (1909–1912), and William A. Stinchcomb (1913–1918). Most of the actual construction was supervised by the latter, and Felgate was again credited as assistant engineer. The new viaduct had twelve reinforced concrete arches, also erected on steel centering, with four ribs each. The length of the structure was 2,656 feet, or 3,112 feet including the approaches from West 9th Street and West 25th Street. The central span over the river was supported by a steel arch of 591 feet, erected as a

136

cantilever from each abutment until the two ends met at the center. The minimum clearance for vessels on the river was 96 feet. The bridge was built with two decks, the upper one for four lanes of traffic and the lower with room for six street car tracks. There was an underground station at each end, and the tracks surfaced on Superior Avenue at West 6th Street and on Detroit Avenue at West 29th Street. The first street car crossed the bridge on December 24, 1917, and it was fully opened to traffic in 1918. A statement published upon the completion of the bridge, despite its Chamber of Commerce tone, gives a fair indication of the significance of the structure to the city. "Nowhere in America does there exist at the present day any bridge or viaduct that can rival, in artistic design, usefulness and permanency of construction, this massive span which binds together the two most populous sections of the metropolis of the middle west."[37]

The opening of the High-Level Bridge encouraged an immediate development of the West Side residential district, and houses of the same general class as those in Shaker Heights were built along Edgewater Drive and Lake Avenue westward into Lakewood. Like the completion of the Superior Viaduct in 1878, the "binding together" of the East and West Sides in 1918 was symbolic. The era was passing when streets and neighborhoods belonged to the carriage, the street car, and the pedestrian. The far-reaching effects of the automobile were about to be felt, as "motoring" ceased to be the hobby of the rich man. Henry Ford had built one of his Model T branch plants in Cleveland in 1913, and the first electric traffic signal anywhere was installed at Euclid Avenue and East 105th Street in 1914. As much as any other single factor, the automobile would shape the postwar city of the twenties.[38]

Playhouse Square, Euclid Avenue at East 14th Street, looking east in 1926.

# 1921: Playhouse Square

The upper Euclid commercial district beyond East 9th Street reached a high point in its development with the cluster of theaters in the area known as Playhouse Square. Their architectural interest does not lie in their unusual style but in their functional and planning arrangement. If the concentrated grouping itself was not unique, its survival over half a century later was very unusual indeed. The Stillman Theater had opened at Euclid and East 12th Street in 1916. Joseph Laronge, an important real estate developer, envisioned the possibility of making the portion of Euclid Avenue east to 17th Street into a street of theaters and fine shops. He presented his plan to businessmen in the theater world and offered choice locations. Together with Marcus Loew of the New York theater syndicate, Laronge and others formed Loew's Ohio Theatres, and as the concept developed, the planned entertainment district was created within five years.[1]

The early years of the century had been a period of consolidation in the theatre world. The employment of actors was centralized by the formation of booking agencies which developed the star system and sold talent on a commercial basis. The stock company, which had been a group of independent actors who managed their own plays, was a casualty of this era. The theater syndicates owned and built their own theaters all over the country. At the same time, the motion picture was becoming a major industry. The first complete narrative film, *The Great Train Robbery*, was produced in 1903, and in 1915 D. W. Griffith's full-length masterpiece, *Birth of a Nation*, was released. By 1917 motion pictures brought in $175,000,000 annually in admissions, and new theaters were being built specifically for the movies, though in 1921 the "talkies" were still six years away.[2]

The first two theaters to open at the 14th Street location in Playhouse Square were built by the Loew Theatres on a lot with only an 85-foot frontage on Euclid Avenue, but 500 feet in depth. The State and Ohio Theatres were built at the back of the property, with unusually long lobbies giving them the desired frontage on Euclid Avenue. Both theaters opened in February, 1921. The account of the opening called Loew's State "one of the most pretentious undertaken by the management outside of New York City." According to the architect of both theaters, Thomas W. Lamb, its lobby, 45 by 180 feet, was the largest of any theater in the world. It is Italian Renaissance in style, with an elaborately coffered ceiling and giant walnut Ionic columns. The auditorium seats 3,400 persons and has excellent acoustics. It was used for motion pictures and popular orchestras for many years. The Ohio Theatre, reached by a lobby parallel to the State's, had a smaller auditorium of 1,400 seats and was used for legitimate drama. It was also Italian in style. Architect Lamb, a specialist in theaters, designed nearly three hundred and was credited with developing the idea of the modern theater, eliminating the upper gallery and creating a form which was at once grand and intimate in feeling.[3]

Two months later, the Allen Theatre opened in the Bulkley Building next door. The eight-story commercial and office building contained an innovative enclosed parking garage behind the theater. Both the building and the theater were

Ohio Theatre lobby, 1921, Thomas W. Lamb, architect. (*Playhouse Square Foundation*)

designed by C. Howard Crane. The Allen Theatre was planned specifically for motion pictures and had no backstage space. Since the angle of the spectator's view was more important than the distance from the screen, the motion picture theater became longer and narrower. This created more wall space for architectural treatment, and the Allen had groups of false windows illuminated from behind. An observation on this architecture by Talbot Hamlin gives an indication of the distance between traditional and progressive criticism of the period. "It is quite possible that the careful and beautiful detail of the best 'movie' theaters, such as . . . the Allen Theater . . . may do much toward the education of the American people to higher standards of architectural taste."[4]

Although it is doubtful that many modern critics would agree with such an observation, it is now generally agreed that the motion picture palace was an authentic part of American architecture. The State, Ohio, and Allen Theatres did not yet display the "weird inventiveness . . . [and] fantastic illusions [of the mid-1920s] . . . stolen from every conceivable architectural style of the past."[5] It was only later that movie palaces flowered into Romanes-

que cathedrals, Aztec temples, and Moorish palaces. The relatively early Playhouse Square theaters came at a brief moment of equilibrium in this architectural type. Being Adam or Renaissance in style, with the lavish use of marble, expensive woods, murals, brocaded tapestries, and gilded plaster relief, they paid homage to European court theaters. As such, they were still representative of the late nineteenth century symbolic use of architecture.

In March, 1921, the Hanna Theatre opened in the annex of the Hanna Building across Euclid Avenue from the Bulkley Building. The sixteen-story office building was erected by Dan R. Hanna, Sr., in memory of his father Marcus A. Hanna. The buildings were designed by Charles A. Platt, the architect of "Gwinn" and of the Leader-News Building. The latter had also been erected by Dan Hanna in 1912 on Superior Avenue, and the Hanna and Leader Buildings are very similar in design. In both buildings, the divisions of the facades were purposely handled in such a way as to minimize the verticality of the structure. The general severity of the design is relieved by the cornices and monumental arched entrances, which are Renaissance in style. The acute angle of Euclid Avenue and East 14th

Street affected both the exterior design and the floor plan of the Hanna Building, requiring a truncated corner and an unusual interior corridor plan. The Hanna Building and its annex are linked by a bridge above the first story. The Hanna Theatre was a legitimate theater seating 1,535 persons and was operated by the Shubert theater syndicate of New York. Compared to the other theaters, the Hanna has a diminutive lobby, which I. T. Frary found "refreshingly sane and appropriate." The auditorium itself is Pompeian in its decorative treatment, with a richly polychromatic effect to the coffered ceiling, the boxes, and the proscenium arch.[6]

The capstone of Playhouse Square was the Keith Palace Theatre, which opened on November 6, 1922. It was built to house the performances of the Keith vaudeville circuit. According to a contemporary account, Edward F. Albee planned to build a "palace" which would be a memorial to his partner B. F. Keith. Early publicity called the completed theater "The Most Beautiful Playhouse in the World." The Palace Theatre is nested in front of Loew's State on East 17th Street, and above the lobby and foyer rises the B. F. Keith Building, a twenty-one story office tower and the tallest building in Cleveland in 1922. Itself a good example of the prewar classical skyscraper, the Keith Building boasted another superlative on its rooftop, a three-story electric sign proclaiming "B. F. Keith Vaudeville" to the entire city. The building and theater were designed by George L. and C. W. Rapp, a noted firm of Chicago theater architects.

The Keith Theatres had always led the other agencies in believing that the provision of beauty and comfort was good for business. Albee conceived this theater as a palace for the ordinary people. It was furnished with marble and bronze fittings, crystal chandeliers from Czechoslovakia, mulberry brocade wall coverings, Louis XVI style furniture, original paintings, and in some cases actual antiques. The three-story lobby has two curving marble staircases, perhaps suggested in this case by the Paris Opera, and paired columns of simulated ivory-colored marble. The colors of ivory and gold predominated throughout. In spite of the fact that the auditorium has a capacity of 3,680, it was comfortable and appeared modest in size. The greatly improved backstage design included a Green Room and facilities for the actors—a drawing room, nursery, barber shop, and kitchenette, as well as forty-eight dressing rooms with baths. The stage has a seven-story fly space. Connections between the various

Palace Theatre lobby, 1922, Rapp & Rapp, architects. (*Playhouse Square Foundation*)

buildings make it possible to go from the Palace stage into Loew's State, and thence into the Ohio, and finally into the Bulkley Building and the Allen Theatre. This connected plan was one of the most unusual features of the Playhouse Square development.[7]

At the time of its completion, the Keith Palace was considered the greatest of the vaudeville theaters. A contemporary description pointed out that this "most beautiful" of playhouses was not for opera, or drama, or spectacle, but for vaudeville, the theater of the common people. As an index of the popular culture of the immediately postwar years, and in the provision of a feeling of luxury for the masses, theaters like the Palace were a remarkable and uniquely American phenomenon.

At Euclid and East 102nd Street, the opening of Loew's Park Theatre preceded the opening of the downtown State by two weeks. The Park was also

Palace Theatre, Euclid at East 17th Street, 1922, Rapp & Rapp, architects (*Playhouse Square Foundation*)

designed by Thomas W. Lamb in the Italian Renaissance style and featured a foyer extending the width of the theater with marble stairs leading to a mezzanine. The theater seated 3,600, and its ivory and gold decorations, murals, and majestic proscenium arch equalled the splendor of Loew's other theaters. The East 105th Street district soon came to rival Playhouse Square and included Keith's East 105th, the Circle, the University, the Alhambra, and the Park Theatres. They were neither so concentrated nor so connected as the downtown group, but they offered the same motion pictures, vaudeville, and orchestra music. The district was an uptown shopping center, with specialty shops, professional offices, banks, markets, and apartments, but unfortunately it did not survive the years as well as Playhouse Square. By 1976, due to changing social patterns and economic conditions, three of the four corners at Euclid and East 105th Street had been leveled, and Loew's Park Theatre was abandoned.[8]

Union Trust Building (Union Commerce Bank), banking lobby, 1924, Graham, Anderson, Probst & White, architects. (*Dalton, van Dijk, Johnson & Partners*)

# 1921–1930

## Consolidation and Prosperity

The decade is an artificial division of history, but if there is any decade which seems to have had a coherent and identifiable character, it was the twenties. The inauguration of Warren G. Harding in 1921 and the great stock market crash in 1929 seem to bracket an era. It was an era of economic expansion and business consolidation, of nationalist reaction, of the "jazz" age and a "return to normalcy." If there was an underlying principle to the age, it was the domination of all segments of life by the ideals and the credo of "big business." The businessman was the new hero of the age.

A favorable atmosphere for business growth was ensured by a succession of Republican administrations. It was believed that a stable economy had been achieved, with an end to cycles of inflation and depression. More efficient methods of production which had been developed in wartime were further enhanced by the application of the principle of scientific management. The standardization of production methods and parts and the planning of research, marketing, and accounting all contributed to the phenomenal expansion. The decade was typified by the combination of businesses into giant corporations, and the greatest effects of consolidation could be seen in industries such as radio communication, chemicals, retail merchandising, and especially the automobile, where Ford, General Motors and Chrysler assumed their ascendancy over the dozens of earlier independent automakers. The mass availability of the automobile demanded the construction of a network of paved highways, as well as the growth of all the industries and services dependent on the automobile. Due to the mass migration to the suburbs which this made possible,

the real estate business prospered as never before. However, in spite of the widespread faith in continuing growth and prosperity, the wealth was in reality unevenly distributed, for large groups of society did not share in the commercial expansion of the cities.[9]

In Cleveland, a structure which symbolized the business character and financial ambitions of the twenties perhaps more than any other was the Union Trust Building, erected in 1923–1924. The Union Trust Company was the result of the merger in 1920 of three major banks with their subsidiaries and other companies, comprising twenty-nine financial institutions altogether. The total assets were $322,500,000, making it the fifth largest trust company in the United States. The purpose of such a merger was to provide the capital for Cleveland's growing industrial needs without going to another financial center. The Union Trust Company, for example, acted as trustee for the bond issue and mortgage to build Keith's Palace and East 105th Theatres.[10]

The Union Trust Building (later Union Commerce Building) is a twenty-story office building. Measuring 146 feet on Euclid Avenue, 258 feet on East 9th Street, and 513 feet on Chester, it was the second largest office building in the world, containing more than thirty acres of floor space. The chief architectural feature is the grand L-shaped three-story banking room, the largest in the country in 1924. Once again the precedent was Roman, a style expressing not only grandeur and permanence, but also organization. The basilican halls are on a truly Roman scale, with a giant Corinthian order of Italian marble columns on both sides of the fifty-foot wide

Bingham Company Warehouse, 1278 West 9th Street, 1915, Walker & Weeks, architects.

rooms. The barrel-vaulted ceilings are double skylights, and the side "aisles" have elaborately coffered ceilings. In the lunettes at the ends of the room are colorful murals by Jules Guerin, muralist for the Pennsylvania Station in New York and the Panama-Pacific Exposition of 1915 in San Francisco. The building was designed by the Chicago firm of Graham, Anderson, Probst & White, which had used the same barrel-vaulted scheme in the Continental and Commercial Bank of Chicago. The firm was planning the Union Terminal for the Van Sweringens at the same time, and their 1919 prospectus for the Terminal referendum showed a sketch for the grand concourse with still another variation on the vaulted skylight and colossal Corinthian colonnades. However, since the Terminal concourse as executed was below the street, this favorite scheme was not used.[11]

The firm of Graham, Anderson, Probst & White exemplified one of the most important phenomena in architectural practice in the twentieth century. Projects on the scale of the Union Trust or the Terminal demanded a kind of architectural organization and management comparable to that of the architect's corporate client. The development of large scale offices with several partners, which continued to function under the same name for decades, was necessary to organize and handle the complex design problems, as well as the enormous amounts of routine drafting. At the same time, the chief partners in such firms still had the classical training which gave them a breadth of vision when they were not made myopic by a narrow eclecticism.

Fortunately, Cleveland possessed a firm for the spirit of the twenties in Walker and Weeks. Frank R. Walker (1877–1949) and Harry E. Weeks (1871–1935) were both natives of Massachusetts who had studied at the Massachusetts Institute of Technology. Walker graduated in 1900 and spent two additional years studying in Paris and Italy. Upon returning he worked in the office of the prominent Boston architect Guy Lowell, architect of the Boston Museum of Fine Arts and the New York County Court House. Walker subsequently became Lowell's office manager in New York. After a brief period working in Pittsburgh, he came to Cleveland in 1905 at the suggestion of John M. Carrere of the Group Plan Commission. Weeks also came to Cleveland in 1905, having known Walker in Pittsfield, Massachusetts. Both young men joined the office of J. Milton Dyer and were associated with him during the planning of the Cleveland City Hall and the Athletic Club. In 1911 they formed their own partnership.[12]

Like most young firms, Walker and Weeks in their early years did some residential work, including, in 1913–1915, two homes on Fairmount Boulevard for Orville and William H. Prescott. Planned in two different eclectic styles, the houses shared a common garden laid out by the Olmsted Brothers. One of the firm's finest early achievements, however, was a utilitarian structure built in 1914–1915 which clearly revealed the architects' apprenticeship under the progressive influence of J. Milton Dyer. The Bingham Company warehouse, built for a pioneer Cleveland hardware company founded in 1841, was the largest single unit for wholesale hardware merchandising in the world. The form of the L-shaped warehouse is especially interesting because of the difference in grade levels between West 9th and West 10th Streets. The block-long building was a sophisticated design related to the Sullivanesque idiom reflected in the Rockefeller Building. The simple repetitive nature of a massive steel and concrete structure is given architectural character by grouping the windows in vertical ranks between warm brick piers with recessed spandrels. The roof line consists of an utterly plain concave cornice reminiscent of Root's Monadnock Building. But it is the unusually subtle refinements of proportion and detail that raise the architecture of the Bingham Company warehouse above that of its neighbors in the warehouse district. A recent evaluation paid the warehouse the highest tribute: "It demonstrates the distinction between building and architecture."[13]

Before long, however, Walker and Weeks joined the foremost exponents of the continuing classical revival. They soon specialized in bank design, eventually planning over sixty banks in Ohio. One of their earliest commissions was the remodeling of the New England Building for the Guardian Savings and Trust Company in 1914–1915. Working around the existing structural columns, they designed a new street facade of three-story engaged Corinthian columns. The banking room is a majestic basilica-like interior with a flat, coffered ceiling, similar in general style to that of the Union Trust. While nobly expressing the standard image of a bank, the facade does not truly harmonize in style with the upper stories by Shepley, Rutan & Coolidge, but its street scale is so large that the discrepancy is seldom noticed. The Guardian Building was joined with the older Garfield Building on the corner by the National City Bank in 1946.[14]

Walker and Weeks' richest work in homage to the world of finance was the Federal Reserve Bank of Cleveland, erected in 1922–1923. Cleveland was the home of the Fourth District of the twelve semiautonomous regional banks. As the Federal Reserve system established a centralized bank in order to provide more flexibility for the currency and more government control over banking administration, the regional banks served primarily as depositories of member banks and did not accept the accounts of individuals. For this reason, few people have become familiar with the gorgeous interior of the Cleveland bank.

It would be hard to imagine how a building could better represent the intended security and stability of the centralized banking system. Standing at the southeast corner of the area being developed for the Group Plan, the bank was designed to harmonize

Guardian Building (National City Bank), facade altered in 1915, Walker & Weeks, architects.

with the Beaux-Arts classicism of the other Mall buildings. The twelve-story foursquare structure stands on a base of pink granite, and its upper stories are clad in a pinkish Georgia marble with textures that are graduated toward the top of the building. In the early twentieth century tradition of symbolism, the majestic arcade of the lower stories is complemented with decorative and allegorical sculpture by Cleveland's Fischer-Jirouch Company and Henry Hering of New York.[15]

The experience of entering the bank has been compared with walking into the interior of a bar of gold. The public lobby of the main floor has high vaulted ceilings which are deeply coffered and gilded, with a low dome on pendentives at the intersection of the transverse and axial halls. The walls are faced with a rich, gold-veined Sienna marble, and each arched bay is screened by high, black wrought-iron gates which, by contrast, intensify the golden

147

Federal Reserve Bank, main lobby, 1923, Walker & Weeks, architects.

atmosphere. Because of its symbolic and expressive design and its successful relationship to the Group Plan, the Federal Reserve Bank must be considered one of Walker and Weeks' major triumphs.

Not surprisingly, most of the banks of the twenties were designed in the classical idiom associated with conservatism and stability. The largest structure of this kind on the west side of Cleveland was built in 1926 by the United Banking and Trust Company. For the nine-story building at Lorain and West 25th Street, Walker and Weeks chose a more restrained Italian Renaissance classicism with an elaborately pedimented entrance on the east facade. The building was intended to be enlarged so that the six-bay arcade on the north would be centered on that side, but the plan was never carried out. The bank merged with Central National Bank in 1929.

Toward the end of the decade the work of Walker and Weeks began to display current Modernistic tendencies. The simplified geometric forms of the

style were not uncongenial to the classically trained architect; the Modernistic idiom was symmetrical, it provided for the use of sculptured embellishment, and building masses were treated in a way appropriate to the traditional use of masonry. The difference was that it was frankly a style of surface ornament and geometric simplification. The Pearl Street Savings and Trust Company is a good example of this transition from classicism to modernism. Built in 1929, the bank was consolidated with the Cleveland Trust Company during construction and became a branch of that bank. Its facade displays fluted limestone piers with geometric capitals. The metal window spandrels with relief designs are another typical Modernistic device. The entrance is framed by ornamental bronze pylons from which light fixtures project on metal standards. The interior is much more traditional, with round arches and a deeply coved ceiling. Later we shall see that certain elements in the design of Severance Hall, planned by Walker and Weeks at the same time, reveal evident similarities.

By 1930, Walker and Weeks had achieved a regional reputation because of their important works in all major Ohio cities as well as in other parts of the Midwest. Their achievements included not only the Indiana World War Memorial in Indianapolis, but even an Ohio War Memorial Bridge in Belgium. The entire issue of a new journal in the summer of 1930 was devoted to their work, with an introductory note stating that "the firm of Walker and Weeks is recognized as being instrumental to a large degree, in the development of a fine style of architecture in the Mid-West."[16]

In the mid-twenties, the most immediate and obvious application of the Modernistic style appeared in the "setback" skyscraper. The New York zoning law of 1916, enacted to enable light to penetrate the canyons of lower Manhattan, required the forms of the tall building to be stacked in receding layers like the tiers of a wedding cake. For various reasons this became a stylistic manner even in places where the zoning requirement was unnecessary.

The skyscraper had always been considered the typical building of twentieth century America. It was seen not only as symbolic of the business society, but also as the structure most expressive of the new materials of steel and concrete. In the early skyscrapers, however, some critics found that "stupendous achievements" of engineering and function were being masked by eclectic styles. The

United Banking & Trust Company (Central National Bank), West 25th Street at Lorain, 1926, Walker & Weeks, architects.

Pearl Street Savings & Trust, West 25th Street and Clark, 1929, Walker & Weeks, architects.

problem of skyscraper style was sharply focussed in the 1922 competition for the Chicago Tribune Building, in which the second place design by Eliel Saarinen was generally recognized as a far more logical and powerful expression of the building's height, structure, and function than the winning Gothic design. The simple vertical lines and set-back masses of Saarinen's design soon influenced many other buildings. Sheldon Cheney observed that "[the architect] has been quick to grasp the possibilities of proportional massing, and the opportunity for play of light and shade, in these jutting crags and receding terraces."[17]

Cleveland had few such buildings for a city of its size. The most impressive was the Ohio Bell Telephone Building, erected in 1925–1927. The architects were the Hubbell and Benes Company. A number of preliminary schemes were made in various styles, among them Romanesque and

Gothic. Even after the Modernistic treatment was decided upon, old associations could not be abandoned, and the company called the chosen style "Modern American Perpendicular Gothic." The actual design was very similar in mass, treatment, and detail to some of the important buildings of Voorhees, Gmelin & Walker in New York. In turn, their New York Telephone and Western Union Telegraph Buildings clearly reflected the Saarinen solution. The characteristic features were the slender vertical piers with recessed spandrels, the round-arched windows at the top of each setback, and the more massive corner piers with their slightly blunted tops. The twenty-two story Ohio Bell Telephone Building reaches to 365 feet, with three stories below the street level. The structure stands on a concrete pad five and a half feet thick, believed to have been the largest continuous job of concrete pouring ever undertaken in the country, and the

Ohio Bell Telephone Building, 700 Prospect Avenue, 1927, Hubbell & Benes, architects.

steel framework is faced with Indiana limestone. Costing $5,000,000 and containing equipment worth $6,000,000, the building was constructed to house the company's business offices, dial telephone equipment, long distance and toll switchboards, executive offices, service areas, and employee restaurants.[18]

The Modernistic building erected by the Town and Country Club was also designed to answer a more specialized set of functions than the typical office building. As suburban life flourished, the country club came to supplement the city club of the successful businessman, and new town and country clubs proposed to provide two centers for one membership, a centrally located clubhouse with complete social and indoor athletic facilities, plus a rural golf and country club. On this basis, the Cleveland Chapter of the National Town and Country Club financed and constructed its $1,672,-000 building at Euclid Avenue and East 24th Street in 1929–1930. Among the representative members were Edmund S. Burke, Jr., John C. Calhoun, Jr., Leonard C. Hanna, Jr., and Francis F. Préntiss. George B. Post and Sons were the architects. The building's first eight floors housed club activities and included meeting rooms, dining rooms, and athletic facilities. The next ten floors had 122 bedrooms with baths, and the upper three floors contained service areas and a solarium. The insistent vertical lines of the tower are unbroken over its entire height, so that the set-back design was only developed in the lateral dimension. In this case the setback clearly expressed the building's functions, as the windowless walls of the lower blocks enclosed the gymnasium, pool and ball courts. The ornament is concentrated above the monumental entrance, on the window spandrels, and at the top of each rank of windows.

The origins of the abstract geometric Modernistic ornament have not been fully studied. It sometimes combined the stylized plant and animal forms and dynamic rectilinear lines of what is now called Art Deco, American and Mexican Indian motifs, Cubist planes, and even vestigial patterns from the Arts and Crafts and Art Nouveau movements. Many of these influences could be discerned in the National Town and Country Club; the relief panels crowning each tier of windows are especially suggestive of Mayan sculpture.[19]

The National Town and Country Club did not survive the Depression, and the building was acquired by Fenn College in 1937. Organized under that name in 1929, the college's origins could be traced to YMCA night courses begun in 1881 under the inspiration of Sereno P. Fenn, and the later development of the Cleveland YMCA School of Technology. When the building was converted for college use by Herman Dercum, a noted Cleveland residential architect, it housed twenty-seven classrooms, a library, six laboratory spaces, an assembly room, complete physical education facilities, and 122 residence rooms. In 1965 Fenn College became the nucleus of Cleveland State University.[20]

The failure of the National Town and Country Club, as well as the closing or reorganization of many banks during the 1930s, seemed to symbolize

National Town and Country Club (Fenn College Tower), East 24th Street at Euclid, 1930, George B. Post & Sons, architects.

## The Municipality

It is sometimes forgotten that throughout the twenties Cleveland continued its reputation as one of the most progressive cities in the nation. The momentum of the Group Plan was maintained, and several of the buildings in the Mall area were completed during these years. Other cities watched with interest as Cleveland became the largest municipality in the country to experiment with the city manager plan of government, the objective of which was to remove the chief executive from partisan politics. As part of the plan, the city council was chosen by proportional representation from several large districts, and the traditional ward system was abolished. Two able city managers, William R. Hopkins and Daniel E. Morgan, served from 1924 to 1931, when the experiment was discontinued because it undermined the influence of political party leaders, and because the citizens did not understand the advantages of proportional representation. Hopkins was an energetic and efficient administrator who is best remembered for having proposed the municipal airport in order to give the city a position on the United States coast-to-coast air mail route. The field, which was called a "pioneer institution," opened on July 1, 1925 at the Brookpark Road site. Another mark of national recognition was the choice of Cleveland as the site for two political conventions in 1924. The Republican National Convention which nominated Calvin Coolidge and Charles G. Dawes was held in June, and the Socialist Party met in July to nominate Progressive candidate Robert M. LaFollette. Holding the conventions in Cleveland was made possible by the recent completion of the city's Public Auditorium.[21]

The need for a large auditorium and convention hall had been forcibly demonstrated by the necessity for a temporary structure at the Industrial Exposition of 1909. In 1916 the hall was financed by a bond issue passed through the efforts of a committee which organized the support of 116 civic groups. Because of the war and subsequent inflation, construction did not begin until 1920, and the Public Auditorium was dedicated on April 15, 1922. It was the fourth building completed in the Group Plan, although it had not been given a high priority in the original scheme. The Music Hall seating 2,800 was added at the south end of the Auditorium in 1929.

The Public Auditorium was the largest such

the end of a cultural era. From the perspective of nearly fifty years, it is clear that there was never again to be such a consensus of social and aesthetic values. While the World War had marked the end of the nineteenth century in political and social terms, many of the artistic ideas persisted nearly twenty years longer. The transition from classicism to modernism marked the last phase of the nineteenth century aesthetic of eclecticism which had dominated architecture since the 1880s. After 1930 it would become increasingly difficult to build seriously in the historical styles; after 1939 it would be virtually impossible. The social and economic changes wrought by a generation of depression, war and urban renewal would find the look of architecture and the face of the city altered beyond recognition.

Public Auditorium, 1922, J. Harold MacDowell, city architect, and Frank R. Walker, consulting architect. (*Cuyahoga County Archives photo by David Thum*)

convention hall in the country at the time of its opening. Statistics indicate the magnitude of the structure. Over 300 feet long, the auditorium proper had a clear span of 215 feet. The seating capacity of the main floor and the long U-shaped galleries combined was over 11,500. The stage at one end was 60 by 104 feet, with a proscenium opening 72 feet wide and 42 feet high. In spite of its size, the auditorium's acoustical properties were excellent. The hall was illuminated by indirect lighting diffused through glass panels in the ceiling. The basement Exhibition Hall contained over 28,500 square feet of exhibit space and was accessible by numerous ramps and stairways. The circulation plan was designed so that 13,000 people could be evacuated from the building in four and a half minutes.

One of the significant features of such a building is the degree to which the mechanical systems supplemented the relatively simpler needs of shelter and attractiveness in earlier buildings. Their complexity is an indication of the state of the technical arts in the twenties. The ventilating system of the auditorium was able to supply 18,000,000 cubic feet of fresh air per hour, cooled in summer and heated in winter, for which air ducts up to ten feet square were required. The auditorium had an automatic spinkler system, provision for an automatic sheet of water across the stage proscenium in case of fire, a central vacuum cleaning system, back-up electrical systems,

and steam heating for the offices and corridors. The hall was equipped for motion picture projection from a distance of 330 feet and was furnished with one of the largest pipe organs in existence, with 10,010 pipes and 150 direct speaking stops.[22]

The official architect of the Public Auditorium was J. Harold MacDowell, City Architect, with Frank R. Walker as consulting architect. The style of the building is Italian Renaissance, and the auditorium achieves a classical simplicity with its wide ceiling of curving arches. The entrance lobby displays an impressive, if somewhat heavy, use of classical ornament, executed in marble, tile, and decorative plaster. On the exterior, the problem of making architectural sense of such vast stretches of wall was admirably handled by the arrangement of the arcaded windows, the high rusticated podium, and the cornice line which conformed to the recommendations of the Group Plan. The inscription on the frieze spells out the ideals of the period:

A Monument Conceived as a Tribute to the Ideals of Cleveland, Builded by Her Citizens and Dedicated to Social Progress, Industrial Achievement and Civic Interest.

While the Auditorium was not included in the original Group Plan scheme, the planners had always intended that a building large enough to balance the Federal Building would be erected at the south end of the Mall. The City gave the land, which was the

152

former site of Charles Heard's 1875 City Hall. In 1916 a competition was held for a design for the Cleveland Public Library. Fifty-eight firms indicated an interest in the competition, and eight of these were chosen to submit plans, including Abram Garfield, Hubbell & Benes, and Walker & Weeks. The other architects were John Russell Pope, Robert D. Kohn, Edward L. Tilton, Holabird & Roche, and Allen & Collins. Two independent juries in New York and Cleveland chose the plan of Walker & Weeks. Construction was not begun until 1922, and the Library was opened to the public in 1925.[23]

In order to conform with the requirements of the Group Plan, Walker & Weeks produced a design which was nearly identical in size, shape, height, and general style with the Federal Building, but which was different in its treatment of detail. The five-story building, plus basement, has the same arcaded and rusticated ground story, the same colossal colonnades for the middle stories, and the same entablature height. The differences in stylistic detail are subtle and complementary. The library's function demanded more daylight for the reading room, and the plan achieved a 40 percent greater window area on all sides of the building. The interiors were done in the Roman Beaux-Arts idiom which had been used in the Courthouse and City Hall. The vaulted lobby, with its painted ceilings, and the main

reading room, whose three bays with groin-vaulted and coffered ceilings are reminiscent of a Roman bath, are truly impressive public spaces. As a functional building, the Library was widely praised and established a precedent for subsequent library designs. With forty-seven miles of shelving, its capacity was the third largest in the country. There were fifteen reading rooms for various subjects. The arrangement of the departments and the provisions for circulation, storage, and retrieval were efficiently and painstakingly planned. An unusual feature was the architectural treatment of the light court, which was usually left very utilitarian in appearance. Designed in the early Florentine style, its towers and battlemented parapets were executed in buff brick and provide interesting views from every part of the building. Walker & Weeks' mastery of the problems posed by the Public Library within the framework of the Group Plan showed that their civic work was the equal in every respect of their commercial buildings.[24]

In 1930 the Board of Education Headquarters Building, also designed by Walker & Weeks, completed the east side of the Mall between Rockwell and St. Clair Avenues. The six-story E-shaped sandstone building conformed to the height requirement of the Group Plan and had the same building line as the Public Auditorium, but its design is rather

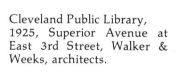
Cleveland Public Library, 1925, Superior Avenue at East 3rd Street, Walker & Weeks, architects.

Central Police Station, 2001 Payne Avenue, 1926, Herman Kregelius, city architect. (*Cuyahoga County Archives photo by David Thum*)

Criminal Court Building, 1560 East 21st Street, 1930, Franz C. Warner & G. Evans Mitchell, architects. (*Cuyahoga County Archives photo by David Thum*)

ordinary compared with the best work of the firm. It seems certain that without the constraints of the Group Plan formula, the Board of Education building would have been more modern. This hypothesis is borne out in the other buildings Walker and Weeks were designing by 1929–1930 as well as in other municipal buildings of the same time.

The Central Police Station and the Criminal Court Building illustrate the transition. The former was erected earlier (1926) and is a somewhat heavy-handed cross between a decadent classicism and the Modernistic idiom. The two columns surmounted by eagles would not have been out of place in the megalomaniacal projects of Albert Speer a dozen years later. Whether they may be taken as symbolic of the exaggerated nationalism on both sides of the Atlantic at the time is open to question. The Criminal Court, on the other hand, was built in 1930 and is a good example of the Modernistic style, with its vertical piers, set back design, and geometric entrance lamps.

Another structure erected in 1930–1931 was the

Municipal Stadium on the lakefront north of the Courthouse. Although it was considered a part of the Group Plan, such a building had not been dreamed of in 1903, when recreation was still a relatively private and small-scale activity. Only after the war did it become such an integral part of society that it could no longer be considered incidental. Golf, tennis, and winter sports became extraordinarily popular, in part because of the increased mobility made possible by the automobile. College football helped to make America a "nation of spectators" and was responsible for the construction of many magnificent stadiums. Professional baseball continued to attract increasing numbers, and prize fighting enjoyed a new popularity. The first event held in the Cleveland Stadium was the Schmeling-Stribling heavyweight fight on July 3, 1931.[25]

The Stadium was projected in 1925, and city manager William Hopkins had plans drawn in 1926. Although a bond issue was passed in 1928, construction did not actually begin until 1930. The completed structure had permanent seating for 78,000, and

Municipal Stadium, 1931, Walker & Weeks, architects, Osborn Engineering company, engineers.

with chairs placed on the field this was increased to 92,000. The plan is oval in shape, with the narrow end toward the west and the superstructure open to the east. The Stadium covers an area of twelve acres, enclosing a four-acre playing field. The outer walls of the structure are made of a mottled gray brick with terra cotta trim. They are not curved, but consist of a series of flat planes, hence the form of the Stadium is actually an oval polygon.

The engineering design was done by the Osborn Engineering Company and the architectural design by Walker and Weeks. The planning of large amphitheaters had been susceptible of architectural treatment since the days of the Romans—in fact, it is a further proof of the decline of eclectic attitudes by 1930 that the Stadium was not Roman in style. Nevertheless, it is doubtful whether many such structures were subject to the subtle artistic considerations expressed by Frank R. Walker in an interview at the time of the Stadium opening. The structure was 116 feet tall (ten stories), and Walker explained the devices used to minimize its height. The outer brick wall was only 61 feet high, and the superstructure of steel and aluminum was set back above the walls. The aluminum louvered facing and roof of the superstructure were planned to reflect the color of the sky, thus making them appear less obtrusive when seen against the lake. According to Walker, the use of structural aluminum was the most extensive to that date and one of the earliest in

the country. There were four masonry towers which functioned as entrances and booths but which were also architecturally necessary "visually to anchor [the structure] to the ground," according to the architect. Such visual considerations make the difference between building and architecture, and exemplify the strength of Walker's traditional training. The decision to place the Stadium on the lakefront as a part of the Mall was accompanied by the hope that eventually the railroad tracks would be eliminated or bridged. In 1930 the Progressive vision of Cleveland was intact.[26]

Another significant example of the collaboration between engineer and architect was the Lorain-Carnegie Bridge, a product of the twenties although it was not opened until 1932. A high-level crossing connecting Lorain and Central Avenues was envisioned at least as early as 1911, when it was advocated in a proposal by H. D. G. Parsons and published in a map issued by the Carnegie Extension Association. In 1925 a special committee of the City Plan Commission recommended that a high-level Central-Lorain Bridge should "be built immediately," and an $8,000,000 bond issue was approved in 1927. A realignment of the streets meant that it was Lorain and Carnegie that were actually connected by the new steel and concrete structure, nearly a mile long, consisting of thirteen cantilever truss spans varying in length from 299 feet over the river to 132 feet at the ends. A lower deck intended to carry four

155

Drawing of a pylon for the Lorain-Carnegie
Bridge, Walker & Weeks, architects.

The architect's contribution should not be understood merely as a matter of adding ornament to an engineered structure. Frequently the engineer has more than one solution available when he confronts a construction problem but has no particular criteria for his final choice. The architect, on the other hand, with his training in design and his sensitivity to relationships of form and materials, is able to select and define the forms which would be the most distinctive and significant. For example, one of the variations from strict engineering necessity on the Lorain-Carnegie Bridge was the curving of the lower edge of the trusses to give a more pleasing arched appearance.

However, the major architectural feature of the bridge was the four massive pylons with conventionalized figures representing Guardians of Traffic. Designed by Walker and sculptured by Henry Hering of New York, they illustrate the simplified classicism which was becoming Modernistic in style. The figures hold in their hands vehicles representing the spirit of progress in transportation: a hay rack, a covered wagon, a stage coach, a passenger automobile, and four types of motor trucks. While there were several bridges designed with approach pylons during these years, the Lorain-Carnegie sculptures are unique because of the integral character of the figures and the pylons, the appropriateness of the symbolism, the consistency of the style, and the scale of the figures. A historical precedent for the pylons existed in the winged guardian figures of the Assyrian kings, which imparted a kind of magical protection. Such a conception seems remote or even absurd nearly fifty years later, but it still conveys an imaginative power of a sort which has become almost lost in an increasingly technocratic society. The brief moment of Watson's "critical public," if it ever existed, seems to have passed all too soon.[29]

This mid-twenties consideration of art in utilitarian structures was demonstrated in a most unlikely building. Of stadiums, bridges, and waterworks, the last would seem to be the least likely to demand architectural treatment, but the Baldwin Filtration Plant was conceived at the outset as a municipal amenity not only practically but also visually. In 1919 a commission was appointed to study the future development of the city water system. Their report recommended that the East Side plant for treating raw lake water should be located above the old Fairmount Reservoir, where a new underground reservoir was already under

lanes of vehicular traffic and two lanes of street car tracks was never completed.[27]

The bridge was designed by engineers Wilbur J. Watson and Associates, with Frank Walker as architect. Watson wrote several books in the twenties and thirties in which he reiterated his philosophy concerning the importance of artistic collaboration. With reference to the Lorain-Carnegie Bridge, he noted that

> Great care was taken to obtain a pleasing architectural creation, demanded by a public that is becoming more and more critical in this regard. This is a manifestation that modern civilization is not satisfied with structures of utility alone, but desires that art shall be considered. As a result of this insistence of a more enlightened civilization, there is an increasing tendency for collaboration between engineers and architects in the design of the more important bridges . . ."[28]

156

construction. On this assumption, the report further advised:

> Owing to the location of the Baldwin filtration plant being adjacent to park property, and in consideration of its commanding site on the elevation overlooking the city, it is certain that it will attract great attention and will be inspected by many visitors. Due attention should be given to the architecture of the buildings and the landscaping of the surrounding grounds, so as to provide for this plant an attractive setting, which its use seems to demand and the topography of its location makes possible.[30]

A site plan was prepared in 1920 by Cleveland landscape architect Albert D. Taylor, using the prominent location and distant view to the best advantage. The structure itself was completed in 1925, half a dozen years before the Stadium and the bridge, and was still classical in conception.

The basic principles of the filtration process were not complicated. Raw lake water was brought to the Fairmount Reservoir from the East 49th Street pumping station. It would be raised to the filtration plant, where chemicals would be added for settling suspended matter, disinfecting, and controlling taste and odor. The treated water would be placed in settling basins and then transferred to a series of sand filters. From there it would be discharged into the clear water reservoir for distribution to the service area.

The underground clear water reservoir was a separate engineering marvel whose architecture is invisible. Five hundred feet wide, 1,000 feet long, and thirty-five feet deep, it has a capacity of 135,000,000 gallons. It is roofed by a thin groin-vaulted concrete slab supported by 1,196 columns which are thirty inches in diameter and spaced eighteen feet apart. Before the reservoir was filled, the underground space had the appearance of a vast and mysterious cathedral. The roof was covered with soil, making a park-like lawn adjacent to the

Underground reservoir, Baldwin Filtration Plant, Fairhill Road, 1925, Frazier-Sheal Company, engineers. (*Cleveland Landmarks Commission*)

157

Baldwin Filtration Plant, Fairhill Road, 1925, Herman Kregelius, architect.

plant. A lengthy appraisal of the aesthetic effect of the underground space appeared in *The Nation* in 1927. A brief excerpt gives its central conclusion.

> No architect ever lived who would not stand in silent wonder in this Hall of Six Hundred Columns. It is an abstraction, a song in some nameless mother tongue that everyone understands. It is the work of a law, of a formula ruling over space and mass—rather, perhaps, a law brought into the range of our feelings by being stated in the most fundamental, most simple terms of human need for formal perfection. It is the product of man's desire for order, freed from the old conventions of architecture by the new conventions of engineering.[31]

To accommodate the working of the filtration plant, city architect Herman Kregelius devised a plan whereby the administrative functions were grouped in a central block three stories high, with offices on the first floor, laboratories on the second, and large tanks on the top floor to supply water for backwashing the filters. Two axial wings contain central galleries with two rows of ten filters each. The entire length of the building is over 750 feet, and the whole is set on a balustraded terrace. The chemical treatment building is a separate structure across the reservoir lawn.[32]

The arrangement of the waterworks thus became an exact demonstration of the principles of Palladio.

First was the principle of hierarchy, or the building up from dependent parts to a focal core, producing the triadic composition which is the essence of a Palladian building. The main entrance became a grand Palladian arch, approached by a double dog-leg Renaissance staircase. A second principle was the coordination of exterior and interior design by representing the interior organization on the facades. The entrance block represents not only the core of the plant, but also the main axis, which leads through to the reservoir lawn. The flanking wings represent the secondary axis, which intersects the central one. The third principle, the expression of civic function, was achieved by the unbroken horizontal continuity of the facades. The classical ornament of the exterior is simple and refined, sufficient to accentuate the dominant elements but not excessive enough to be absurd on a utilitarian structure. The interiors of the filter galleries are light, open, and humane in scale, and slender metal trusses are curved to make a more pleasing design.[33]

It is perhaps ironic that the grand Beaux-Arts ideals of architects like Hubbell and Benes should have been best realized in a waterworks. But it may be fitting that the last and most perfectly Palladian structure for a great industrial municipality was a building like the Baldwin Filtration Plant.

# The Cultural Center

In the postwar atmosphere of the 1920s, the country was gripped by a nationalist reaction which caused a disintegration of the Progressive crusade of the previous decades. A fear of political subversion created hostility to radicals and ethnic and racial minorities. For this reason new immigration was severely restricted by a series of acts passed by Congress during the 1920s, some of which were specifically directed against peoples from southern and eastern Europe. Thus there were no immigrant groups comparable to those of the prewar period to be accommodated in newly created neighborhoods.

However, members of the older Jewish community settled in the area along East 105th Street north of the theater district and east of Rockefeller Park. The mobility of the Jewish community can be traced by the location of their synagogues over the years. From their beginnings around Eagle and East 9th Street, the Jewish congregations had moved steadily eastward along Woodland and Central Avenues. In 1921–1922, both the Oheb Zedek and Anshe Emeth congregations, which had built at East 37th and East 38th Streets less than twenty years before, erected new synagogues north of Superior Avenue. Oheb Zedek built a "modernized" Gothic structure on Parkwood Drive, and Anshe Emeth erected an imposing classical edifice at East 105th Street and Drexel. The latter was part of a million-dollar building for the Cleveland Jewish Center.

From its small beginning in 1869, the Jewish Center had become an institution of national reputation. The new building housed religious, educational, social and cultural activities, with public forums, classes in Americanization, and the Hebrew School. The block-long structure contains an ornate two-story auditorium with arched windows and a vaulted ceiling, numerous classrooms and meeting rooms, a gymnasium, and a swimming pool. The tapestry-brick building has a frieze of stone inscribed with the names of ancient and modern Jewish prophets and scholars. The Anshe Emeth synagogue, now the home of the Cory United Methodist Church, is a fine example of conservative classical style. The sanctuary itself has a central plan, with four great arches leading up to the circular dome. A rectangular U-shaped balcony increased the seating to 2,400 and made it the second largest synagogue in capacity in the country. Arched windows around the room contain stained glass with various Jewish symbols. The building was planned by Cleveland architect Albert F. Janowitz.[34]

The new building of Congregation Tifereth Israel was unusual and modern by comparison. The congregation had moved from its first temple on Huron and East 6th Street to East 55th Street in 1894, and the new Temple on East 105th Street at Ansel Road was begun in 1923. The site occupied a commanding position overlooking the Rockefeller parkway, so that the building became a prominent

Anshe Emeth Congregation and Cleveland Jewish Center (Cory United Methodist Church), East 105th Street at Drexel, 1922, Albert F. Janowitz, architect.

The Temple, East 105th
Street and Silver Park,
1924, Charles R. Greco,
architect.

visual landmark in the University Circle district. The narrow triangular property required an unusual planning solution, and the architect, Charles R. Greco of Boston, devised a seven-sided plan with a circular dome. The Gothic and classical styles gave way to the specific kind of eclecticism already noted in St. Theodosius Russian Orthodox Cathedral. In this case, since the Jewish faith did not have any specific architectural tradition, the eclectic architect turned to the styles of the Near East, the birthplace of Judaism. The Temple was called "modified Byzantine."[35]

The neo-Byzantine design is an interesting set of variations on the arched forms of that style, but it is not a strictly archaeological Byzantine. The round arch provides the basic motif for all of the forms of the interior, both structural and decorative. The sanctuary is ninety feet in diameter (only seventeen feet less than the dome of Hagia Sophia) and eighty-eight feet high. The domed ceiling, a thin masonry vault constructed on the Guastavino system and supported by seven radiating ribs, was one of the largest Guastavino domes built.[36] The seven-sided room is focussed on the Ark and the choir, which is framed by a deep arched masonry vault. The walls are made of cement blocks, some of them precast in curvilinear Near Eastern abstract patterns. A warmth is imparted to the sanctuary by the dark wood of the Ark and the balconies occupying four

sides of the room. The overall impression is one of sombre, heavy richness, illuminated partly by the clerestory windows, but depending largely on artificial lighting. The exterior of the Temple is much more simplified than many eclectic Byzantine buildings. In fact, the severe geometry of the central mass and the twin entrance towers resemble the stripped-down historical forms best exemplified in the early twenties by Bertram Goodhue's Nebraska State Capitol, begun just the year before.

Just around the corner on East 107th Street, the merger of two older Protestant churches produced the commission for another landmark structure, designed by Goodhue himself. The Epworth Memorial Methodist Church, which had built on East 55th Street in 1893, was combined in 1920 with the older Euclid Avenue Methodist Church, which had been founded in 1831. As they outgrew the 55th Street church, the congregation made plans to build at the University Circle site. According to church records, the plan was conceived by Bertram Grosvenor Goodhue shortly before his death in 1924, making it his last work. Walker and Weeks completed the plans and supervised the construction, begun in 1926. The church was dedicated in 1928.[37]

The tapering tower and fleche of the church are so dominant that one tends not to realize that the structure is a nave church which widens into a great

160

octagonal crossing. The massing of the building has often been compared to Mont Saint Michel, and even apart from the central fleche, the grouping of the various rectangular blocks of chapel, offices, minor towers, stairways, and basements does indeed suggest the fortified monastery on the mount. The sloping site above Liberty Boulevard and the Wade Park lagoon reinforces this impression and was clearly a major factor in the architect's conception. The simple masses of the exterior are constructed of a warm golden Plymouth seam-faced granite, contributing greatly to the monumental character.

In spite of the spire and the use of pointed arches, however, Epworth-Euclid was almost as much a Modernistic as a Gothic conception. It epitomizes the simplification and modernizing of historical forms toward which Goodhue and others were working. Goodhue's attitude toward the use of style was expressed in a letter to Paul Cret in 1918:

> Contrary to what I suppose is the generally accepted view, I hold no brief for Gothic as opposed to any other style. Gothic seems to be the generally accepted spirit in which churches should be built; also, I find its forms attractive, therefore a good deal of Gothic work must be laid to my door; but I assure you I dream of something very much bigger and finer and more modern and more suited to our present-day civilization than any Gothic church could possibly be.[38]

The Gothic detail of the Epworth-Euclid Church was kept at a minimum. There are no flying buttresses, crockets and finials, and a minimum of tracery. The ornament displays the scheme which was so successful on the Nebraska State Capitol and which anticipated the Lorain-Carnegie Bridge pylons. Massive blocks of masonry terminate in sculptured figures which grow out of the architectural mass, becoming more three-dimensional and less planar toward the top. Forty-eight sculptures were created by Leo Friedlander, a New York sculptor whose work includes four pylons at the entrance of the RCA Building in New York City.[39]

The church is far more successful as an exterior composition than as interior space. The ambiguous relationship between the nave and the octagon is intensified on the interior. The crossing is a lofty domed space with three small openings, the glowing rose window on the east and two arched transept windows, plus four tiny lancets in the tower. The use of the sanctuary depends entirely on artificial illumination, and that fact is probably the best indication of the church's essentially non-Gothic character. It is significant that by the 1920s both the Temple and the Epworth-Euclid Church were

Epworth-Euclid Methodist Church, East 107th Street and Chester, 1928, Bertram Goodhue and Walker & Weeks, architects.

planned as modern structures to this degree. The two historical styles which provided the most light, Byzantine and Gothic, were completely modified by the mechanical convenience of controlled lighting.

The transmutation of classical forms into modern ones was even more graphically demonstrated across the lagoon at Severance Hall, which fulfilled another part of the Wade Park cultural plan. Designed by Walker and Weeks and erected in 1930–1931, the home of the Cleveland Orchestra was the gift of John L. Severance, prominent businessman from a distinguished Cleveland family. His gift was made on the condition that Cleveland citizens would raise a permanent endowment and maintenance fund. The campaign was led by Dudley S. Blossom, and one of the major contributors was John D. Rockefeller, Jr. The final cost of the building was

161

Severance Hall, Euclid Avenue at East Boulevard, 1931, Walker & Weeks, architects. *below*: Grand foyer.

$2,500,000. The orchestra, an outgrowth of the Musical Arts Association, had been formed in 1918 and so was only eleven years old when Severance announced his gift in 1929. Upon its completion, Severance Hall was seen not only as a home for music, but as a background for social display and as "an exhibit of architectural imagination and grace and beauty."[40]

The unwary might be led into thinking that Severance Hall is a classical building in the same spirit as its neighbor, the Cleveland Museum of Art. At the opening, traditionalists were pleased to call it "Georgian." However, there seems no reason to take issue with the *Plain Dealer* critic who wrote: "Architectural courage and a rare imagination have gone into it. It is audacious in its architectural variety, in its combination of the conventional and the modernistic, in its splashing use of brilliant color and contrast."[41] The building is first apprehended from the East Boulevard corner as a regular polygon, perhaps hexagonal. In fact it is not regular, and the stepped central mass has eleven sides. The cardinal principle of modern architecture, that the external form must reveal the interior plan, was daringly and consistently flouted. The central roof is not over the auditorium, as a viewer might have conceived, nor yet over the foyer. Actually, its apex is over the junction of the foyer and the auditorium, which stretches back on a straight line from the entrance. The auditorium is flanked by triangular wings containing lounges, library, offices, and circulation areas. At its opening the building contained not only the main hall seating 1,844, and a 400-seat chamber music hall on the ground floor, but also a radio broadcasting studio for the orchestra. On the stage there was a lift in the orchestra pit, a cyclorama, and a skydome for operatic productions. The auditorium and stage had a system of color spotlights operated by a clavilux or "color organ" console to produce innumerable constantly changing effects. One of the most unusual features was the automobile drive-through at the street level, enabling concertgoers to be deposited at a lower lobby.[42]

The classical exterior of Severance Hall was intended to complement not only the Museum of Art but—perhaps even more—the Allen Memorial Medical Library directly across Euclid Avenue, also designed by Walker and Weeks. The corner portico on a high base had its precedent in Palladio's *I Quattro Libri* and the Villa Foscari, Malcontenta, but the architects' disregard for precedent is betrayed by the lack of stairways which would give the upper porch a functional meaning. The entrance leads into the

Wade Park Manor, East 107th Street and Park Lane, 1923, George B. Post & Sons, with W. Sydney Wagner, architects.

two-story grand foyer, elliptical in shape, whose pillars, balconies, and grand staircases are superficially reminiscent of lobbies such as those in the Palace Theatre. But the bronze ornamental detail, chandeliers, and stylized reliefs are Modernistic or "Art Moderne." Even more daring was the use of color in the carnelian jasper columns with their gilded capitals. These transitional stylistic forms prepared the concertgoer somewhat for the style of the auditorium, but not for its color, which was a cool silver and gray. The flaring reeded frame of the proscenium arch and the filagree floral pattern of the ceiling were called "French modernistic" by one critic. The ceiling is unusual in that its curved shape and overall pattern are unbroken to the last row of the balcony, unlike the irregular or stepped ceilings of older halls. This feature expressed a democratic spirit rare in a hall of this type.

While Severance Hall might be considered from one point of view as a series of stylistic compromises, it should also be seen as a brilliant solution to a set of demanding requirements, and as a conscious and original design executed in a kind of modern Mannerism. Even a modern critic can sympathize with the early appraisal that "Severance Hall is one of those singular and complete triumphs which come to an American community infrequently, if ever."[43]

Appropriate to the cultural development of University Circle was the construction of a group of three luxury residential hotels. The concept of the residential hotel was common in other parts of the country, but it was relatively new to Cleveland, where this type of housing need had been satisfied by apartment buildings. All opened in 1923, the Park Lane Villa, Fenway Hall, and the Wade Park Manor reflected the striking prosperity and generally higher standard of living which characterized the twenties.

Just across East 105th Street from the Temple, the Park Lane Villa overlooks Rockefeller Park. Styled in a French Renaissance eclectic idiom, it was designed by Reynold H. Hinsdale, a Cleveland architect who had worked with J. Milton Dyer. Hinsdale was also associated with George B. Post & Sons in the planning of Fenway Hall, located on East 107th Street at Euclid Avenue.[44] But the precedent-setting residential hotel for Cleveland was the Wade Park Manor, also planned by G. B. Post & Sons, whose expertise in hotel design was well known, with W. Sydney Wagner as principal designer. Wagner, who had worked in the offices of Warren & Wetmore and John Russell Pope, became a partner in the Post firm in 1920 and designed large hotels in Buffalo,

163

Cleveland Play House,
2040 East 86th Street,
1927, Small & Rowley,
architects.

Syracuse, Seattle, and New York City. The $4,000,-
000 Wade Park Manor is an eleven-story structure in
the Georgian Revival manner. It had 400 rooms, of
which forty were single and others were grouped
into two, three, and four-room suites. Every suite
was different, many containing furnishings which
were authentic reproductions of historical pieces.
The large public rooms on the first floor were
designed and furnished in the English style. The
furnishing contract was $500,000, said to be the
largest ever made for a hotel of that size. It enabled
the Manor to provide an atmosphere of luxury and
exclusiveness which was appropriate and contributed to the tone that was being established for
the cultural center.[45]

The Cleveland Play House was not strictly in the
geographical orbit of the University Circle center,
but its new building of 1926-1927 was very much a
part of the cultural spirit of the twenties. Established
in 1916, the Play House Company in just ten years
had become a landmark in the development of the
independent repertory theater movement
throughout the country. This movement, especially
active outside New York City, was a reaction against
the domination of the theater field by booking
syndicates such as Keith's and Shubert's. As new
plays were produced, entire productions, including
scenery and costumes, would be saved for a

repertory of later productions. Not only did this
economize on production costs; it also eliminated the
long run phenomenon, replacing it with several
revivals over a period of years. In addition, the
repertory movement fostered experimental and
laboratory productions for professional growth.[46]

The site of the new Play House on East 86th Street
between Euclid and Carnegie Avenues was given by
Mr. and Mrs. Francis E. Drury, members of a
Cleveland manufacturing family—a happy coincidence that permitted the side street to be called
Drury Lane, after London's famous street and
theaters of that name. Since the new building had to
be planned to accommodate a varied program and
the many special-purpose rooms it required, the
architects, Philip Lindsley Small and Charles Bacon
Rowley, were faced with special design problems. To
begin with, they had to confine the multi-purpose
building to a relatively small site. The plan they
devised was considered unique in that it required
two auditoriums and two stages. The main
auditorium seated 522 and the smaller studio theater
had 154 seats. Furthermore, all of the special-
purpose facilities had to be accessible to both
theaters. More than half of the building was
"backstage" and seldom seen by the public. Consisting of three floors, it contained large shop areas,
scene docks, property and costume rooms, dressing

rooms, a Green Room, a staff room, a rehearsal room, and a lunch room and kitchen.

Architecturally, the exterior of the brick and tile-roofed building is a clear expression of the various units enclosed within. The auditoriums and their tall stage houses are treated as simple rectangular blocks—masses suggestive of the late Italian Romanesque style, but with very little ornament. The design was called "an admirable example of the dignity, character and beauty obtained by well-studied mass, line, texture, color and silhouette without use of embellishment." Only the little groin-vaulted entrance loggia and the charming inner courtyard, used for intermission refreshment, have any specific historical reference. The two lobbies are connected, yet each has its own identity. The interior design of the auditoriums is spare almost to the point of functional modernism. The main proscenium is a simple rectangle thirty feet wide and twenty-eight feet high. All parts of the room, including the ceiling beams and wood paneled walls, are composed of straight lines, in contrast to the rococo movie theaters being built in the same years. The Green Room, designed, furnished, and given by Cleveland's premier interior designer, Louis Rorimer, was an exquisite essay in Art Moderne. In its overall plan and execution, the Play House was a marvel of compactness, economy, logic, and taste.

In Rockefeller Park north of the cultural center, a commemorative project particularly appropriate for Cleveland had its inception in this decade. A unique series of cultural gardens was begun, recognizing the contributions of various nationality groups to the life of the city. They later became unified into an integrated chain that symbolized the fusion of the distinct nationalities into one American culture. The group was one of the last examples of commemorative landscape architecture and of the prewar type of comprehensive organic planning which had its roots in the nineteenth century. Begun in 1926, the project continued throughout the Depression years of the thirties and was not completed until the eve of the Second World War.

A Shakespeare garden had been built in 1916, continuing an old tradition of gardens in the Elizabethan manner and containing plants referred to in Shakespeare's plays, but the idea of a series of gardens was not conceived until 1926 with the creation of the Hebrew Garden. The Cleveland Cultural Garden League was established under the inspiration of Leo Weidenthal, editor and publisher of the *Jewish Independent*, and by 1930 German and Italian gardens had also been completed. Land was donated by the City of Cleveland, and the gardens eventually occupied the eastern half of Rockefeller Park between St. Clair and Superior Avenues. During the Depression years labor was provided by the WPA, while funds for materials were raised by the garden groups. In 1936 the City Department of Parks and Public Property created the Division of Landscape Architecture, and the City provided general supervision of the planning. A unified plan was prepared, with walks connecting the various gardens in a continuous chain, and in 1939 the series of eighteen nationality gardens was dedicated as a unit.[47]

The cultural gardens combined elements of formal planning from the Italian and French traditions with the more informal English practice. The steepness of the slope from East Boulevard to Liberty Boulevard

Plan of the Cleveland Cultural Gardens, 1937.

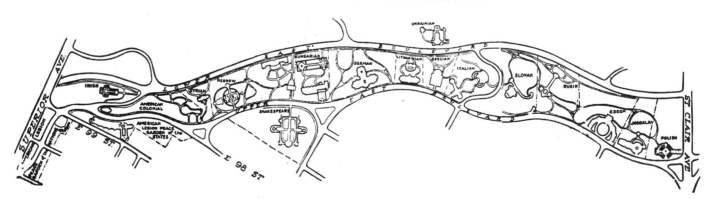

165

German Cultural Garden, with sculptures of Goethe and Schiller, East Boulevard and North Boulevard, 1929, Herman Dercum, architect.

provided an opportunity for contrast, variety, and complex formal and organic relationships. Most of the gardens contain some elements of the formal kind of planning which was characteristic of architects trained in the older Beaux-Arts tradition. The majority of them feature an axial or centralized plan, with paved terraces and commemorative sculpture. A few of the plans display an obvious and

Lower plaza of the Italian Garden, 1930.

specific symbolism, such as the six-pointed star of the Hebrew garden and the Celtic cross of the Irish garden, but a general pattern also seems to be discernible, in that the gardens of the Slavic and Eastern peoples are centralized, while those of the Latin and Western European groups are axial or cruciform. Some are very European in flavor; especially notable in this respect are the Italian garden's long esplanade ending in a circular fountain and overlook, the curving baroque staircases to the lower boulevard in the Lithuanian garden, the sunken rectangular patio framed by Ionic columns at the Greek garden, and the wrought iron gates of the German and Hungarian gardens. A few of the plans were laid out by European architects from the respective nations, but Cleveland landscape architects, including A. Donald Gray, Ashburton Tripp, and Maurice Cornell, were responsible for several designs.[48]

From the point of view of the nationality groups, the commemorative sculpture, representing scholars, authors, poets, artists, and national heroes, was an essential part of the plans. Several of the sculptures were created by Frank L. Jirouch, the noted Cleveland sculptor whose firm executed the decorative sculpture for virtually all of Walker & Weeks' buildings. William McVey was another Cleveland sculptor represented, while in the Ukrainian garden there were three busts by the internationally known sculptor of the Cubist generation, Alexander Archipenko. In an attempt to maintain high artistic standards, each plan was submitted to the City Plan Commission for comment. When a proposed design for a bust of Chopin in the Polish garden was rejected by the society responsible, the decision was approved by Commission member Abram Garfield with the comment: "Our gardens can be so easily made a repository for indifferent statuary if we are not quite critical."[49] The sculpture is installed in various fashions. There are busts mounted on pedestals, some relief plaques attached to stones, and several life-size figures. The most monumental work is the heroic bronze of Goethe and Schiller, a replica of the original sculpture in Weimar, Germany.

With their combination of formal architectural elements, organic landscaping, and commemorative sculpture, the cultural gardens represented a unique effort at integrated landscape architecture. Half a century after its inception, however, the commemorative motive was nearly forgotten and all but incomprehensible to the generation of the 1970s.

# The Van Sweringen Years—II

It is unnecessary to point out that the accomplishments of the Van Sweringens epitomize the organization and prosperity of the twenties, but they were hardly typical. Their projects were breathtaking even in an age of superlatives. The vision of Shaker Heights was followed by plans to extend the rapid transit and suburban development all the way to the Chagrin River. Meanwhile Shaker Square became a reality, and the Union Terminal group was completed, climaxing the decade.

The Village of Shaker Heights was soundly established and its success assured when the rapid transit opened in 1920. By 1923, 887 houses had been built. There was a great demand for homes that offered the advantages of suburban living coupled with strong restrictions and easy transportation to the center of the city. In 1927 a promotional advertisement stated that "Shaker Village is said to be the largest residence development under single control in the world." The commitment of the developers to private home ownership was shown by the fact that in 1930 eighty-seven percent of the houses were single-family dwellings, twelve percent were two-family, and only one percent were for three or more families. The primary appeal lay in the "permanency" to be found in a planned suburb so controlled and in homes "so defended that they might retain the comfort for which they were built, throughout the century, without change or interference" from commercial and social "invasion." By 1976 the century of permanency was more than two-thirds accomplished.[50]

The architecture of the suburban houses of the twenties held few surprises. Progressive experimentation subsided, and eclecticism was the accepted manner. Most architects and clients would have concurred with the art editor who said,

> Our turning to the three accepted models for monumental architecture in the construction of our skyscrapers [Greco-Roman, Renaissance, Gothic] is precisely what we have done, more frankly perhaps, in domestic architecture. We have recognized our limitations. We are no longer trying to be inventive. We have accepted certain things as standardized, and are now striving correctly to interpret the standards.

This expression of the desire for stability and security may also be understood as a concomitant of the tendencies of the period toward isolationism, a narrow nationalism, and intolerance. The World War decade was described by the same critic as resembling other ages

> of great material prosperity, overlying, as always, a background of menace. Such conditions always breed efficiency and sophistication and an underlying mental tiredness . . . By the time a nation or an individual . . . has become saddled with problems of administration on a big scale, whether of armies and colonies or of vast industrial enterprises, domestic architecture trends inevitably to be a solace and a refuge . . .[51]

To express the ideas of solace and refuge, architects turned to styles from ages and countries which had developed satisfying and comfortable forms of domestic architecture. There might be half a dozen to choose from: American Colonial, an English manner (either Adam or Georgian), Italian, French, Elizabethan, Spanish, or Cotswold, from the cottages of the hills of southwest England. Almost none of the plans were an exact copy of a historical building. The livable domestic plan which had been evolved in the previous decades was enclosed in massing, materials, and details which recalled the desired style. The similar plans and common scale, differentiated mainly in detail, resulted in the familiar streets where Tudor, Colonial, and Renaissance homes stand side by side without jarring in the least. The most successful eclectic architects had enormous libraries of historic style reference books, the likes of which have never been gathered together before or since. The architect was a skillful practitioner in playing variations on a theme. The ingenuity and sophistication with which these variations could be handled were his reason for being, and within their own framework, compel a certain admiration.

Few of the homes in Shaker Heights were built by the Van Sweringen Company itself, but the restrictions dictated the price range of homes for each street. Thus there were enclaves of diverse character within the village, from mansions to medium-sized residences to more humble houses. Virtually all were architect-designed, but any attempt to describe all of the good eclectic architects and the several styles they used in Shaker Heights and other suburbs would only result in a catalogue. On the other hand, it is impossible to be selective without also being quite arbitrary. A list of outstanding examples of residential architecture might include the Tudor house for Alfred Fritzsche by Meade and Hamilton on Parkland Drive, the Classic Revival mansion of Edwin Motch by Charles Schneider on South Park

Alfred Fritzsche house, Parkland Drive, Shaker Heights, 1923, Meade & Hamilton, architects.

E. R. Motch house, South Park Boulevard, 1924, Charles Schneider, architect.

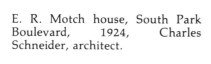

Georgian Revival houses, 13834 and 13840 Lake Avenue, Lakewood, Clarence Mack, architect.

*left:* First Baptist Church, Fairmount Boulevard and Eaton Road, 1929, Walker & Weeks, architects. *right:* Plymouth Church, Coventry and Weymouth Roads, Shaker Heights, 1923, Charles Schneider, architect.

Boulevard, the French provincial villa for Salmon P. Halle by Corbusier, Lenski and Foster on Park Drive, and the Georgian Revival houses of Clarence Mack. The list of accomplished eclectic architects could be extended indefinitely, including, among others, Howell and Thomas, Bloodgood Tuttle, Abram Garfield, Philip Small, Harold Burdick, Antonio di Nardo, Frederic Striebinger, and Dercum and Beer.[52]

Churches for the suburban community were designed to relate to the domestic architecture and were conceived in the same eclectic spirit. The two favorite styles were American Colonial and English Gothic. When the new Plymouth Church of Shaker Heights was planned, "it was concluded that the Colonial or Georgian, sometimes called the 'late Renaissance,' provided through its simplicity, adaptability and homelikeness the characteristics that seemed most suitable for the community of Shaker Heights."[53] It is also significant that although the church assumed the name of the old Plymouth Congregational Church downtown and remained affiliated with the Congregational Church, it was organized and planned as a united community church. The congregation was first established in 1916 and the church was erected in 1920–1923 at Coventry and Weymouth Roads on a site given by the Van Sweringen Company.

The architect was Charles S. Schneider (1874–1932), one of Cleveland's most brilliant eclectics. Having studied with Meade and Garfield and later at the Ecole des Beaux-Arts, he had also worked in the office of George B. Post. A comparison of Plymouth Church with "Stan Hywet," the great Tudor mansion of F. A. Seiberling in Akron, reveals the range of Schneider's versatility. His design for Plymouth Church is an excellent example of the eclectic revival of the Wren-Gibbs type of London church transplanted to America. Its Ionic entrance portico and the 150-foot steeple above are admirable in proportion and detail, and the interior has the characteristic U-shaped gallery.[54]

The Walker and Weeks firm was responsible for two of the most typical suburban churches in the Gothic style—the First Baptist Church and St. Paul's Episcopal Church. St. Paul's moved from its old Euclid Avenue building to Fairmount and Coventry in Cleveland Heights, where its parish hall was erected in 1927–1928, and the 150-foot bell tower in 1929. The firm's designer was J. Byers Hays. After many delays and changes in plan, the main sanctuary was added in 1949–1951, but the changes caused by reduced financial circumstances worked serious compromises on the original concept, and the earlier parish hall and tower remain the most successful

Shaker Heights City Hall, Van Aken Boulevard and Lee Road, Shaker Heights, 1930, Charles Schneider, architect.

portion of St. Paul's design. The First Baptist Church moved from its Prospect Avenue location to Fairmount Boulevard and Eaton Road, dedicating its new building in 1929. Its tower, although similar in many respects to St. Paul's, shows more of the Modernistic simplification which has already been noted in other Walker and Weeks buildings of the late 1920s. As with much eclectic work of the period, the ultimate aim was not to create a replica, but to provide sufficient style reference to convey a convincing atmosphere.[55]

The consistency of the domestic vision and style in the planned suburb was remarkable. School, store, library, hospital, fire station, and even the gasoline station were designed in the Georgian and Tudor idioms. The Shaker Heights City Hall and fire station, built in 1930 and designed by Charles Schneider, was one of the last such efforts. Its slightly angled facade addresses the intersection of Lee road and South Moreland (Van Aken) Boulevard. The building states its civic role with a semi-circular two-story portico and an octagonal cupola with elliptical fanlights. This compulsion for consistency produced few architectural master-pieces, and the use of style elements to cloak different functions may be questioned. Yet such a view produced a pleasing and satisfying ambience which maintained the illusion of the English village, and which enhanced the desired feelings of stability and security. In the terms of eclectic architectural thinking, such consistency could only be obtained through the repetition of historical styles.[56]

The spirit of private initiative which produced Shaker Heights was manifested in a more personal way in a unified group of houses built at the western edge of the suburb. A group of artists, decorators, architects, musicians, and writers who had created a distinctive neighborhood on Hessler Road near University Circle decided to build a private village of semidetached houses on the Heights. A site of about five acres was obtained, located between Fairhill Road and the deep ravine of Ambler Park. The original scheme of a group of double houses was

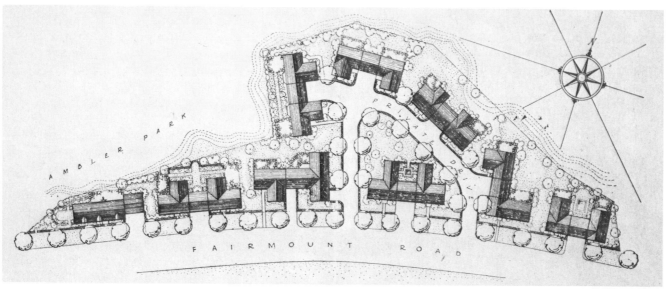

planned by architect Antonio di Nardo in 1928, although the houses as actually built were designed by Harold O. Fullerton, with A. Donald Gray as the landscape architect. Some units were situated directly on Fairhill, while others were placed around a driveway yard. The living rooms overlooked the ravine, and the garages faced the street. The architecture followed the tradition of the Cotswold cottages, the houses being constructed of stone and stucco with steep slate roofs.

By the time the houses could be built and occupied in 1931 the complexion of the occupants had changed somewhat. Gray and Fullerton lived in the group, and other residents included a newspaper editor, an interior decorator, several business executives, and Russell and Rowena Jelliffe, founders of the social settlement which became Karamu House. This private residential development represented a kind of social, financial, and artistic collaboration which would become increasingly rare after the twenties.[57]

The evolution of Shaker Square, not far from the Fairhill "village," reveals the volatile nature of the financial world of the twenties. The Square was not the original conception of the Van Sweringens, but the final outcome of earlier developments and failed plans. In March, 1922, a $30,000,000 development for a model apartment community was announced for the area at Shaker Boulevard and Moreland Circle. According to the newspaper announcement, the plan was "said to be without parallel in building history." The land was acquired from the Van

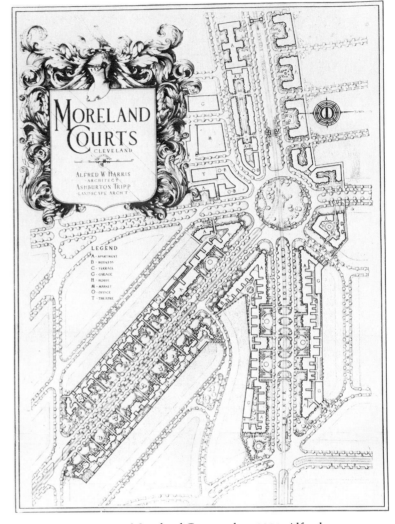

Moreland Courts plan, 1922, Alfred W. Harris, architect. (*Alfred W. Harris, Jr.*)

*opposite*: Plan of the Fairhill Road village, 1928, Antonio diNardo, architect. (*The Bystander*) *left*: Fairhill Road village, 1931, Harold O. Fullerton, architect.

171

*left:* Moreland Circle, before 1927. Moreland Courts at the left. *below:* Architects' plan for the redevelopment of Moreland Circle (Shaker Square), 1927, Small and Rowley, architects. Rendering by William C. Grauer.

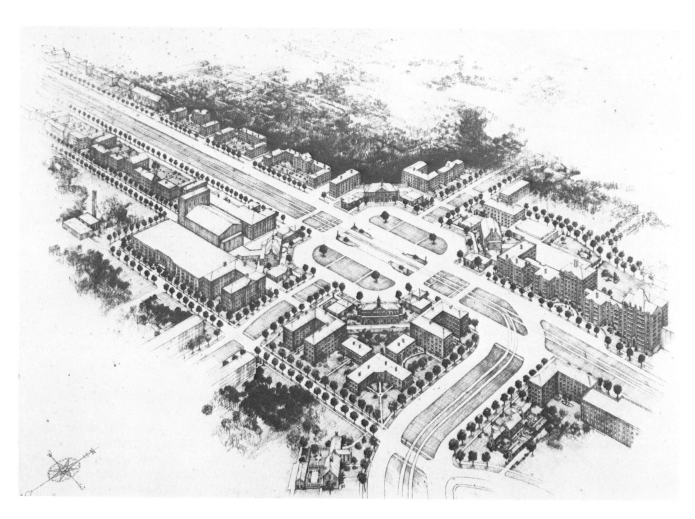

Sweringen Company by Josiah Kirby, president of the Cleveland Discount Company, on the assurance that the development would be appropriate for the western edge of Shaker Heights. The Moreland Courts would include two apartment structures 1,500 feet long on Shaker Boulevard between Moreland Circle and Coventry Road, terrace homes on South Moreland (Van Aken) Boulevard, business buildings, stores, and a theater on Moreland Circle, and a market house, central heating plant, and parking garage on Williams Avenue southwest of the Circle. The entire architectural concept was the work of Alfred W. Harris, who spent fourteen months on the preliminary planning.

Only the great apartment block on the north side of Shaker Boulevard was begun. As the newspaper account stated,

> While the mere thought of a single brick wall 1,500 feet long, four to ten stories high and dotted with a series of doors and windows would at first seem to suggest the pinnacle of monotony, this 1,500 foot stretch of building promises to be a revelation. In this solid wall, Alfred W. Harris, the architect for the entire project, will have written the entire history of English architecture when the last brick is in place.[58]

The journalistic tribute was not exaggerated. The vast stretches of the Moreland Courts ought not to work architecturally, but they do. Each unit was treated differently, with stylistic idioms from successive periods of English architecture ranging from the Elizabethan to the Georgian. The connecting link between the two eight-story towers was treated as a screen, and the relationships between mass and ornament are surprisingly effective. Harris' drawings for the office and store buildings show an equally great variety of form and detail, mostly Elizabethan, creating the general feeling of a medieval street. The effect of the architect's intentions can be gauged in the irregular block of apartment houses south of Shaker Square and bounded by Drexmore, South Moreland, South Woodland, and Hampton. Nearly all of them were designed by Harris, although they were built by different developers. Every building is different, and the juxtapositions of round towers, bay windows, steep slate roofs, half-timbered gables, and brick, stone, wood, and stucco create a picturesque arrangement of great variety.

Less then a year after the announcement of Moreland Courts, in February, 1923, the Cleveland Discount Company failed and went into receivership, its stock worthless. During 1923 and 1924 O. P. and M. J. Van Sweringen had several discussions with architect Harris for a scheme to develop Shaker Boulevard west to East 93rd Street, and by the end of 1924 they had decided to complete Kirby's development of Moreland Courts. However, in the end the Harris plan was not carried out, and the Van Sweringens engaged Philip L. Small and Carl Bacon Rowley to complete the Moreland Courts apartment and to plan Shaker Square on the site of Moreland Circle.[59]

Shaker Square was built in 1927–1929. Contrary to local opinion, it was not the first planned suburban shopping center in the United States; that distinction seems to belong to the Country Club Plaza in Kansas City. However, Shaker Square did have several unusual features, the most obvious of which was its integration with the rapid transit. The general plan of the Square has often been compared to a New England village green, but it owes a great deal more to the concepts of mid-eighteenth century Neo-Classic town planning as seen in the royal squares at Nancy and Paris. A contemporary account recognized other precedents:

> Viewed in its entirety and from the standpoint of scale and architectural character, the Shaker Square gateway development will be without a counterpart. During the past three years, Philip L. Small, architect, has made a study of shopping centers and apartment developments in many parts of the country. No combination development was found on an extensive enough scale to serve as a pattern. The inspiration itself is old, coming down from the Agora of Greek cities, the Forum of Roman towns, and the commons of New England.[60]

In any case the Square illustrates a continuing dependence on European models, although it is interesting to reflect that it exists as a setting, not for a royal statue, but for a railway line.

The buildings in the four quadrants of the Square are more significant as a backdrop for the space than as architecture. The two-story center block of each quadrant is flanked by one-story symmetrical wings and accented by square corner pavilions. The materials of red brick and white trim, with slate roofs, give an overall harmony. The classical Neo-Colonial ornament consists of delicate pilasters and capitals, broken pediments, dentilled cornices, semicircular fanlights, and small-pane sash combined to create an attractive—if not completely convincing—unity. These references to Georgian domestic building, including the Mount Vernon portico on the restaurant, had an expected kinship with the architecture of the Shaker Heights

Shaker Square, 1927-1929, Small and Rowley, architects.

community. They seem to support the assertion of Marcus Whiffen that such Georgian Revival facades "constitute the last consistent street architecture America has had."[61]

The Colony Theatre, designed by John Eberson, a Chicago and New York theater architect who was called "the master of the atmospheric star-and-clouds house," was not completed until 1937. The later date accounts for the fact that its interior displays a streamlined Modernistic style completely different from the eclectic facades. In the decades since the Second World War, Shaker Square has been criticized for the original lack of planning for parking and later expansion, but these very factors have served to maintain its intimate pedestrian scale. Nearly fifty years after its construction, the Square retains to a remarkable degree the character of the upper-class residential neighborhood which brought it into being.[62]

Projecting the further extension of the rapid transit, the Van Sweringen Company made plans in 1926 for the residential development of the land east of Green Road. To be known as "Shaker Country Estates," the area ran from Green Road east almost to the Chagrin River, and from Kinsman Road north to Gates Mills, encompassing roughly the later villages of Beachwood, Pepper Pike, and Hunting Valley. Parcels of land were offered for residential development, subject to the same Van Sweringen restrictions as Shaker Village, including the approval of architectural plans. The area was platted by the F. A. Pease Engineering Company, and most of the main roads were carried out. Shaker Boulevard was extended to Brainard Road, where Gates Mills

Boulevard branched to the northeast and a Chagrin Falls Boulevard (not the present extension of Kinsman Road) was to have branched to the southeast. Kinsman "Boulevard" would have become a divided continuation of South Moreland (Van Aken) beyond Warrensville Center Road.[63]

The land parcels were sold only for residential use. In order to ensure their development as country estates and to prevent speculative development, a schedule for the subdivision of each parcel was stipulated. There could be no subdivision for a certain period of years; a period followed during which an estate could be divided into two sites; and eventually further subdivision would be permitted. The process required a time span of as much as twenty-five years, and under no circumstances could a subdivided lot have less than a 100-foot frontage.

The most remarkable feature of the development, from the point of view of modern planning, was the conception of Shaker Boulevard beyond Warrensville Center Road as a depressed four-lane divided highway with the rapid transit in the center of the right-of-way. The roads which eventually became Shaker Boulevard would have been marginal roads. Viaducts for grade separation were constructed at Warrensville Center, Green, and Richmond Roads. The rapid transit would have been extended out the length of Gates Mills Boulevard. This concept of a depressed four-lane divided highway with grade separations, marginal roads, and rapid transit in the center has never been improved upon, and was still a part of planners' thinking in the 1970s.

The story of the Van Sweringen enterprises has

174

been called an "improbable tale." In a dozen years, the two brothers created a real estate development which comprised a complete community with its own government, a rapid transit system, a transcontinental railroad system worth two billion dollars, and finally the Cleveland Terminal group. W. H. Alburn observed in 1932 that

> Any competent financier could have proved, a decade and a half ago, that the Van Sweringen project was impossible. And as a matter of fact, all of them did, just as they could prove today that such an accomplishment would not be capable of repetition unless it were so outrageously favored by Fortune that it would confound all the laws of economics and probability. It is quite evident that the brothers themselves would have agreed, in 1916, that no considered program could have been so well ordered as to result in the achievements shown in 1932, and it is equally evident that they had no such program in mind. They were too intelligent to project a plan of such complexity into a future so invisible.[64]

The Terminal project preoccupied the Van Sweringens throughout the decade. Although the actual design was begun in 1922, it was not until 1924 that the acquisition of property, demolition of structures, and excavation began in earnest. At the end of 1924 the revised plans for a monumental entrance portico and a skyscraper "as high as the building code will permit" were announced, and the actual design for the Terminal Tower was first shown in February, 1925. In the midst of constant legal and political battles, site preparation continued, eventually costing some $20,000,000. Foundation work was begun in 1926, and the construction of the steel framework started at the end of that year. The structure rose rapidly throughout 1927, and the structural work on the Tower was completed in August. Early in 1928, plans for the department store and the Medical Arts Building were announced, and work began on the depot itself, beneath and south of the Terminal Tower building. The first train entered the Terminal on October 23, 1929, a locomotive and two coaches carrying the Van Sweringens and Erie Railroad officials. Regular passenger service began in June, 1930, and the formal opening of the Terminal group, including the Hotel Cleveland, and the Builders Exchange (later Guildhall), Medical Arts (later Republic), and Midland Buildings, took place on June 28, 1930.[65]

Six-hundred-feet-wide Shaker Boulevard, as it is planned east of Center Road

*above:* Proposed Shaker Boulevard rapid transit extension beyond Warrensville Center Road, as shown in *Peaceful Shaker Village* (1927). *below:* Warrensville Road viaduct, Wilbur J. Watson & Company, engineers.

175

Terminal Tower under construction, 1927, etching by Louis Rosenberg.

# 1930: The Terminal

The significance of the Terminal group for the life of the city was profound. There had been a pronounced lag in property values on the site south and west of Superior and Ontario. The district was called "the city's worst disfigurement," a drab area of commonplace structures, dives, and squalor. In addition, the center of business activity had moved out Euclid Avenue to Playhouse Square and beyond, and the Mall development was becoming a civic focal point. The Terminal project served to make Public Square once more the focus of the downtown.

When the Union Terminal opened, it was recognized nationally as a facility "which ranks in magnitude and completeness with the best in the country."[1] It was unique in several respects, but the idea which attracted the most attention was the commercial development of the air rights over the depot. All of the office buildings were superimposed over the railway station proper. While the concept was not new, the Cleveland Terminal was distinctive in that the plan provided for the complete utilization of the space above the street level for commercial purposes. All of the passenger facilities were below the street level, and only the Public Square entrance and the upper part of the passenger concourse were above. The station consisted of two levels, the concourse twelve and a half feet below the level of Public Square, and the track level twenty feet below that. This arrangement was made possible in part by the topography, which allowed the tracks to be brought in at the lower level, an advantage that was in fact among the reasons for locating the Terminal on Public Square.[2]

The project was also unique in its need for elaborate engineering. Although the southern part of the site sloped down toward Canal Road, extensive grading was still required, and 2,500,000 cubic yards of earth were excavated. More than one thousand buildings were razed in the area needed for the entire development. The approaches required the construction of many bridges over streets, and bringing the tracks from the south and west made it necessary to build a 3,450-foot high-level viaduct over the Cuyahoga Valley. The structural engineering of the project caused special interest because of the complex framing required for the various levels and buildings, the heavy loading and special foundations, and the many bridges and retaining walls. The piers of the tower were carried to bedrock 250 feet below street level, making them the deepest foundations in history. The street plan was rearranged, and the extensions of Prospect Avenue and Huron Road were built over the station on viaducts.

Another unusual feature was the electrification of the steam trains before passing through the urban area. Apart from situations involving tunnels, this was the first installation in the United States in which electrified engines were used to haul the main line trains through the city. The electrified track extended over seventeen miles of route between Collinwood and Linndale.

The Terminal handled two classes of service, the through traffic on the steam railroads, for which twelve tracks were provided initially, and the rapid transit, for which there were six tracks. Provision was made for future development of the complete east-to-west rapid transit service. Three major railroads, the Nickel Plate, the Big Four, and the New York Central, used the Terminal from the outset, to be joined later by the Baltimore & Ohio and Erie Railroads. The trackage was sufficient to accommodate all of the major railroads that might wish to enter the depot, but the Pennsylvania never did.

The cost of the $179,000,000 project could be divided into four parts: the construction of the passenger terminal and its approaches by the Cleveland Union Terminals Company, $88,000,000; the improvement of existing railway properties and their freight and engine facilities, $40,000,000; the rapid transit, $20,000,000; and the air rights buildings erected by the Cleveland Terminals Building Company, $31,000,000. The chief engineer of the project was H. D. Jouett, who had been an engineer for the Grand Central Terminal. The contractor for the Terminal Tower was John Gill & Sons, and the Lundoff-Bicknell Company built the Medical Arts and Builders Exchange Buildings.

The passenger terminal was a model of efficient planning. Five portals at the Public Square entrance open into a vaulted portico 153 feet long and forty-seven feet high. The three center entrances lead to the Terminal building and its elevator lobbies, the others to ramps descending to the station. At each end of the portico are entrances leading to the rapid transit lobbies. On the concourse level, the 450 foot length of the room is divided into three units, an entrance lobby, a ticket lobby, and the passenger concourse. The first two units have a groined ceiling twenty feet high, supported on piers which also carry the superstructure of the Tower building. The concourse, containing the stairways to the lower track level, has a segmental arch ceiling forty-two feet high with a skylight.

A distinctive feature of the station was the amount of commercial space assigned for shops and concessions. The layout provided wall frontage for all the necessary services—ticket office, waiting room, lunch room, barber shops, rest rooms, dining room, parcel checking, baggage counter, and taxicab entrance. The large amount of remaining space was allotted to retail stores and show windows, including

Union Terminal, floor plan of the station level. (*The Architectural Work of Graham, Anderson, Probst & White*)

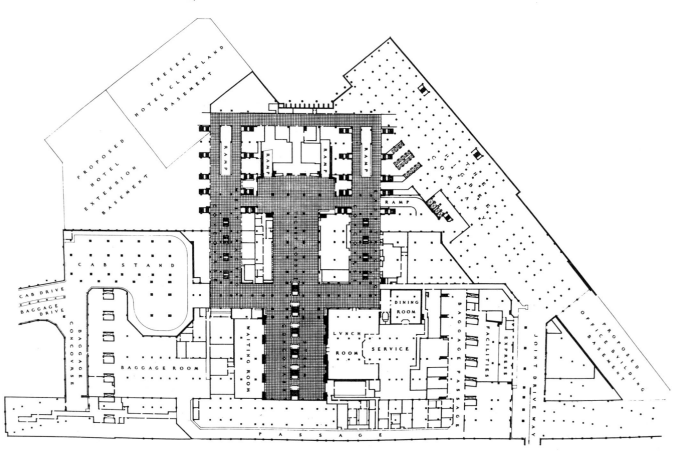

The Terminal Group. Left to right: Builders Exchange (Guildhall), Medical Arts (Republic), and Midland Buildings; Higbee's Department Store, Terminal Tower, and Hotel Cleveland; United States Post Office.

six restaurant facilities and every kind of shopping desired by the traveler. Operated by Harvey, Inc., the merchandising services eventually occupied 175,000 square feet (four acres), making the largest unified service in connection with a union passenger station. The restaurants accommodated 9,000–10,000 persons during the lunch period. In addition, and unseen by the public, were the express and mail facilities, and baggage, maintenance, and employees' areas.[3]

In a variety of ways, the Terminal group invites comparison with Rockefeller Center in New York.

The area covered by the station, and hence the air rights buildings, is seventeen acres, exactly the same as Rockefeller Center. Without going out-of-doors, the public could go from the depot to a 1,000-room hotel and a twelve-story department store, and via underground concourses to three large banks and four office buildings. The Builders Exchange Building contained a nine-story parking garage, whereas the Rockefeller Center garage, the first indoor office building garage in Manhattan, was not completed until 1939. As a planned commercial "city-within-a-city," the conception of the Terminal group

Republic Building plaza, Ontario Street.

"polarize the forces of growth" and to stabilize the center of the city. Combining features of the commercial center and the station, the Terminal group acted in much the same way. Although its role later declined with the cessation of railroad passenger traffic, the Terminal became the central station of the east-west rapid transit in the 1950s, and later of the pioneer rapid transit link to the airport. Both the New York and the Cleveland project were planned for further expansion, but while Rockefeller Center has continued to grow by the addition of new structures, especially across Sixth Avenue, the Terminal group has seen only the addition of the United States Post Office in 1934, and a State Office Building in the late 1970s.[5]

Rockefeller Center has been called "the first landscaped skyscraper." Winston Weisman was undoubtedly correct when he stated that "in office building the [economic] factors militate against the use of landscaping," and further that Rockefeller Center tended to supply the necessary precedent for the landscaped plaza for post-World War II buildings and architects.[6] Yet it is significant that the monumental entrance portico of the Terminal faced Public Square and thus embraced the entire expanse of landscape as its front yard. This relationship was an intentional part of the planning from the beginning. The Terminal group even had a "mini-plaza," located in the open court between two wings of the Medical Arts (Republic) Building facing Ontario Street. It contained a paved and planted area, sculptured fountain, and benches for pedestrians. The little plaza was still intact, but unfortunately not maintained, in the 1970s.

An important difference between the two projects, however, was the relative lack of decorative art in the Cleveland Terminal. With the exception of the seven murals by Jules Guerin in the lunettes of the entrance lobby, there was no attempt to incorporate a decorative program like the Rockefeller Center sculpture by Lee Lawrie, Paul Manship, Isamu Noguchi, and Leo Friedlander, or the murals of Diego Rivera and José Maria Sert.

The Terminal Tower, "as high as the building code would permit," reached fifty-two stories and 708 feet in the air. At the time of its completion, it was the second tallest building in the world, surpassed only by New York's Woolworth Building. Unfortunately the magnitude of the conception was not matched in daring by the architectural style. At the time of the final design in early 1925, the modernistic evolution had taken place, a fact clearly illustrated by

preceded Rockefeller Center by several years, and the group was virtually complete just as the construction of Rockefeller Center was begun. Henry-Russell Hitchcock's 1958 observation on Rockefeller Center may seem to apply as well to the Terminal group: "a more urbanistic grouping, extending over a considerable area, replaced the earlier ideal of building single structures of ever greater height. . . . This change in approach, recognized ever since as a turning point, has yet to be significantly followed up."[4] However, because of the existing hotel, the depot requirements, and the evolution of building plans, the final arrangement of the Terminal buildings was the result of an additive process rather than a comprehensive scheme.

In a recent critical analysis of Rockefeller Center and Grand Central Station, James Marston Fitch has pointed out that both of those projects worked as significant generators of activity, serving to

*left:* New York Municipal Building, Manhattan, 1911-1913, McKim, Mead & White, architects. 580 feet tall. (*Municipal Archives of the City of New York*) *right:* Terminal Tower, 708 feet tall, to the same scale.

181

Cleveland's Ohio Bell Telephone Building. Yet Graham, Anderson, Probst & White borrowed directly from a prewar precedent, the New York Municipal Building, for the double peristyle crown of the tower.[7] Designed by McKim, Mead & White and begun in 1911, the Municipal Building embodied an excellent design and was a perfectly respectable model for a Beaux-Arts skyscraper, but by 1925 it belonged to another generation.

The Terminal's interiors were also executed in a discreet Beaux-Arts classicism. They were rich and scholarly in detail, but enervated in spirit, like much of the domestic architecture of the period. The most impressive architectural space is the entrance

Midland Building entrance, 1930, Graham, Anderson, Probst & White, architects.

Lobby of the Union Terminal. (*David Thum*)

portico with its richly coffered ceiling, and the Union Trust Company branch (later National City Bank) at the entrance is a finely detailed classical interior. On the concourse level, because of the large amount of commercial space, the architectural treatment was limited to the marble columns and floors and the ornamental bronze frames surrounding the shop fronts and show windows.

One of the main reasons for the conservative style was the necessity of incorporating the Hotel Cleveland of 1918 into the group. When the department store was added in 1931, its symmetrical placement required that it also be designed to match the hotel. On the other hand, the three office buildings on Prospect Avenue (they are separate buildings in spite of being connected) were planned in 1928–1929, and the Modernistic style was by then an acceptable alternative to complement the classical group. The columns, arches, and cornices of the upper stories were dispensed with, and the buildings were simple masses rising sheer from the base for eighteen stories. Indented light courts gave the Builders Exchange Building three shafts on the south, the Midland Building three on the west, and the Medical Arts Building two on the east. The surface ornament of the lower stories was Modernistic (later called Art Deco) and combined geometric, naturalistic, and figurative motifs. Especially on the Prospect Avenue facades, it had the lushness and a sculptural quality that was characteristic of many buildings in those years.

Thus part of the Terminal group looked backward to the Beaux-Arts, and part of it more nearly caught the spirit of its own time. If the architectural style of the entire group had been as forward-looking as the concept of the commercial development, the Cleveland Terminal would probably still enjoy a deserved national reputation.

Colony Theatre foyer, Shaker Square, 1937, John Eberson, architect. (see page 174)

# 1930–1950

## Greater Cleveland

By 1930, Cuyahoga County was a metropolitan area. The great increase in suburban population was shown by the fact that Bedford, Berea, Euclid, Garfield Heights, Maple Heights, and Rocky River all achieved the status of cities in 1930, followed by Shaker Heights and Parma in 1931. Previous to that time, only Cleveland Heights, East Cleveland, and Lakewood were large enough to be separate municipalities. In 1940 these cities were joined by South Euclid and University Heights.

Describing Cleveland in 1940, William Ganson Rose wrote that "avenues of traffic and trade reached out to the boundaries of thriving cities and villages that nestled close to the sprawling, fan-shaped mother city, content in their municipal independence and the charm of the residential sections. This was Metropolitan Cleveland . . ."[8] The development of a network of state and federal highways in the 1920s had brought urbanization to the villages in a way that the railroads were never able to do, but in spite of the forces for change many of the cities and villages in Cuyahoga County retained some features of their early nineteenth century New England character until the Second World War. This was true, for example, of Strongsville, where the notable Greek Revival Pomeroy house stood; Olmsted Falls, with its many modest early houses lying sheltered in the Rocky River Valley; Brecksville, whose 100-year old Congregational Church had been built by Charles Heard's partner Simeon Porter; and Chagrin Falls, with its handsome brick Town Hall (two stories tall before the fire of 1943) and numerous Greek Revival, Gothic, and Italinate houses. Even a city like Bedford, which had been industrialized by the advent of the railroad, had its old village green with the nearby home of settler Hezekiah Dunham, the mansard-roofed Town Hall of 1874, and the splendid Queen Anne mansion of Holsey Gates. Likewise, Berea centered around the Victorian store fronts along Bridge and Front Streets and the grave sandstone structures on the campuses of Baldwin-Wallace College.

The local history of these villages was regarded with new interest in the 1920s and 1930s, as people could now look back on three or four generations of continuous settlement. Cleveland architect Albert Skeel, who had been associated with Frank Barnum early in his career, sponsored the restoration of early historic buildings in Ohio in the 1930s and restored and remodeled the Brecksville church in 1929.[9] The historicism of the early twentieth century had also created a nostalgic attitude toward the eighteenth and early nineteenth century village which finally culminated in the beginning of the Williamsburg restoration in 1927. In the Greater Cleveland area, Gates Mills could serve as a case study of the way in which the "quaint" village was viewed from the metropolis. Gates Mills had already become a commuter town in 1900 with the opening of an electric interurban railroad between Cleveland and Chardon. Within a few years the nineteenth century mill town was re-created as a village in the "New England tradition" as it was understood in the early twentieth century. Most of the small nineteenth century houses were "improved," generally by the addition of roof dormers, porches, or completely new wings, while many of the new residents built homes in the classical revival styles. This group included S. Prentiss Baldwin, the first Clevelander to

Gates Mills Town Hall, Gates Mills, 1930, Frank R. Walker, architect.

"discover" Gates Mills, and Walter C. White of the White Motor Company, whose famous "Circle W" estate with its great dairy barns was designed by Walker & Weeks and built in 1917–1924. Frank R. Walker was president of the Gates Mills Improvement Society in 1917–1919, and when the village was incorporated in 1920 he was the first mayor, serving for four years. The Gates Mills Methodist Church of 1853 was acquired by the Episcopal Church in 1927 and became St. Christopher's-by-the-River, after which it was restored and altered for the Episcopal service by Walker. The Town Hall, built in 1930 in a simple Georgian Revival idiom, was also designed by Walker.[10] The involvement of traditional architects in this kind of historic re-creation was the final and perhaps one of the most lasting phases of eclecticism, as Alan Gowans has pointed out so succinctly: "Now people are not merely content to preserve relics of the past, they intend to bring the past back to life, physically and literally, with every resource modern technology can command; it is to this late Victorian impulse that we owe Williamsburg and Winterthur, Old Sturbridge and Greenfield Village."[11]

However, the challenges of the growing metropolitan area could not be met by what was essentially a kind of escapism. Many people were aware of the need for some kind of regional planning. At an Ohio State Planning Conference in 1928, Abram Garfield, chairman of the City Plan Commission, called attention to the blighted areas of the city and the need for housing studies. One outgrowth of these studies by architects Garfield

and Walter McCornack was some of the pioneer public housing of the early and mid-thirties.[12] In 1937 the Regional Association of Cleveland was formed, with Garfield as president, to concern itself with "the development of comprehensive regional plans for land use in Cleveland and its environs; the promotion of better housing conditions for the people of Cuyahoga County, and the exercise of governmental powers in respect of land use and housing conditions." The association correlated surveys and research by others and conducted the studies that were necessary to develop regional planning in such areas as zoning revision, housing problems, highways, and the development of the lakefront.[13]

Even earlier, a significant development in regional planning had taken place in the years during and immediately following the First World War, with the creation of the Metropolitan Park System. The Cleveland Metropolitan Park District was created in 1917 under the inspiration of William A. Stinchcomb, county surveyor at the time of the completion of the Detroit-Superior bridge and first director of the Metropolitan Park System. Stinchcomb, in a discussion of the park system, made it clear that regional planning was seen as an extension of the principle of scientific management as it was applied in business and industry. Developed in response to the haphazard growth of cities, the essential principle of such planning was the allocation of land for the best social and economic use. New ways of thinking about the relationship between urban and rural areas were demanded by the same factors that were changing every area of life, namely, increased leisure and improved transportation. In the late nineteenth century, 70 percent of the population lived in rural areas. Two generations later, the ratio had been reversed, and it was understood that urban man still needed contact with natural and open spaces.[14]

The Metropolitan Park System began as a series of parks and reservations, with the park board attempting to acquire areas which had peculiar scenic and topographic features, which were accessible to the public, and which could be easily coordinated into a planned system. It is significant that part of the justification offered for acquisition was that the land was unsuitable for residential or industrial development. It was also assumed that industry would move southward in the Cuyahoga Valley, and that provision should be made for industrial growth and river improvement perhaps as far as Brecksville. As

186

conceived by Stinchcomb from the beginning, the plan contemplated the development of connecting parkways and boulevards to make a continuous chain of parkland which would completely encircle the park district. By 1930 the park district included all of Cuyahoga County plus Hinckley Township in Medina County, and the basic nuclei of the chain were established. From west to east they included Huntington Park in Bay Village, the Rocky River Reservation, part of the Big Creek Reservation, the Hinckley Reservation, the Brecksville Reservation, the Bedford Reservation, South Chagrin and North Chagrin Reservations, and the Euclid Creek Reservation. The connected chain of green parkway was later given the poetic sobriquet of "Emerald Necklace."[15]

The creation of the Cleveland Metropolitan Park System was part of a general movement throughout the country, but the Cleveland system, in both its extent and its conception, was one of the finest. Such plans were created for "the promotion and preservation of social values." They were motivated by objectives such as the improvement of community living and a better home environment, the provision of recreational opportunities, and the cultivation of "the cultural side of our natures" through nature study and quiet reflection. These aims were considered to constitute the essence of the best kind of city planning.

The Cleveland Metropolitan Park System, as illustrated in *Cleveland Engineering*, 1929.

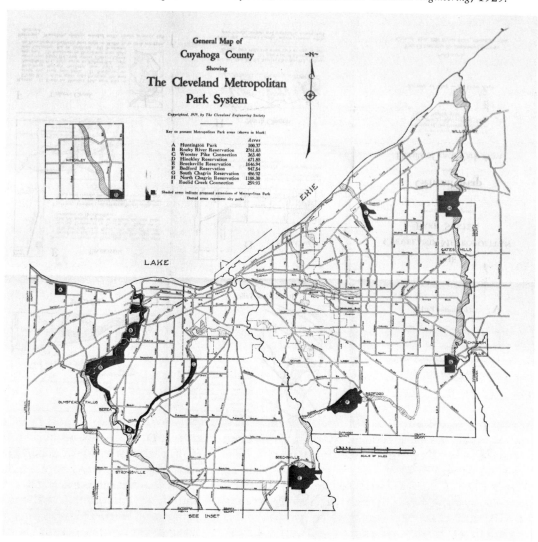

# Modernism

> Modern! Modern! Modern! We have it drummed into our ears at every turn. And why not? Is this not the age in which the new replaces the old with the rapidity of thought? The radio—the airplane—talking motion pictures—all modern—all indications of the age in which we live.[16]

While this quotation from an architectural magazine of 1930 hardly has the intellectual rigor of a philosophic creed, it shows the extent to which popular acceptance was ready for modernism. The Crash of 1929 and the ensuing Great Depression shook the confidence of Americans in the old system and its established values. The old academic theories now seemed impractical, and people were more receptive to the ideas of the early progressives like Frank Lloyd Wright, and more important, to the new ideas from Europe. While America had retreated into isolationism and "normalcy" in the twenties, the European countries had already undergone a devastating disillusionment with the old order in the wake of the First World War. Groups appeared in Germany, France, Holland, and other countries with a vision of rebuilding society and its physical setting on "realistic" foundations. Several architects working independently developed the common characteristics of a style which was later defined as "international."[17]

The International Style was above all a reaction against everything Victorian. Complexity and picturesqueness were replaced by simplicity and severity; texture, color, and ornament by smoothness and plainness. Instead of being disguised, structure was deliberately exposed, and the effect of monumental solidity gave way to a sense of volume, transparency, and reflective surfaces. The evolution of these qualities was based on certain assumptions. First, it was an article of faith that the scientific attitude could solve all problems and produce a better way of life. The prestige of science and technology were enormous, and the machine was elevated as the symbol of the age. Le Corbusier called the home a "machine for living," by which he meant that it should provide "a complete, flawless answer to a clearly articulated question." This humanistic demand was misunderstood by generations of younger architects. The incorporation of technological achievements was complemented by the firm belief that a rational order could be applied to both society and art. Analysis, followed by the conception and application of a master plan, would enable the expert to reorganize everything from an office to a city. This belief, which was the counterpart of the trend toward scientific management and efficiency studies in American business, meant that the ideal architect would become little more than an efficiency expert. Finally, good architecture must be "functional," which implied that architecture grows out of community resources and is determined by economic forces and technology. Thus the new materials and techniques of the twentieth century demanded a new style based on machine technology and rational order. As narrowly interpreted, this principle came to mean that a purely "functional" building was necessarily a better one. By the third quarter of the century, most of these assumptions had become so generally accepted that few people could remember when they were not taken for granted.[18]

The work of the European architects first became well known in the United States through the epoch-making exhibition of *Modern Architects* at the Museum of Modern Art in 1932. Arranged by Philip Johnson and Henry-Russell Hitchcock, Jr., the exhibition concentrated on the four founders of the International Style, Le Corbusier in France, J. J. P. Oud in Holland, and Gropius and Miës van der Rohe in Germany. Six American architects were also given special emphasis. One member of the exhibition committee was Philip Johnson's father, Homer H. Johnson, a well-to-do Cleveland attorney and advocate of the arts. The exhibition was brought to the Cleveland Museum of Art in October, 1932.[19]

In the late 1930s, after the rise of Hitler, many of the pioneer artists, architects, and intellectuals of the modern movement came to the United States, where they helped to make the International Style dominant by the 1940s. However, these factors were probably less important than the fact that the style itself spoke to the prevalent mood of the 1920s and 1930s.

Cleveland's response to modernism was, characteristically, less one of style than one of technical experimentation. During the single month of July, 1932, for example, half a dozen projects were under way in which modern forms or new construction techniques were demonstrated. One architect published the plans for a house with a flat roof, virtually a trademark of the International Style. Its asymmetrical composition and the horizontal banding of the windows also suggested the European style. According to architect Louis R. Leonard, in a

Porcelain enamel house, 2077 Campus Drive, South Euclid, 1932, Charles Bacon Rowley, architect.

remark which must have seemed incomprehensible to the older eclectics, "In the past the design of the house has given too much prominence to the roof and copied without reason homes which do not fit in with the life of the modern American family." The next week a house design was shown in which the exterior walls were made of hard pressed fiber board, and the interior walls of insulating wall board nailed directly to studs, with no lath or plaster. It was only later that this system became standard building practice. Another house was to be constructed of brick-on-tile walls, with interior floors made of tile arches on junior steel beams, and interior partitions of tile. The design, however, was a conventional Georgian pattern. Still another plan also utilized a combination of masonry and steel; undoubtedly some of these methods were intended to stimulate the depressed steel industry.[20]

A design that caused nationwide attention was the world's first house of porcelain enamel on steel. Designed by Charles Bacon Rowley (partner of Philip L. Small in the planning of Shaker Square), the house was built by the Ferro-Enamel Corporation and erected in South Euclid. The structure consisted of a welded steel frame and was sheathed with russet-colored porcelain enamel shingles. The walls were insulated with mineral wool and fiber board, and the windows had steel frames. The house was

advertised as being fireproof and needing no painting. Its cost was comparable to that of a masonry house. At the same time a second steel house was erected in Solon whose walls were not framed, but were made of sheet steel panels prefabricated at the factory, making each room virtually a steel box. This house, too, was faced with porcelain enamel shingles.[21]

What could be done in South Euclid or Solon apparently could not be done in the City of Cleveland. Early in July, 1932, Walter McCornack testified before the housing committee of City Council, arguing that it was essential to revise the city building code to permit the use of new materials. The chief argument was the reduction of costs that the new materials would make possible. Much of the emphasis on new methods was directed toward the possibilities of economical housing. One speaker described the construction of government low-cost housing projects in Vienna. It was pointed out that such buildings would satisfy the safety, fire, and sanitary provisions of the existing code just as well as conventional construction. Two methods mentioned in the report were light steel construction and the use of fireproof plaster.[22]

The fact that all of these developments took place within one month in the early 1930s shows that Cleveland was in the forefront of experimentation

189

with new building methods. While they did not demonstrate a preoccupation with the functional aesthetic, they shared the modern assumptions concerning new systems, materials, and technology.

The International Style and the decade of technical experimentation came together in a house built in 1938–1939 by architect Harold B. Burdick for his own residence. Burdick had worked in the firms of Meade & Hamilton and Walker & Weeks, assisting in the design of the Federal Reserve Bank. The majority of his work was in the traditional idioms, but his own house, like many other experimental houses, was planned as a prototype for a quality house in an economical price range. The external form consists of a twenty-eight foot square and is basically symmetrical. It is framed with steel columns, and the three walls of glass block are the most unusual feature. There are also large plate glass windows in the elevations, while the second story windows have steel casement frames. The exterior stucco of the second story is laid on Armenite, a trade name for a pressed wood fiber board. The roof decks are flat, except for a third story studio or "dog house," which has a hipped copper roof. The attached garage has a deck with a curved railing, suggesting an ocean liner. This was a common usage of the "streamlined" look of the thirties, as it expressed the beauty of functionalism in commonly understood terms.[23]

In March, 1939, Burdick opened the house for public showing for two months. The General Electric Company assisted in the showing, since the house used the new flourescent lighting and had an all-electric kitchen. This was probably the first domestic use of flourescent lighting. Although the actual size of the interior is small, it appears larger because of the simplicity and continuity of the space, as well as the large window area. None of the interior partitions are bearing walls, and several of them consist of bookcases or closet units. The walls are paneled with Philippine mahogany and fir plywood, thus eliminating the painting and cleaning of plaster. The floors are also constructed of Armenite, over which linoleum with inlaid patterns was laid. The streamlined ocean liner aesthetic recurs in curved walls over the central fireplace and in the upper hall. In several respects the finished house differed from early plans and specifications, undoubtedly for economic reasons. Some difficulties in maintenance were later encountered because of the unproven building materials, but these are far outweighed by the convenience and significance of the design.[24]

A perfect opportunity for the display of the modern style and new building techniques was presented by the Great Lakes Exposition of 1936 and 1937. It was planned to celebrate the industrial trade empire of the eight states bordering on the Great

Burdick house, Stratford and Scarborough Roads, Cleveland Heights, 1938, Harold B. Burdick, architect.

View of the Great Lakes Exposition, 1936, showing the Hall of Progress and the Automotive Building.

Lakes, which constituted one of the greatest manufacturing, financial, and marketing areas of the world. Moreover, the year 1936 was the centennial of Cleveland's incorporation as a city. The Exposition was not called a "World's Fair," and it was smaller in scope than the better known fairs of the thirties, Chicago's Century of Progress in 1933–1934 and the New York World's Fair of 1939. However, the Cleveland Exposition benefited from the experience of Albert N. Gonsior, who was in charge of construction at the Chicago Fair, at which much experimental work with quick and inexpensive construction was done. The architects of the Exposition described the style of the buildings as "simple, straight-forward, colorful and severe" and prophesied that they would "establish a trend in modern design just as did the buildings of the Columbian Exposition and the Century of Progress."[25] However, the chief achievements of the Great Lakes Exposition were to be in areas other than architectural style.

Among the more lasting benefits were the public improvements that resulted, including the completion of the Group Plan. The last building remaining in the area designated for the Mall was removed in 1935. The entrance to the Exposition led to a plaza occupying the Mall north of St. Clair Avenue, an area of five acres. The large underground exhibition hall, which had been constructed in 1932 at the end of the Mall north of Lakeside Avenue, was used for

the Exposition, together with the Public Auditorium. The lakefront exhibition area was reached by a 350-foot long bridge over the railroad tracks and stretched from the Stadium to East 9th Street, where much of the lakefront had been a public dump. Additional land was filled, creating the lakefront site, and a portion of the Lakeland Expressway was rushed to completion. To the east of 9th Street was a Midway amusement area and an international village called "Streets of the World." Some three dozen nationality groups offered refreshments, entertainment, and crafts in settings representing the various countries.[26]

Five major structures were erected, in addition to many notable smaller buildings and industrial exhibits. The five were the Horticulture Building, the Hall of Progress, the Automotive Building, an amphitheatre for the transportation pageant "The Parade of the Years," and the Marine Theatre, which was rebuilt in 1937 for Billy Rose's Aquacade. The main entrance on the Mall was marked by seven seventy-foot simple square pylons with three horizontal planes at the top. The bridge to the lower exhibition area was called the Court of the Presidents, honoring the sixteen Presidents who were natives of Great Lakes States. It was lined with gilded eagles sculptured in the debased classicism which was the favorite bureaucratic style of the thirties, whether democratic or fascist.

The Horticultural Building on the lakefront

Automotive Building, Great Lakes Exposition, 1936, Antonio diNardo, architect.

Hall of Progress, Great Lakes Exposition, 1936, Hays and Simpson, architects.

Court of the Presidents and "aurora borealis" lighting, Great Lakes Exposition, 1936.

exemplified the streamlined functionalism already alluded to in the Burdick House. Rising in three tiers, its stepped terraces facing the lake were rounded, intended to resemble the forward decks of an ocean liner. The architects were Franz C. Warner and G. Evans Mitchell. The three and a half acres of varied horticultural gardens and pools on the nearby hillside were designed by A. Donald Gray. The great stage of the transportation pageant, 250 feet wide and 100 feet deep, was capable of carrying locomotives. Planned by stage designer Richard Rychtarik, it had a 4,500 seat amphitheatre designed by the Osborn Engineering Company. The architect of the Automotive Building was Antonio diNardo. It was 541 feet long and 228 feet wide and constructed with so-called scissor trusses forming two long, steeply-gabled buildings separated by an interior landscaped court. The roofs had four continuous lines of horizontal louvers for ventilation. Surrounding the structure at the entrances were thirty-two pylons over seventy feet tall. The Hall of Progress, 540 feet long and 180 feet wide, was constructed with a new and unique system of rigid wooden trusses, utilizing a principle heretofore employed only with steel and concrete. Designed by the firm of J. Byers Hays and Russell Simpson, the frames combined columns and beams in a rigid continuous unit. The wooden framework was constructed of lumber in two by six-inch and two by ten-inch sizes and covered with 5/8-inch plywood, making a rigid box truss. The beams thus created were used to span thirty-foot aisles in the exhibition hall. The utter simplicity of these buildings, their frank expression of interior structure, and their generally "realistic" or factory-like appearance were eminently suitable for providing economical exhibition space and were also expressive of the industrial theme of the Exposition.[27]

On the other hand, the festival atmosphere was largely created through color and light. In fact, the use of light as an architectural element was one of the major contributions of the Exposition. The mastery of dramatic artificial illumination was relatively new in the 1930s, and engineers and visitors alike took delight in its application. There was the precedent of the exposition lighting at Chicago's Century of Progress, and another spectacular example of the concept of light as an architectural element was Albert Speer's "cathedral of light" for the Nazi Party Rally in Nuremberg in 1934. Because Cleveland was recognized as a center of the lighting industry both in research and in practice, primarily because of the presence of Nela

Park, the planners of the Exposition set out to make it the best lighted exposition ever seen. They achieved the goal of providing a greater intensity of light—the power used was sufficient for a city of 50,000 people.[28]

Lighting balance was a primary concern, in order to display the buildings to the best advantage while avoiding direct glare. Masts and pylons throughout the grounds carried indirect spotlights. Some were covered with corrugated materials which caused the light to scintillate with movement. The planes at the top of the entrance pylons were made into reflective surfaces by indirect spots. Around the grounds 200 eight-foot standards provided general illumination, and mercury lighting was used in certain areas to approximate the effect of daylight. The fountain in the horticultural gardens, consisting of a vertical center jet, four cylindrical jets, and an eight-foot dome of water, was illuminated with underwater floodlights producing eight color combinations in two-minute cycles. The roof louvers of the Automotive Building were indirectly lighted to give the impression of horizontal streamers of light. The Marine Theatre displayed "Aurora Borealis" lights, moving beams projected into the sky and radiating from a center. At the lakeshore stood a thirty-foot lighthouse with a searchlight of 14,000,000 candlepower, said to be the most powerful beacon in the world. Engineers from Westinghouse, General Electric, and Nela Park cooperated with the Exposition engineers to achieve these varied effects, for which all of the electric wiring was underground. As a demonstration of the modern faith in scientific systems and functional design, the lighting and the architecture of the Great Lakes Exposition gave ample evidence of Cleveland's position in this movement.[29]

Although the ambition of the Exposition planners to "establish a trend in modern design" was not fulfilled, J. Milton Dyer, who had been working only sporadically since World War I, reappeared in 1940 at the age of seventy to give Cleveland one of its rare instances of functionalism raised to the level of art. The United States Coast Guard Station was called the finest and "most beautiful" in the nation when it opened in August, 1940. Built at a cost of $360,000, the two-story reinforced concrete structure was erected on filled land in the Cleveland harbor at the end of a narrow causeway. It consists of three distinct units plus a sixty-foot tower. The main L-shaped structure contained the communications room, officers' quarters, mess hall, recreation room, store rooms and on the second floor, crew and staff

Cleveland Harbor Station, United States Coast Guard, 1940, J. Milton Dyer, architect.

quarters. At the northwest corner of the "L" stands the lookout tower, its platform reached by an interior spiral staircase. Connected to this building on the south is the boat house with three slips, maintenance space, and a tackle and work shop. The third unit is a separate garage building to the east.[30]

The building was called "streamlined" in 1940. As in some of the Exposition buildings, the architectural design combines smooth flat and curved surfaces analogous to those of a ship. The two curved masses facing one another between the main structure and the boat house suggest the bulkheads of a liner, while the tower shape was derived from a funnel or mast. The resemblances to a ship are even more obvious on the interior. The various areas connected by passageways are small and irresistibly convey the labyrinthine experience of finding one's way about below decks. The stair rails are pipe railing and form a semi-circular curve at the bottom of the flight. The mess hall, located in the curving bay at the south end of the building, has curved windows like those of a liner's saloon. From almost every aspect one looks out over the water. The entire design shows an awareness of the International Style architects,

Greyhound Bus Terminal, 1465 Chester Avenue, 1948, W. S. Arrasmith, architect.

particularly Le Corbusier and J. J. P. Oud. Yet the building is an original work of art, clearly intended to convey the experience of being on shipboard, and succeeding more by symbolism and evocation than by imitation.

Although the amount of actual construction during the 1930s and 1940s was circumscribed, first by the economic deprivations of the Depression and then by wartime shortages, the spirit of modernism had made its permanent impact. As Alan Gowans observed of the postwar era: "What had once been [a] revolutionary emphasis on flat roofs, horizontal window strips, wide plain expanses of wall, exposed steel and concrete and glass, and general lack of ornament was now commonplace for offices and apartments in every city, schools and churches and drugstores in every town, diners and motels and gas stations along every highway."[31] Two of the best examples of this trend were built in downtown Cleveland in 1947 and 1948.

The Greyhound Bus Terminal on Chester Avenue was a classic statement of the modern style. Built in 1948, it was identical in spirit, if not in exact detail, with the typical Greyhound bus terminal everywhere. The set-back stories, rounded ends, horizontal windows, glass block, and the insistent vertical of the pylon, which acted not only as a sign but as a strong foil to the long horizontal lines, epitomized the assimilation of the International Style. The simplicity of the design achieved a timeless appeal, so that after nearly thirty years the building still seems contemporary.

The Bond Store, which opened in October, 1947, on the site of the old Hickox Building, was called with characteristic local pride "the most modern and most beautiful apparel store in America." The owners also stated, "We have great faith in the future of Cleveland . . . we want to take our place in Cleveland's progress."[32] By now the idea of progress was synonymous with modernism. Whether appropriate or not for a retail store, the entire building was conceived in the idiom of commercial advertising display. The awkwardness of the acutely angled site at Euclid and East 9th Street was solved by a cylindrical corner element which was topped by a "floating" roof canopy pierced with circular holes and illuminated by spotlights. At the third floor level a curved solarium and display area projected from the corner. The saw-tooth plan of the side elevations made angled show windows so that shoppers were taken out of the sidewalk traffic. These theatrical and seemingly somewhat temporary aspects of the

Bond Store, Euclid Avenue at East 9th Street, 1947 (demolished), Walker & Weeks and Herbert B. Beidler, associated architects.

design were balanced by the use of solid permanent materials—pink granite and plaid terra cotta, steel and aluminum.

The interior seems to have been conceived in the spirit of the world's fairs and film musicals of the thirties. There were four sales floors, and the spectacular open space could have been a setting designed for Busby Berkeley. Illuminated mirrored columns extended from the main floor through a second floor ceiling well to the third floor. A curving staircase, as suitable for descending showgirls as for ladies' apparel shoppers, soared to the upper floors. All of the interior trim was aluminum, finished either natural, satin, or black.

The application of technology for comfort and attractiveness was complete in the Bond Store. The interior was entirely air-conditioned. There was indirect lighting in several colors, and fifty-two pastel shades were used in the interior decoration. Flourescent lighting was controlled in three degrees of intensity and enhanced by spotlights. The storefront show windows were lighted through louvered ceilings. The architects were Walker &

Bond Store interior, 1947. (*Cleveland Press*)

Weeks in association with Herbert B. Beidler, an architect practicing in Chicago who had worked briefly in Cleveland in the mid-1920s. As a dramatic and consistently designed setting for the retail sales function, their Bond Store represented the climax of the 1930s brand of modernism in Cleveland.

## Public Works

During the 1930s the advent of large-scale federal public works had a revolutionary effect on building in the United States. It was facetiously said that Harold Ickes, administrator of the Public Works Administration, "proved to be a builder to rival Cheops." Between 1933 and 1939 the PWA helped to construct 70 percent of the country's new schools, 65 percent of the courthouses, city halls, and sewage plants, 35 percent of the hospitals and public health facilities, and many bridges, tunnels, and highways.[33] A new federal building in Cleveland had already been projected since the late 1920s. The United States Post Office, replacing the old Federal Building of the Group Plan, was completed in September, 1934. The *Plain Dealer* cynically remarked that the cornerstone laying on February 16, 1933, was rushed so that the outgoing Republican administration would get the credit.

As the last building in the Terminal group, the Post Office was also erected on the air rights over the property of the Cleveland Union Terminals Company. The architects were Walker & Weeks and Philip L. Small & Associates, although the titular architect was James A. Wetmore, Architectural Supervisor of the U.S. Treasury Department. The design was intended to harmonize with the Terminal buildings, but Frank Walker stated that he understood it was not to be monumental in the sense that Brunner's Federal Building was. The Modernistic exterior of the five-story rectangular block was very simple, with fluted piers between each rank of windows providing the basis for the design. In the mid-1970s it was discovered that the sandstone facing had never been secured to the wall structure as specified by the architects, and the Post Office was forced to re-face the entire structure, using precast concrete panels for the fluted piers. The only public space in the $5,000,000 building is the 228-foot long lobby where the postal windows are located. Because of the location over the railroad, a unique system of chutes and conveyors was designed to carry mail directly to and from the railroad platforms. The Cleveland architects conferred frequently with government officials, so it is not surprising that the Post Office bears the stamp of the 1930s official architectural style.[34]

An equally important revolution of the thirties was the change in historic assumptions concerning social responsibility. The passage of the Social

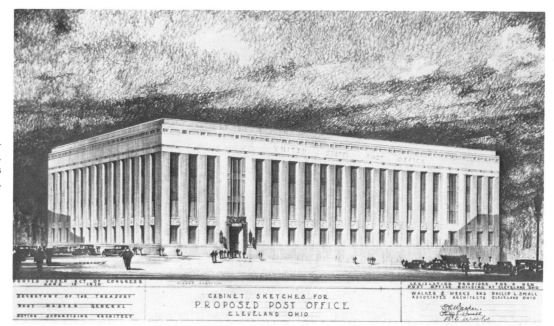

United States Post Office, Prospect Avenue, 1934, Walker & Weeks and Philip L. Small, associated architects.

CABINET SKETCHES FOR
PROPOSED POST OFFICE
CLEVELAND OHIO

Security Act in 1935, which established the principle of clear-cut social rights for individuals, was merely the most obvious manifestation. A public obligation was also recognized at every level of government for providing housing for those who could only afford low rents. The State of Ohio adopted the first public housing law in the nation, under the influence of Ernest J. Bohn, director of the Cleveland Metropolitan Housing Authority from 1933 to 1968. Bohn achieved a national reputation for his work in public housing in Cleveland, and the various Depression, wartime, and postwar housing estates built under his assistance or direction included 9,537 housing units.[35]

An important stimulus to the design of public housing in the United States was the European housing shown in the Museum of Modern Art exhibition of modern architecture in 1932. When the exhibit was brought to the Cleveland Museum of Art in the fall of that year, the "presence, energy, and power" of the new architecture was recognized by the *Plain Dealer* critic, who gave the housing examples special comment. Plans were also shown of a proposed housing project for the area between Central and Scovill Avenues from East 22nd Street to East 38th Street in Cleveland. The architects were Joseph L. Weinberg in association with William H. Conrad & Wallace G. Teare. The plans showed the influence of German architects and exhibited the standardization and simplification which were characteristic of the modern functional style.[36]

The Cleveland proposal had been designed for a private developer in anticipation of receiving funds from the Reconstruction Finance Corporation. Created in 1932, the RFC was authorized to provide 85 percent of the required capital for housing construction by limited-dividend corporations which would supply the other 15 percent. Many projects were planned across the country, including three others in Cleveland, for the area between Cedar and Central Avenues, designed by Walter McCornack, for the Outhwaite homes by Maier, Walsh & Barrett, and for the site popularly known as Whiskey Island on the near West Side, also planned by Weinberg, Conrad & Teare. When none of the developers could raise the necessary capital, the Public Works Administration entered the field of construction with federal funds in 1933. From the point of view of the Roosevelt administration, the PWA housing projects were primarily a means of providing employment and a stimulus to the construction industry. Because of the advanced planning on the Cleveland projects, three of them were chosen—Cedar-Central, Outhwaite, and the Whiskey Island project, called Lakeview Terrace. The first three public housing projects authorized and begun by the federal government, all were started in 1935 and occupied in 1937.[37]

Lakeview Terrace is especially notable because of its successful adaptation to a difficult site, and it became internationally known as a landmark in public housing. The twenty-two acre site at West

Lakeview Terrace, 1935-1937, Weinberg, Conrad & Teare, architects. (*Ohio Historical Society*)

28th Street lay between the lake and the proposed location of the Main Avenue Bridge. It was an irregular hillside with an eighty foot drop in elevation, an average slope of 10 percent, and a slope of 20 percent at the steepest parts. Frederick Bigger was the site planning consultant. The project planners developed two schemes, the final one being adapted to the hillside by a curving road with many of the housing units arranged in a fan-like pattern. There are forty-four residential buildings of three types—apartments, row houses, and a combination of the two. The latter contain row houses on the first and second floors, with apartments on the third, and form retaining walls where the slope is steepest. The buildings are oriented, as much as possible considering the topography, to provide daylight and unobstructed views of the lake. They cover only 23 percent of the site area.

The building construction is entirely fireproof, consisting of masonry walls of brick on tile with concrete roof and floor slabs. Interior partitions are of solid metal lath and plaster, and the windows have steel casements. The design of the building units was clearly influenced by European precedent. The curved end walls, the windows arranged in horizontal bands, the iron railings, and especially the disinctive downturned hoods over the doorways reflect the housing of J. J. P. Oud and the work of other International Style architects.

Lakeview Terrace also included the first community center in a public housing project. It contained an auditorium, nursery, recreation room, and meeting rooms. A large central playground was provided adjacent to the Community Building. At the West 28th Street entrance to the project there were two buildings containing administrative offices and thirteen shops. When a change in the location of the shoreway exit eliminated any transient traffic, the shops could not be sustained, and the east building was finally replaced in 1973 by a high-rise apartment for the elderly.

The project was also innovative in its use of the decorative arts, made possible by the creation of the Treasury Relief Art Project in 1935. The ornamentation includes sculptured relief panels on the exterior wall of the community center auditorium, and murals in the nursery. While the use of decorative art has often been considered inconsistent with the

198

functional style, the architects of Lakeview Terrace responded positively when the possibility of public-funded art was suggested. The liaison with the federal agency was handled by William Milliken, director of the Cleveland Museum of Art.[38]

Lewis Mumford used Lakeview Terrace as an illustration of public housing in *The Culture of Cities*, with the comment: "Good plan, well-adapted to site, with combination of apartment houses and smaller dwellings. Note the placement of the dwellings at right angles to the roads, the skillful use of contours on the left, the abandonment of useless and costly streets, and ample interior playground."[39] The development was also called "one of the best public housing projects in the country" and "a milestone in the history of American architecture." A recent study of the project concluded that "the architects were able to take advantage of a unique and short-lived combination of circumstances: the stimulation of nation-wide interest in mass housing; the dissemination of the theories and designs of radical European architects specifically concerned with housing; federal government efforts to provide employment through direct funding of housing projects; and the availability of a challenging site."[40]

Lakeview Terrace passed to the control of the Cleveland Metropolitan Housing Authority in 1940. Meanwhile the first genuine housing legislation, as distinct from job-creating bills, was passed in 1937 and continued in effect until the war in 1941. The Valleyview Homes on West 7th Street and Starkweather and Woodhill Homes at Woodland Avenue and Woodhill Road were built and occupied in 1940 under this program.[41]

The first portion of the lakefront highway (later the Lakeland Freeway and more recently Memorial Shoreway) was another major federally assisted project of the Depression years. Built to coincide with the Great Lakes Exposition, the first section from East 9th to East 21st Street was begun in November, 1935, and opened in May, 1936. Much of the roadway was built on filled land and old public dumping grounds. The right-of-way was 100 feet wide. Because the expected settling of the filled soil made it impracticable to pave the roadway for at least two years, the surface was simply covered with oiled cinders. In August the highway was completed to East 55th Street and later to Gordon Park. The Works Progress Administration contributed $3,-000,000 toward the project, and 9,000 workers were employed during the construction period.[42]

In 1938–1939 the "gigantic" Main Avenue Bridge was constructed, linking the shoreway on the east

Lakeview Terrace, 1935-1937.

with Bulkley Boulevard, which became the West Side portion of the shoreway. Less than eighteen months passed between the groundbreaking and the dedication of the structure in October, 1939. The $7,000,000 project was built by Cuyahoga County with aid from the PWA amounting to $2,450,000. The six-lane, cantilever-truss structure is over a mile long, making it the longest of the three high-level bridges. With its approaches the bridge extends from West 6th to West 32nd Street. The girders over the railroad on the eastern approach, over 270 feet long, were the longest span girders ever built in America. John O. McWilliams, county engineer, was in charge of construction, Fred L. Plummer was chief design engineer, and Wilbur J. Watson was consulting engineer.[43]

In 1940 a bond issue for additional highway construction was passed. It covered the extension of the Lakeland Freeway, Rocky River Bridge improvements, the extension of Jennings Road, the Willow Freeway, the continuation of Chester Avenue as a through street to Wade Park, and the Newburgh Freeway. Any rapid progress on these projects was delayed by the entrance of the United States into World War II, the question of priorities with regard to public works, and the preparation of a comprehensive plan for the county. A long-range expressway plan was developed by the Express

Highway Committee of the Regional Association in 1944. The engineers included representatives from the state, city, county, Regional Association, City Planning Commission, and Cleveland Transit System. The plan envisioned an inner belt surrounding the central downtown area and an outer belt around the greater part of the city. The scheme for a $240,000,000 integrated expressway system was considered a solution to the traffic problems of the metropolitan area. All of the expressways which had actually been completed three decades later were anticipated in the 1944 plan, and certain links, such as the Newburgh Expressway, were still being studied by highway planners as a part of the Federal Interstate Highway system.[44]

During World War II there was a statistically enormous amount of government construction in Cleveland, most of it consisting of utilitarian space-enclosing structures of little architectural distinction. In 1941 the National Advisory Committee for Aeronautics (NACA) began the construction of a research center for jet propulsion costing $20,000,-000 on a 200-acre site adjacent to the Municipal Airport. The Cleveland location was chosen from sites offered by sixty-two cities. The facilities included the Engine Propeller Research Building, Engine Research Building, Altitude Wind Tunnel, Light Research Hangar, and Ice Tunnel. The NACA Aircraft Engine Research Laboratory, consisting of twelve buildings covering a floor area of ten acres, was formally dedicated in 1943.[45]

In 1942 one of the world's greatest war factories, the Fisher Aircraft Assembly Plant, was also constructed near the Cleveland airport. Popularly known as the Bomber Plant, the building covered nearly thirty acres. It was built for the assembly of the B-29 bomber and later used for the construction of P-75 escort planes. After the war the plant was used for tank construction for twenty years, and some of its hangars housed various air units. Other government construction during this period included the million-dollar Veterans Administration Hospital in Brecksville, a group of seven buildings opened in 1941, and the Crile General Hospital in Parma Heights, which consisted of eighty-seven connected buildings and was opened in 1943.[46]

## Transformations

Change is fundamental to the growth of a city. Just as the Cleveland of 1876 bore no resemblance to the village of 1796, so the greater metropolis of postwar Cleveland was very little like the city of the Centennial year. Both haphazard development and conscious planning work new patterns; changes in building technology alter the size, shape, and materials of structures; shifting patterns of residential, commercial, and industrial use are inevitable; improvement frequently necessitates demolition; and fashions in taste change. Nevertheless, the forces of metropolitan growth and modernism, as well as the possibility of public funding and the incentive of economic constraints, created a momentum in the 1930s and 1940s for changes of a kind and a magnitude that were unprecedented.

The acceptance of modernism and scientific progress brought about a general attitude that anything old was obsolescent and anything new was necessarily better, and at the same time the fact that historicism and older values had been found wanting caused their complete rejection. The architectural expression of this attitude was frequently to be found in the modernization of old buildings. It was not a new idea, for even in the mid-nineteenth century a Greek Revival house might often be made Gothic or Queen Anne and brought "up-to-date." But rarely was remodeling or "renovizing," as it was called in the 1930s, taken up with such zest. A common manifestation was the widespread remodeling of store fronts, and the most notable example was the alteration of the Euclid Avenue entrance of the Arcade in 1939. The first two stories of the facade were faced with polished carnelian granite. The central arch was replaced by a square entrance and two relief medallions with the profiles of Stephen V. Harkness and Charles F. Brush, the first president and vice-president of the Arcade Company. At the same time steel members were inserted to support the tower. The alteration was supervised by Dan Mitchell for Walker & Weeks.[47]

The reconstruction of the Catholic Cathedral of St. John in 1946–1948 was different in purpose and intention. A new cathedral had long been projected by two earlier bishops, either on the site of Saint Agnes' Church or near Severance Hall, and an enlarged edifice was needed. But the spirit of modernizing motivated instead a decision to encase

The Arcade. Euclid Avenue facade remodeled 1939. (*Martin Linsey*)

the older brick cathedral of 1852 with Tennessee Crab Orchard sandstone. Thus was obliterated the early Gothic Revival church by the most important mid-nineteenth century American Catholic architect, Patrick C. Keely, (1816–1896), designer of several other churches in the Cleveland Diocese and several hundred in the East. The facade of St. John's Cathedral was rebuilt, the tower demolished and a new tower and transept erected on the south side, and the apse was enlarged and altered in design. The interior columns, groin-vaulted ceiling, and stained glass of the original church remained. The architects of the reconstruction were Stickle & Associates.[48]

Suburban growth in Cuyahoga County contributed to an important transformation in the residential patterns of the city. While the older immigrant groups were becoming generally more

dispersed in the 1920s, the black community became more concentrated. Because of economic and social barriers, few blacks were able to join the suburban exodus. The first great migration of Negroes to Cleveland had taken place during and following World War I, and between 1910 and 1930 the black population increased from 8,000 to 72,000. By 1930 the concentration of the black community was consolidated as a ghetto in the area between Euclid and Woodland Avenues from East 14th to East 105th Streets.[49]

As with the earlier immigrant communities, the church was a dominant institution in the black community. An early building erected by a historic black congregation was St. John's African Methodist Episcopal Church. The first Negro congregation in Cleveland, St. John's had been founded in 1830 by a group of fugitive slaves from the South. The church built its new red brick Gothic building on East 40th Street in 1908. In the 1920s it was unnecessary for most Negro congregations to build new churches; they usually bought the buildings of white congregations which were relocating away from the city center. In this manner several historic congregations acquired equally historic buildings. Shiloh Baptist Church, for example, was the first Negro Baptist congregation in Cleveland, having been formed in 1849. In 1923 Shiloh purchased the classical temple of the B'nai Jeshurun congregation at East 55th and Scovill. In 1934 Antioch Baptist, one of three other churches which originated out of Shiloh Church, purchased the brick and stone Romanesque building which had been built for the Bolton Avenue Presbyterian Church in 1896. The First Church of Christ Scientist, a Neo-Classic building designed by George F. Hammond, was occupied by the Lane Metropolitan Colored Methodist Episcopal Church in 1919. Other institutions also acquired older buildings and thus ensured their continuing usefulness. For example, the Universal Negro Improvement Association, founded in 1911 by Marcus Garvey, a Negro nationalist and reformer from Jamaica, to promote Negro welfare, occupied the Jacob Goldsmith house on East 40th Street in 1923.[50]

Two secular institutions which erected new buildings in the black community offer an interesting comparison in style. From the point of view of architectural design, the two decades which brought about the acceptance of the modern style were spanned by the Phillis Wheatley Association and

Antioch Baptist Church (Bolton Avenue Presbyterian Church). Cedar Avenue at East 89th Street, 1896, William Sabin, architect.

Karamu House. The Phillis Wheatley Association was founded in 1912 by Edna Jane Hunter, a black professional nurse, in order to provide a residence and job-training center for Negro girls. Among other functions, the association served the purpose of protecting unattached young women in the expanding ghetto. It was largely dependent on white financial support, which some people interpreted as a means to keep the YWCA segregated. Mrs. Levi T. Scofield, who was the first president of the Board of Trustees, was at the same time president of the city's YWCA. In 1918 Edna Hunter was able to purchase an old mansion on Cedar Avenue for expanded facilities, and in 1924 a $500,000 fund raising drive was conducted for a new nine-story building. Completed in 1928, the new building contained schools for instruction in music, cooking, and cosmetology, and could accommodate six times as many girls in residence as the old home. Designed by Hubbell and Benes, it was one of the most simple and sophisticated designs by the architects of the Cleveland Museum of Art. In a way, however, the handsome building could be seen as a symbol of what was considered by some to be white paternalism.[51]

In 1915 the Playhouse Settlement, a vehicle for new racial consciousness and an interest in black folk culture, was founded by two white social workers, Russell and Rowena Jelliffe. Its chief purpose was to establish a multipurpose social center and biracial community theater. In 1927 its first permanent auditorium was given the name Karamu Theatre. The name was derived from a Swahili word meaning "a place of joyful meeting" and symbolized the interest in African culture. The first theater burned in 1939, and although the programs continued, it was not possible to rebuild until ten years later. The directors chose the architects of the Cleveland Play House, then the firm of Small, Smith, Reeb & Draz, to design the new theater in 1949 and the Community Service building which was completed in 1959. In its asymmetrical plan, cubical simplicity, and lack of ornamentation, the architecture of the combined Karamu House facility was typical of the assimilated International Style which dominated the 1950s.[52]

The acceptance of modernism, the dispersion and concentration of various groups, and the beginning of large-scale public funding in the 1930s and 1940s merely laid the groundwork for profound changes in the shape of the city. The scope of the transformations that could be wrought by public funding were only hinted at in the housing, construction, and highway projects of these decades, although one consequence of public funding, the creation of needless projects by planners and builders only because public funds were available, seemed inevitable. The two government programs which would have the greatest impact on the city, "urban renewal" and the Interstate Highway system, were to flourish in the next two decades.[53]

Phillis Wheatley Building, Cedar Avenue at East 44th, 1928, Hubbell & Benes, architects.

Karamu House, East 89th Street and Quincy Avenue, 1949-1959, Small, Smith, Reeb & Draz, architects.

Park Synagogue, Mayfield Road, Cleveland Heights, 1950, Eric Mendelsohn, architect.

# 1950: Park Synagogue

In the late 1940s and early 1950s there was no single structure or grouping comparable in significance for Cleveland with those of earlier years. Any such selection would be quite arbitrary. However, in 1947–1950, greater Cleveland was graced with a building by one of the old masters of the modern movement. Only Walter Gropius and Eric Mendelsohn are represented in Cleveland, and Mendelsohn's Park Synagogue, one of his last projects, is generally regarded as a major work of twentieth century architecture. It was the largest and most ambitious of four synagogues and community centers designed by him and built in the United States between 1945 and 1953. The others were located in St. Louis, St. Paul, and Grand Rapids.[1]

Eric Mendelsohn (1887–1953) was a member of the World War I generation of architects who set out to bring about a new beginning in architecture. His extraordinary Einstein Tower at Potsdam, designed in 1920, soon became a popular symbol of modernism. A characteristic which it shared with all of his later work was a form in which the parts were integrated by an organic continuity, so that no part could be taken away without destroying the whole. In fact, the term "organic architecture," usually associated with Frank Lloyd Wright, was also used by Mendelsohn. The teaching of Sullivan and Wright appealed to the German architect, particularly the idea that a study of the principles of growth and structure in nature could provide the chief inspiration of architectural design. Mendelsohn met Wright during a visit to the United States in 1924 and helped to make his work known in Germany. While there is no question of attributing influence either way, their mutual appreciation and support were apparent.[2] Wolf Von Eckardt has called Mendelsohn the first successful modern architect. He received commissions for important buildings, won many competitions, and pleased his clients, yet he never compromised his artistic intent. Mendelsohn left Germany in 1933 and worked in France, England, and Palestine for the next eight years. He came to the United States in 1941, where he lived until his death in 1953.[3]

Mendelsohn was only mentioned in passing in the catalog of the *Modern Architects* exhibition of 1932. He was not a sufficient purist to be identified with the International Style and in fact, was not easy to classify as an architect. He was sometimes regarded as an exponent of the cool, impersonal, modern worship of the machine, perhaps because of his successful work with department stores, cinemas, and hospitals, but while he agreed that "certainly, the primary element in architecture is function," he also added that "function without sensibility remains mere construction."[4] Today he is usually called an expressionistic architect—one who believes that architecture, instead of being purely geometric, should express its essential structure and the needs of life which it contains. Like other modern architects, Mendelsohn was intrigued by the structural possibilities of new twentieth century materials, but while the International Style architects were creating new forms dictated primarily by function and the new technology, Mendelsohn sought to use the new materials to express the social and spiritual needs of man. For this reason, the synagogue commissions especially appealed to him.

In 1946 the Cleveland Jewish Center, which had

moved to the Heights from its building on East 105th Street, began plans for a new temple and community center. Mendelsohn was chosen as architect, and Rabbi Armond E. Cohen's admiration for the great master was instrumental in assuring that his artistic concept was carried out.[5] The application of the modern style to a synagogue was still daring in 1946. The "modernized Byzantine" of the Temple (1924) and the Byzantine eclectic style of the Temple on the Heights (1928), both designed by Charles Greco, were still typical of the accepted Near Eastern tradition in synagogue architecture. The basic plan of the four Mendelsohn synagogues was essentially functional, evolving out of the fact that several times as many people attended the services on the High Holy Days as on the average Sabbath. The main sanctuary was joined by a foyer to an assembly hall so that when partitions were opened, the sanctuary size was almost doubled. Mendelsohn's own words best explain his conception of the Cleveland center:

> The Cleveland Park Synagogue is, in fact, a community center, sheltering the three activities of a contemporary congregation: the house of worship—the House of God, the school for the education of the children—the House of the Torah, the auditorium for the assembly and recreation of the adult members—the House of the People. . . .
> The Site at his disposal—30 acres, hilly and densely wooded—demanded and, at the same time, facilitated a bold approach. Along the small axis of the site and across its highest elevation runs a clear stream in a 20-foot deep ravine forming with its branch a peninsula. This fan-

shaped peninsula, clearly visible from the highway—the main approach road, seemed to be predestined to carry the *Temple Area* with assembly, foyer, temple proper, choir-room, chapel, garden-court, and amphitheater which is cantilevered out over the tip of the promontory [not executed].

> The only available space large enough to carry a *School* for 1000 pupils was across the ravine to the North of the peninsula providing, as it does, the needed North-South exposure for the classroom-wings.

> As the *Administration* has to serve both major parts of the building: Temple Area and School Area, a bridgelike structure over the ravine seemed to be the most natural device.

> These were the practical considerations, the factual material with which the architect had to work. Facts and ideas, however, are not separated in our art. They start to interact at the moment the building program is studied and the site visited.

> The work's success depends on the finished building fulfilling its purpose, on its structural and economical soundness, and on being a flower which did not exist before in the garden of Architecture.[6]

The symbolic nature of Mendelsohn's thinking is clear, and all accounts of his creative process indicate that he developed the concept as a complete totality from the beginning. However, the original concept of the Park Synagogue was considerably revised in a second phase. The classroom wing was not placed across the ravine, but around the garden court behind the assembly hall, and the bridgelike structure leading to an auditorium wing was not built until 1969 under the direction of the firm of Bialosky & Manders.

Park Synagogue, Mayfield Road, Cleveland Heights, 1950, Eric Mendelsohn, architect.

The main expressive form of the temple is its vast hemispherical dome, 100 feet in diameter and at the time the third largest in the United States. "Mendelsohn believed that in Judaism, God is not remote or mysterious but rather He is near and the heavens and earth are united in the Spirit of God. He, therefore, constructed a synagogue which is virtually all dome."[7] There are no walls dividing the heavens from the earth. The structural design of the building was equally daring. Having first conceived the expressive form, Mendelsohn then found a way to accomplish it through engineering. The reinforced concrete hemisphere rests on ten supporting points. The curvature begins at a height of fifteen feet and the apex of the ceiling is sixty-five feet above the floor. The beam at the base is 8-1/2 inches thick, but the rest of the dome, which is made of reinforced Gunite concrete sprayed in place over wooden forms, has a thickness of only four inches. During the construction, the forms were supported by scaffolding, and the ribs which maintained the proper curvature were held in place by horizontal rings of welded pipe. When the concrete was set, the roof was covered with felt and then copper sheets, which have been allowed to weather to a greenish color. The interior ceiling is made of acoustic tile applied directly to the concrete dome in horizontal rows. The drum of the dome is entirely glazed with large plate glass windows. Although many members wanted to use stained glass, Mendelsohn rejected the idea, insisting that the views of nature through the clear glass would bring the congregation closer to the Spirit of God.[8]

The synagogue's fan-shaped assembly hall is roofed with clear span trusses, of which the longest measures ninety-three feet. The sanctuary and the foyer may be thrown together by opening sliding doors, and the movable doors between the foyer and the assembly hall jack-knife into a recess. The structure of the educational wing consists of reinforced concrete slabs with steel supports. Most of the interior walls are finished with plywood of birch, maple, and mahogany.

The first impression of the Park Synagogue is one of deceptive simplicity. Most of its forms are common to the vernacular usage of much institutional architecture of the late 1940s. However, careful observation reveals great subtlety in the details and proportions. Furthermore, Mendelsohn's individual use of the modern idiom produced one of the most European of the mid-twentieth century structures in Cleveland.[9]

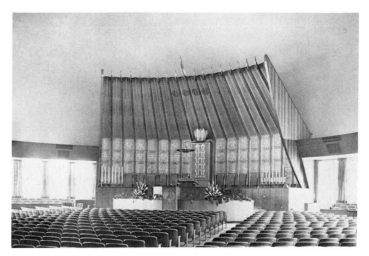

Park Synagogue, interior.

Finally weaned from Near Eastern eclecticism, a distinct style of synagogue architecture emerged in the 1950s. While owing something to several architects, it was probably most indebted to Mendelsohn. Likewise, many of Mendelsohn's early plastic visions, captured in little sketches of fluid and expressive forms, have come to fruition in the work of Saarinen and Nervi, and even in Wright's last works. By providing an alternative to the monotonous cubic austerity of most modern architecture of his era, Mendelsohn made a unique contribution to twentieth century architecture. Cleveland's Park Synagogue is widely recognized as one of the significant landmarks in this accomplishment.

Park Synagogue, education wing.

Interstate-77 interchange to proposed Interstate-90, at Broadway and East 37th Street, 1965.

# 1950–1960

## Consensus and Reawakening

The Eisenhower Years. This characterization of the 1950s suggests the organization man in the gray flannel suit, a period of prosperity and the new upwardly mobile middle class, a comparative harmony in American life, and perhaps a general tone of blandness. But it was also an era of considerable diversity, containing the involvement in the Korean War, the beginning of the civil rights movement, the end of McCarthyism, and in the arts the beginning of abstract expressionism, rock music, and a literature exploring the place of the individual in a mass society. It was especially a period of changing life styles whose essence was a much greater informality.[10]

Frederick Lewis Allen pointed out in 1952 that despite the conventional anti-New Deal rhetoric about "big spending," federal intervention, and threats to private enterprise, there was already "subconscious" agreement that a balance had been struck between government regulation and assistance programs on the one hand, and the efficiency and flexibility of private business on the other. In other words, America was not evolving toward socialism, but *beyond* socialism. The unprecedented affluence and relative stability following two decades of depression, wartime, and recovery led to "consensus" interpretations of society; the conflicts and crises of the preceding years were deemphasized, and there was a more general agreement on the goals and ideals of American life. In this context American architecture of the 1950s clearly reflected a period which was an interlude more than a new beginning, and the buildings themselves expressed the balance of social and individual concerns, as well as the new affluence.[11]

The decade started slowly for significant building in Cleveland, but there was no lack of thought given to the problems of the city. In 1949 a General Plan for the City of Cleveland was prepared under director John T. Howard and adopted by the City Planning Commission under the chairmanship of Ernest J. Bohn. Intended as a thirty-year plan, it set out general guidelines for the growth and development of the city. Separate consideration was given to business and industrial areas, residential land use and neighborhood improvement, lakefront development, traffic thoroughfares and rail transit. The downtown was expected to continue as the "natural" main business and shopping area; in 1949 it was impossible to foresee the enormous impact of the giant suburban shopping centers. Considerable thought was given to the type and density of housing and to the redevelopment and conservation of existing neighborhoods. In order to cope with traffic congestion, the construction of the freeway system drawn up by the Express Highway Committee of the Regional Association in 1944 was made an integral part of the plan. Provision was made for a high-speed rapid transit rail system, which already envisioned a line to the airport. It is significant that projects which would require public funding, not only by the city but also from county, state, and federal sources, were carefully indicated, as were the areas in which private business and individuals could work within the plan.[12]

The Public Square and the Mall were a continual focus of interest. In 1949, Western Reserve University was considering a new building on the site of Cleveland College (the 1898 Chamber of Commerce Building). It was to consist of a vertical block facing

209

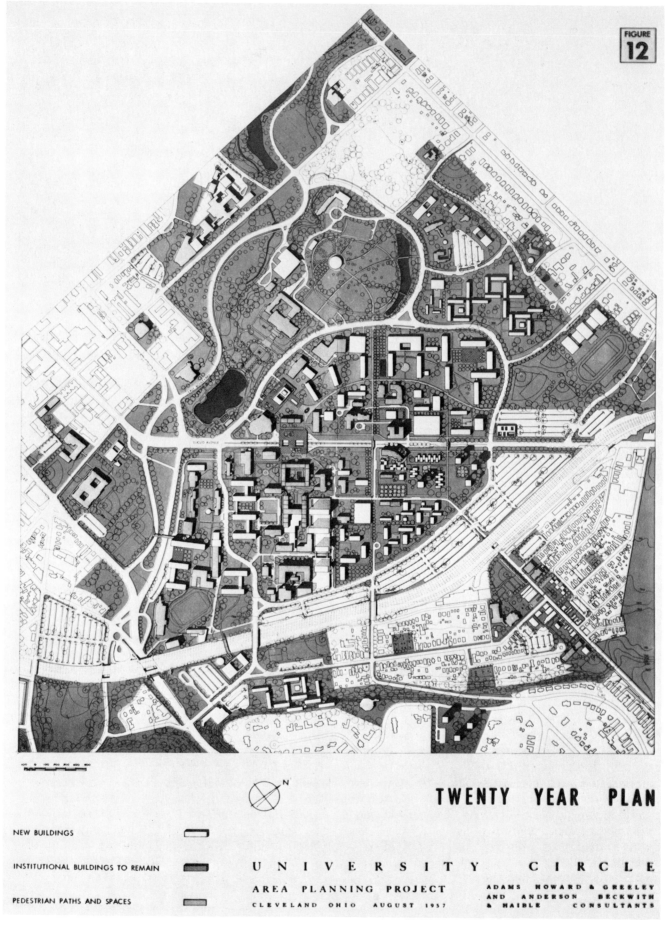

TWENTY YEAR PLAN

NEW BUILDINGS

INSTITUTIONAL BUILDINGS TO REMAIN

PEDESTRIAN PATHS AND SPACES

U N I V E R S I T Y        C I R C L E

AREA PLANNING PROJECT

CLEVELAND OHIO AUGUST 1957

ADAMS HOWARD & GREELEY
AND ANDERSON BECKWITH
& HAIBLE CONSULTANTS

University Circle Development Foundation, Twenty Year Plan, 1957, Adams, Howard & Greeley planning consultants.

Cleveland Institute of Music, 11021 East Boulevard, 1961, Schafer, Flynn & van Dijk, architects. (*Dalton, van Dijk, Johnson & Partners*)

the Square comparable in mass to the Chamber of Commerce, and a long horizontal block facing the Mall with the same height as the Group Plan buildings. The design by Garfield, Harris, Robinson & Schafer, the continuing firm of Abram Garfield and one of the most active architectural offices of the period, was conceived in the International Style idiom. Although the college was not built, the Cuyahoga County Administration Building, a complementary building by the same firm at the northwest edge of the Mall, was erected in 1956.[13]

By the mid-1950s the institutions at University Circle were all embarked on large expansion programs. The great surge in college enrollments, the new prosperity, and the simple fact that no building had been done for twenty-five years were responsible. The Case Institute Electrical Engineering Building was completed. Ground was broken for an addition to the Cleveland Museum of Art, an attached wing creating an open courtyard next to the original Neo-Classic structure. A newly located Museum of Natural History was begun, as well as new buildings for the Cleveland Institute of Art and the Cleveland Institute of Music. The Howard M. Hanna Pavilion of the University Hospitals was under construction. Western Reserve University was building the I. F. Freiberger Library and was now considering the site at the southeast corner of Euclid and Adelbert Road for its Cleveland College building (later called Baker Memorial Building). Most of these were designed in variants of the now-accepted classic modern style, a version of the International Style, with varying degrees of success. In general, the utter simplicity of the buildings, with their plain surfaces, box-like volumes, and total lack of ornamentation, seems from the perspective of twenty

years to give them a bland similarity. Architects had arrived at a consensus that functionalism, whatever its interpretation, was the appropriate guiding philosophy of the age.[14]

In 1957 the University Circle Development Foundation, later the University Circle Foundation and then simply University Circle Incorporated, was created to reinforce the commitment of the cultural institutions to the Circle area and to carry out a twenty-year development plan. The first organization of its kind in the country, it was established by the various institutions, each of which assigned a part of its individual autonomy to the corporation, giving it the authority to do the things that could be better done jointly than separately. A master plan was worked out by planning consultants Adams, Howard & Greeley of Cambridge, Massachusetts, providing for the growth of the member institutions and the development of the entire physical environment. The plan emphasized the aesthetic qualities of the area and proposed the means to create "a unified, beautiful cultural center." Among the common facilities developed were parking, new roadways, a shuttle bus, and a private police force. The application of the principles of urban renewal, with the acquisition and clearance of land for building sites, was designed in such a way as to minimize the inconvenience to individual property owners. Nevertheless, although the objectives were to minimize dislocation and to integrate the area with surrounding neighborhoods, the plan called for the demolition of Adelbert Hall, Case Main, Schweinfurth's science and law buildings, two of the Mather College buildings, Hessler Road (a charming early twentieth century residential cul-de-sac), most of the magnificent architectural museum that con-

Model for the Downtown General Plan (1959),
Eric A. Grubb, director, City Planning Commission. William A. Gould and associated architects, developer of model.

stituted Magnolia Drive, and several other declining
but still livable residential streets. Much of this
demolition was only prevented by economic constraints which developed in the late 1960s. Twenty
years later, the plan was perceived by many to be
outmoded and insensitive to the possibilities of the
pre-existing neighborhood matrix. It was clear that
the entire long-range plan should be restudied in the
light of new rehabilitation and preservation concepts.[15]

In the latter part of the fifties, downtown
Cleveland was also given special study. An article in
*Architectural Forum* in August, 1955, noting the
suburban growth which siphoned off tax income
from the city, asked a fundamental question, "Why
does Cleveland fail to captivate the suburban
imagination?" In spite of the city's progressive

programs in housing and transportation, and in spite
of the individuality and the visually "stirring" quality
of the downtown, there seemed to be no easy
answer. In 1958–1959 the City Planning Commission prepared a study of the downtown as an
amendment to the General Plan of 1949. The
downtown was defined as the area bounded by Lake
Erie, the Cuyahoga Valley on the west, and the
Innerbelt freeway on the east and south. Prepared
under planning director Eric A. Grubb, the
recommendations were far more specific and
detailed than those of the earlier General Plan.
Professional planning consultants from Philadelphia, Chicago, and Cambridge, Massachusetts, were
retained, and local architectural consultants were
Robert C. Gaede, J. Byers Hays and Wallace G.
Teare. The plan was accompanied by a large three-
dimensional model developed by William A. Gould
and associated architects for the purpose of illustrating the proposals.[16]

The study began with an analysis of the function
and the assets of the downtown area, together with
regional growth projections and goals. There was
also a succinct appreciation of the positive visual
qualities of the downtown area. The proposals that
followed reveal the ambitious scope of the planners'
thinking. Further development of the Mall area as a
government center was proposed as substantial
long-term space requirements for governmental
purposes were identified. County functions were
grouped near Ontario and Lakeside, City and State
offices at East 9th and Lakeside, and federal office
buildings on the western edge of the Mall. Proposals
for traffic circulation included the completion of the
Innerbelt freeway and improvement of the
lakeshore expressway. The study also suggested a
subway under Euclid Avenue between East 14th
Street and the Terminal. This was accompanied by a
proposal for the reorganization of Playhouse
Square, including the redesigning of the intersection
of Euclid, Huron, and East 14th Streets. At the other
end of the Euclid Avenue business axis, the
reconstruction of Public Square was shown. It
provided for ramps for buses from Euclid and
Superior Avenues to an underground concourse for
transportation interchange. Ontario Street would
be closed, and the north and south halves of the
Square were redesigned as pedestrian plazas, with
the proposal that the Soldiers and Sailors Monument
be relocated. The major architectural proposal was
the construction of an extended public exhibition
hall at the north end of the Mall which would bridge

the railroad tracks and provide a central structure north of Lakeside Avenue, thus "completing" the Burnham plan. The development of additional commercial office towers and expanded hotel facilities was also envisioned. The plan further suggested the creation of an industrial park in the existing semi-industrial area east of East 18th Street and north of Chester Avenue. Among the remaining proposals, residential apartment development was suggested at two sites, one in the four blocks surrounding St. Clair and East 12th Street and the other near Fenn College. Both sites clearly showed the influence of Le Corbusier's "Ville Radieuse," with widely separated apartment towers combined with lower housing in park-like settings. Once again, the necessary public and private measures were identified. Opportunities were noted for using urban renewal funds under the Housing Acts of 1949 and 1954, which authorized assistance in the assembling, clearance, and preparation of sites for redevelopment, planning assistance, rehabilitation, and public housing.

Meanwhile the first new downtown office building since the Terminal group was erected in 1956–1958. The Illuminating Building was also the first tall building in Cleveland to display the glass curtain wall which became standard in the 1950s. It was begun five years after the pioneer Lever House in New York and was exactly contemporary with the Seagram Building of Mies van der Rohe and Philip Johnson. Like those buildings, it was set back on a small pedestrian plaza. Located just off the northwest corner of Public Square, the twenty-two story tower was designed by New York architects Carson & Lundin. It was built around a central service core, and the ground floor, in addition to the lobby and elevator bank, contained a display and service area for the company's customers. There was also a restaurant, which was the only architectural element to project beyond the sheer rectangular facade. The building was originally planned as a steel frame structure, but a steel shortage required the columns to be changed to reinforced concrete. This caused no perceptible alteration in the external appearance, and the grid of the frame was expressed with aluminum mullions separating the glass and wall panels. As the city's first downtown office building in twenty-five years, its first modern glass-sheathed tower, and its first tall reinforced concrete frame structure, the Illuminating Building was of more than passing interest in the Cleveland of the 1950s.[17]

Illuminating Building, northwest corner Public Square, 1958, Carson & Lundin, architects.

## Connective Tissue

During the 1950s Cleveland maintained a national reputation in its development of city transportation systems—air, transit, and highway. The new terminal at Hopkins Airport, the rapid transit, and the Innerbelt freeway were all completed or well under way by 1961. While a new way of looking at engineered structures and utilitarian buildings was accepted by this time, and a new aesthetic of functionalism had developed, these Cleveland works were not primarily significant for their aesthetic design. The statement of Outcalt, Guenther & Associates, architects of the airport terminal, summarizes the designer's approach in the 1950's: "We purposely avoided a more costly, monumental structure. We designed a building around the problems. Our purpose was to answer specific needs."[18]

The architects' previous experience in airport design was limited to some of the temporary facilities for various airlines at the Cleveland airport. Specialists in schools, they are said to have applied principles used in the planning of the Columbus School for the Blind, which provided for simple, direct, one-way movement. The problem of planning a terminal was likewise seen essentially as one of providing a "pipeline" for a clear, uncluttered circulation pattern. The designers chose a centralized plan with unified ticketing and waiting areas, as distinct from the "unit plan" preferred by some airlines, in which there is a separate terminal for each company. The passenger entered a single ticket lobby with counters for all airlines, then was taken by escalator to the large waiting room and concessions area, and thence was directed to the boarding ramps. The arriving passenger found a single baggage collecting area on the direct route to surface transportation. In other words, according to *Architectural Forum*, the circulation pattern was worked out, and the building was wrapped around it. The possibility of economical future expansion was incorporated, as well as flexibility in the use of space to meet changing needs. All of these factors resulted in the judgment of *Architectural Forum* that the Cleveland airport was close to the "theoretical best" described and recommended by the Civil Aeronautics Administration. The journal also stated that it would "provide the best circulation pattern of any large United States airport."[19]

Two bond issues for the $3,500,000 terminal were passed in 1950 and 1952, and construction actually began in 1953. The building was opened for service in February, 1956. Upon its completion, critical judgment found that the facilities were "ahead of other major air terminal developments anywhere in the country." William Milliken, director of the Cleveland Museum of Art and an experienced world traveler, was reported as saying, "This is the most effective and best designed airport I've seen on either side of the ocean." The architectural design was well within the "contemporary" tradition, "with straight lines, graceful curves, and no unnecessary ornamentation."[20] While the architects insisted on the primacy of functional planning, many qualities of the architectural design epitomize the style of the 1950s: the plain surfaces; the use of enameled wall panels, aluminum, and glazed brick; the curved lines which not only contribute to the circulation but are also expressive of movement; and the feeling of open spaciousness on the interior.

Meanwhile the Cleveland Transit System was building a high-speed, off-street crosstown rapid transit line. For over a decade it remained the only completely new rapid transit installation in the country since World War II. When *The American City* reported the projected program in 1951, it commented that Cleveland was among the cities assuming leadership in attacking the problem of traffic congestion. Projected in 1950, construction on the first thirteen-mile segment began in 1952. The line followed the existing main line railroad right-of-way from Madison and West 117th Street via the Union Terminal to Euclid and Windermere in East Cleveland. From the Terminal to East 55th Street, trains on the Cleveland transit route meshed with cars on the older Shaker rapid line. All intersections were grade-separated, and the double-unit cars discharged passengers at floor level on high-level platforms. Because of the spacing of the twelve stations nearly a mile apart, the travel time over the thirteen-mile route was only twenty-eight minutes. Automobile parking lots were later provided at several of the transit stations, and they were credited with being largely responsible for increased used of the rapid transit.[21]

When the first portion of the transit route was opened in 1955, plans were already under way to extend the line another two miles to Lorain and West 143rd Street. Studies were also made for a proposed extension from the University-Cedar station via Euclid Heights Boulevard to Coventry Road, repeating the idea of Patrick Calhoun's 1896 railway

214

Cleveland Hopkins Airport Terminal, 1956, Outcalt, Guenther & Associates, architects.
*(Rode, Kaplan, Curtis & Woodard) below:* Terminal waiting room.

on the same route. The additional West Side section was completed in 1958, but the extension to the Heights was not built. In 1961 a four-mile extension of the transit line to the Cleveland airport was proposed. As a demonstration project in mass transportation, it was intended to show the feasibility of a high-speed rail line connecting a central city with its major airport. The planning was already completed in 1961, but construction did not begin until 1966. The airport extension was completed in 1968, giving Cleveland the first high-speed rapid transit in the country providing a direct line between the downtown business district and the airport.[22]

These were significant achievements, yet within ten years of the initial opening, the wisdom of the $38,000,000 rapid transit development was seriously questioned. It was pointed out that after an initial increase in passengers through 1960, the numbers

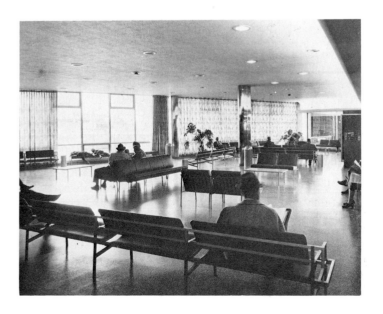

215

steadily declined. It was contended that trends in automobile and fixed railway use had not been projected into the future; that the commitment of the general public to individual private transportation had not been acknowledged; and that the development of transit systems had been skillfully promoted by railway equipment manufacturers. In fact, the major portion of the rapid transit was complete before the competition of the new freeways was made possible by the Federal Highway Act of 1956.[23]

As one of the few large-scale government programs that developed under conservative Republican economic policy, the proposed interstate highway plan provided for federal funding of 90 percent of the construction costs. In Cleveland work began on the Innerbelt expressway which had first been envisioned in the Regional Association plan of 1944. The Innerbelt was expected to remove 50 percent of the traffic from downtown streets and to serve as a distributor for downtown business traffic and later as a connection to other freeways. Late in 1959 the first section from the shoreway to Chester Avenue was completed. The entire three-mile stretch to West 14th Street, which would eventually connect with the Medina freeway to become Interstate 71, was opened in December, 1961. To cross the Cuyahoga Valley, a fourth high-level bridge was constructed, carrying an eight-lane roadway which was the widest in the state. The southern link to East 30th Street was completed in 1962, and the connection to Broadway and the Willow freeway, which became Interstate 77, was opened in December, 1965.[24]

The authority of the highway planners was prodigious, and until the passage of the Historic Preservation Act of 1966 the shortest or most expeditious route was drawn, with little regard for its effect on the quality of the existing surroundings. Two of the most unfortunate losses to freeway construction were the Leonard C. Hanna mansion on Euclid Avenue, Cleveland's only building designed by Stanford White, and St. Wenceslas Roman Catholic Church (1892–1899), the church of the oldest Bohemian congregation in the city. St. Wenceslas stood at Broadway and East 37th Street, near what became a giant interchange which covered some ninety acres and which still led nowhere in 1976.

## Suburbia

The affluence of the 1950s provided the means for thousands of families to seek a better home, and the promise of greatly improved transportation afforded the opportunity to settle farther from the city center. By comparison with the massive exodus to the suburbs in the 1950s, the suburban migrations of the early part of the century had been a mere trickle. In *The Domesticated Americans*, a witty portrait of the manners and the houses of Americans, Russell Lynes calls attention to the mobility and the restlessness of Americans as a national characteristic, in contrast to the rootedness of the European. Furthermore, Lynes observes that "It is part of the basic code of real-estateism to make not merely buildings but entire areas of a city obsolete, to encourage shifts in fashion for residences and for business buildings, and to abandon the unfashionable to deterioration into slums, either human or commercial."[25]

The population of the City of Cleveland dropped from 915,000 in 1950 to 876,000 in 1960, and some of the closer suburbs (Lakewood, East Cleveland) also declined during this decade. However, only 16 percent of the growth in the county metropolitan area could be attributed to these losses, since the population of the county increased by 258,000. Because the lakeshore suburbs (Lakewood, Bratenahl) had developed early, and the closer suburbs (Cleveland Heights, Shaker Heights) were already well built up, the main directions of settlement were south and west on the West Side (North Olmsted, Brook Park and Parma) and southeast (Garfield Heights, Maple Heights, and Warrensville Township), and northeast (Euclid, South Euclid, and Lyndhurst) on the East Side. The most phenomenal growth took place in Parma, where the population grew from 28,897 in 1950 to 82,845 in 1960. The increases in Brook Park and Warrensville Township, while numerically about one-fifth of Parma's, were proportionally 400 percent and over 600 percent.

The houses in the older suburbs were essentially upper-class and upper middle-class homes, and a very large proportion of them were designed by architects. The houses in the suburban developments of the 1950s, on the other hand, were developers' houses, and their repetitious forms and placement on the street were directly descended from the speculative Queen Anne and bungalow vernacular idioms of the older city neighborhoods. Russell Lynes, who observed that they were closer in shape to the log cabin than anything in the intervening years, noted that

> Today's house, however expensive, has become a box again, or a series of boxes. Sometimes the box has a sharply peaked roof and is covered with white clapboards, in which case it is called Cape Cod. If it is a box longer than it is wide and has a gently pitched roof, then it is a ranch house. If it is a square box, it is still a bungalow. If it is a two-story box, it is "colonial." If it is two boxes set next to each other but one a little above the other, then it is a split-level. (It can be either a split-level Cape Cod or a split-level ranch.)[26]

Such "packaged" housing was to be found by the tens of thousands in all of the suburbs of Cleveland's metropolitan area. Perhaps the most obvious external feature which distinguished these houses from earlier ones was the attached garage. Frequently facing the street and dominating the front of the house, it expressed in architectural terms both the affluence of the family and the dependence of the suburban house on the automobile.

Even the luxury high-rise apartment was a series of boxes stacked in layers to make a tall box set on end. Winton Place on Lakewood's Gold coast was the most elegant of these structures in the Cleveland area. Here the box was mitigated by the fact that two parallel rectangular towers were joined side by side and offset at the corners; moreover, fin-like stacks of balconies marked the corner suites. Planned by Chicago architects Loebl, Schlossman & Bennett and built in 1962–1963, the thirty-story structure was advertised as the tallest apartment building between New York and Chicago. Like the Illuminating Building, Winton Place had a reinforced concrete frame, and its soaring vertical lines were emphasized on the exterior elevations. The old garden suburb ideal was reflected in the eight-acre site, of which the tower, set back 500 feet and enjoying unobstructed views of Lake Erie, occupied only 6 percent. Its park-like character was somewhat compromised by the later addition of more parking on the west side of the building.[27]

The automobile created other problems which demanded new and creative solutions. After the war traffic congestion and parking needs rendered the traditional commercial retail center nearly useless as a shopping environment. A few people saw that shopping habits would have to change, but no one could predict what forms would need to be developed to accommodate them. The downtown department

Winton Place, Lake Avenue, Lakewood, 1963, Loebl, Schlossman & Bennett, architects.

stores were uncertain about the advisability of moving to the suburbs. The first major department store in Cleveland to take this step was Halle's, which built a branch store in 1948 at Shaker Square. The site was located on Shaker Boulevard just to the west of the southwest quadrant of the Square. The planners, Conrad, Hays, Simpson & Ruth, with Robert A. Little, had to work with certain existing conditions: the rapid transit, the boulevard, the Colony Theater and the parking lot behind it. They approached the design without preconceived style ideas and arrived at a simple modern rectangular form. The use of red brick and white stone was chosen to harmonize with the existing Colonial Revival buildings, but the approval of the Van Sweringen Company was obtained only after some

217

Halle's Shaker Square store, Shaker Boulevard, 1948, Conrad, Hays, Simpson & Ruth, with Robert A. Little, architects.

difficulty. The Chamber of Commerce, which had been making awards for quality in various building types for many years, called Halle's at Shaker Square "the best retail commercial building of 1948 in Cuyahoga County."[28]

But Shaker Square and older shopping "villages" like it were not originally planned for the vastly increased use of the automobile. Even worse was the congestion in the typical "strip" of small retail stores along a main thoroughfare or secondary street. Various interim solutions were tried. At first parking was provided behind a row of stores which lined a main street, but this meant that the customer entered through a rear entrance, while the display windows and main fronts went unnoticed. To solve this problem, groups of stores were set back from the sidewalk line, and parking off the street was provided in front. The next step was the suburban shopping center of the early 1950s, which was essentially an elaboration of the strip development, with much larger parking lots, sometimes on more than one side of the stores. Examples of this stage in the Cleveland area were Southgate in Maple Heights (1952) and Parmatown (1956). The store fronts were linked by covered walkways. Portions of the parking lot were still placed next to the rear delivery and service entrances, while some of the individual stores had attractive entrances provided from both sides. These developments were not yet very far beyond what Victor Gruen called the "prehistoric" stage of shopping center development.[29]

In the mid-1950s there evolved the concept which Gruen calls the "regional suburban shopping center," a center having at least one full-line department store together with a reasonably wide selection of tenant stores. By the end of the decade the concept was further refined as the enclosed climate-controlled mall replaced the "open" center. The inspiration of the nineteenth century arcades in this evolution is obvious. The first mall in the Cleveland area, Severance Center, was opened in 1963, seven years after the earliest in the country, Gruen's Southdale in Minnesota. Severance Center represents one of the simpler plans of the regional center, with two major stores (Higbee's and Halle's) joined by a single long mall, enhanced by a lower level at certain points. The symmetry of the plan was emphasized by a large square fountain court located midway in the mall and lighted by a clerestory. Except for the department stores, all of the store entrances and display windows opened off the mall, which was reached from the parking lots by arcades at the center and the ends. While this plan might be varied by the introduction of three or more department stores, with the mall varying in shape, direction, or number of levels, the basic concept of the regional suburban shopping center as established in the late 1950s continued into the 1970s, the most recent being the enormous Randall Park Mall opened in 1976.

In stylistic terms, the development of the suburban shopping center is a perfect illustration within a

218

Severance Center, Mayfield Road, Cleveland Heights, 1963, The Austin Company, designers and builders.

Randall Park Mall, Miles Road, North Randall, 1976, Edward J. DeBartolo Corporation, designers and builders.

period of only twenty years of the cyclical theory of classical art history. Insofar as the categories of Heinrich Wölfflin's *Principles of Art History* are of interest to the modern reader, the archaic style is represented by Southgate, the classic by Severance Center, and the baroque by Randall Park Mall.[30]

The planning of Southgate was purely functional; there were few if any aesthetic considerations. The appearance was the simple, direct result of the economic and technical considerations involved. The use of materials was straightforward, with no attempt at embellishment. The artless simplicity of this approach is emphasized by the fact that it was felt necessary nearly twenty years later to "improve" the walkways with shingle roofs and other ornamental alterations.

Severance Center, on the other hand, was clearly designed with a particular point of view. The straight line of the mall makes the interior space immediately comprehensible. All of the surfaces have clear-cut, tangible boundaries, and there is a crispness and a completeness to all of the forms. The depth of the space is perceived as a sequence of planes. The various parts—display windows, walls, ceiling forms, and clerestory—are all clearly articulated. These are the qualities of the classic style.

Even more strikingly different is the Randall Park Mall, where the space is not immediately—perhaps never fully—comprehensible. Instead of tangible, clear boundaries, there is apparent movement and change. Instead of one-point perspective, non-frontal views are urged upon the spectator. The system of stairs and ramps between levels increases the feeling of flowing forms and limitless space. The various parts are swallowed up in a total unity and submit to the dominating motive of the angular lines and prismatic solids. The play of light through and around the stalactite-like columns represents a remarkable technical achievement and increases the feeling of baroque space. The sensation of spaciousness desired in a shopping environment has been greatly enhanced by this imaginative treatment.

For all of its virtues in simplifying a part of the retail commercial process, the regional suburban shopping center of the fifties created secondary problems. In addition to drawing off income from the urban center, it increased the need for mobility and complicated the lives and circulation patterns of people. Moreover, Gruen suggests that the shopping center was only one of several kinds of centers, each serving a special purpose, so that people were forced to travel ever greater distances to work, to shop, to be entertained, to do business, or to enter into civic activities. Thus attention began to turn more and more to the possibility of multi-purpose centers.

The skills necessary for the planning and coordination of such centers had been an increasing part of American enterprise since the 1920s, and by the 1950s they were being refined to a science. They included understanding the economic factors in profitable development, analysing the supporting population, encouraging long-term enlightened self-interest on the part of developers, and ensuring the availability, accessibility, and proper characteristics of a site. More complex coordination was necessary between the development organization (perhaps in itself consisting of several departments), architects, consultants in engineering and transportation, landscape architects, and others. The limitations of the suburban center and the evolution of new planning concepts and systems were among the factors which contributed to a new downtown Cleveland plan in 1960. More important were the concern over the deteriorating urban core and the availability of federal urban renewal funds. Together with the existence of the earlier planning studies such as the General Plan of 1949 and the Downtown Plan of 1959, these factors produced a major urban renewal plan—Erieview.

Erieview Tower, 1964, Harrison & Abramovitz, architects.

# 1960: Erieview

The Erieview urban renewal plan was first presented to the public on November 22, 1960. It was a plan designed to eliminate much of the existing blight and decay in the aging district northeast of the downtown core. The plan was conceived to generate excitement for the downtown, to enable the city to work within the federal urban renewal program, and to encourage private capital investment. Because the emphasis was on economic redevelopment, the plan was created by the Cleveland Department of Urban Renewal with the understanding that the newly formed Cleveland Development Foundation would ensure the backing of the financial and business community.

Although Erieview was a specific urban renewal project in contrast with the general guidelines and more theoretical proposals of the City Planning Commission, much of the analysis of future needs and many of the recommendations with regard to land use evolved out of earlier studies by various city departments. The project area of 163 acres extended roughly from East 6th to East 17th Street between Chester Avenue and the lakefront and linked the office core at Euclid and East 9th Street with the waterfront to the north. The plan was designed to be completed in two phases, with the 96-acre western portion designated for public and commercial use and the 67 acres east of East 14th Street to be residential. The published plan stated that "in terms of the combined factors of scope, variety and its impact on the city, Erieview is undoubtedly the most ambitious project so far undertaken under the Federal Urban Redevelopment Program."[1]

In order to qualify for urban renewal funds, the buildings and the environment of the project area had to be so seriously deficient that public action was needed to remedy the deterioration. A building inspection determined that 71 percent of the 237 buildings in the area were substandard in structure, facilities, or safety. Although sixty-eight buildings were found to be in good condition, only ten were proposed for retention, as the rest did not conform to the proposed uses of the area. The clearance of structures for reasons of land use as well as poor condition was one of the most controversial features of the plan. Fifteen years later this kind of wholesale demolition became inconceivable with the movement toward preservation.[2]

Under the federal guidelines, the land was acquired by the city, tenants relocated, structures demolished, and necessary site improvements installed; assembled parcels of land were then sold to private developers at a fraction of the cost. The federal legislation was originally written so that redevelopment of the land would be primarily residential, but it had been revised to permit commercial use. Urban renewal standards were established in the form of design controls, and the proposals of private developers had to conform to the overall plan. In the Erieview plan specific design objectives were set with regard to land use, building height and setback, population density, amount of site coverage for various uses, and parking.

The plan was prepared for the City of Cleveland by I. M. Pei & Associates. The internationally known Pei was the architect of the Mile High Center in Denver and had planned redevelopment projects for New York, Philadelphia, Washington, and Pittsburgh. At the presentation of the Erieview plan, Pei described the proposals as "bold, aesthetic and

Erieview plan, perspective rendering, 1960, I. M. Pei & Associates, planners.

realistic."[3] The planners conceived a group of buildings with low silhouettes accented by vertical towers. More than 50 percent of the land would be open space to be developed as parks and malls. A forty-story tower placed directly on the axis of East 12th Street at St. Clair Avenue was the hub of the plan. A reflecting pool to the west was planned to create "a setting unequalled by any office building in the U.S." Also west of the tower an entire block bounded by East 6th, East 12th, St. Clair, and Lakeside was designated for a massive federal office building with a central court, while to the east was a shopping center. North of Lakeside, East 12th Street was shown as a new mall flanked by two office buildings and a motel. South on East 12th Street at Chester Avenue there was an open square for pedestrians, shoppers, and leisure activities, and across the street was a twenty-story apartment building and another apartment hotel.

The residential community planned for the second stage of development included seven thirty-story towers arranged to form two vertical groups. These were placed among two six-story structures of immense length which faced inward on landscaped courts whose ground plans formed geometric Greek fret designs. The largest would have stretched across two city blocks and had an uninterrupted facade over 1,000 feet long. *Architectural Forum* referred to Pei's housing as "highly mannered superblocks."[4] Like the residential area in the City Planning Commission's Downtown General Plan, this apartment arrangement was clearly foreshadowed by Le Corbusier's "Plan Voisin" for Paris.

Thus the Erieview plan provided for public and commercial office space, hotels and entertainment, and various classes of multi-family housing. In addition it proposed a new street and circulation pattern within the project area, with some of the older streets closed and the creation of a few new connecting ways. A final element of the plan caused a certain sense of *déjà vu*. This was a terrace across the

224

railroad tracks north of Lakeside Avenue and reaching from East 9th to East 18th Street. The possibility of obscuring the unsightly railroad tracks while at the same time providing direct access to the lakefront, or at least a viewing platform, had been a recurring dream in Cleveland planning since the nineteenth century.

This master plan for downtown urban renewal by an internationally known architect has inevitably been compared with the Group Plan of Daniel Burnham. The similarities were indeed more than superficial. Even though Erieview had important asymmetrical elements, both plans were essentially classical. Like the Group Plan, Erieview was arranged around major and minor axes. There were specific design controls for uniform building heights on certain major streets and enclosing plaza areas. The clear articulation of building masses and open space was characteristic of both plans. But the most intriguing similarity lay in the fact that much of the groundwork and many of the basic conceptions with regard to function and placement had been done by local planners, and the master architect was brought in to give them an aesthetic form with his own stamp.

The success of Erieview must be judged according to two sets of criteria—the one economic and social and the other aesthetic. In terms of its own goals of clearing blighted land and attracting private capital investment, the plan was a mixed success. The most vociferous critic was Philip W. Porter, a retired editor of the *Plain Dealer*, who called Erieview "the mistake that ruined downtown."[5] According to Porter, Erieview tended to pull office occupants and commercial and entertainment business away from Euclid Avenue, thus contributing to its decline. This interpretation ignored the role of the regional suburban shopping center in the decline of the downtown commercial district. Another criticism maintained that because so much of Cleveland's urban renewal effort was channeled into Erieview, another large urban renewal project for the deteriorating Hough-Wade Park area on the East Side was ignored. It is true that sixteen years later several of the new Erieview office buildings and especially the large apartment complexes were not filled to capacity or operating profitably. However, to blame everything from the closing of the downtown movie palaces to the Hough riots of 1966 on the Erieview development seemed tenuous.

By the mid-1970s a more serious set of criticisms had developed concerning both the entire concept of urban renewal and the kind of architecture represented by Pei's plan. It became clear that total clearance, by destroying the existing context of buildings and streets, took with them the variety, complexity, color, and sense of continuity which gives an urban area its character. In the process, furthermore, the existing population was displaced, and although the urban renewal program provided for relocation, many low-income people frequently could not find comparable economical housing elsewhere. A third criticism of urban renewal concerned the acquisition of land with public funds and its cheap disposal to private developers, which was seen as symptomatic of the increasing cooperation and interdependence of government and business interests.

Pei's architectural scheme represented the apogee of modernism, but fifteen years later the entire philosophy had undergone a thorough revisionism. Architects no longer had faith in the potential of architecture and planning for shaping society. The fundamental character of the Erieview project—a classical plan with calculated asymmetries, major axes, uniform building heights, and the clear articulation of spaces—was no longer perceived as ideal. On the contrary, it was criticized for producing a boring consistency. The isolated towers and apartment superblocks inspired by Le Corbusier appeared inhuman in scale and frighteningly anonymous as places of habitation. A newer view of architecture replaced the Modern ideal of functionalism with the desire to invoke historical references, variety, ambiguity, and a kind of poetic evocation. In 1960 Erieview could not have had the "complexity and contradiction" which Robert Venturi later found at Las Vegas and which many others rediscovered in the Victorian Main Street. Nevertheless, any assessment of the plan, in addition to judging it on its own terms, must take into account these new attitudes.

The architecture of the buildings, even judged on its own terms, was not uniform in quality. Fortunately, the forty-story tower at the hub of Pei's plan was erected first, providing a dramatic symbol for the entire project. The building was undertaken by an owner-architect-builder team consisting of the Galbreath-Ruffin Corporation, Harrison & Abramovitz, and Turner Construction Company. The same group was responsible for similar office building projects in New York, Boston, Pittsburgh, and Milwaukee, and Wallace Harrison had been associated with the design of Rockefeller Center, the

Erieview Plaza. One Erieview Plaza, 1965, Schafer, Flynn & van Dijk, architects. Bond Court office building, 1971, Skidmore, Owings & Merrill, architects.

United Nations Building, and Lincoln Center in New York.[6] The development of such building teams, which enabled the expertise of economical business operations to be brought to building, was characteristic of the period and once again illustrates the growing nature of architecture as a commercial "package."

The design of the Erieview Tower caused wide comment. According to an appraisal in *Architectural Record*, the building achieved superior architectural quality within the limitations of a speculative venture. The article credited the building with "an almost institutional look, secured at rental-market cost."[7] It was pointed out that the structure consisted of durable but not costly materials which created visual appeal and would keep the maintenance costs low. The walls consisted of greenish-gray spandrels and glass with a grid of dark anodized aluminum, and the vertical lines of the external structural members were emphasized. The treatment of the lobby materials of marble, glass, stainless steel, and terrazzo produced the kind of anonymous standardized elegance that came to seem characteristic of the corporate package. The widely spaced structural columns and the central elevator core provided an open and efficient floor space.

The location of the Erieview Tower was an immediate indication that I. M. Pei's concept would

not be followed slavishly. It was not placed directly on the axis of East 12th Street, but was moved to the west. The plaza and reflecting pool were well designed and created a pleasant open space, but it would not be possible to assess their impact fully until the lower buildings flanking and defining the space were erected to the north and south of the plaza. Likewise, the building height limitations were not observed. The block to the west of Erieview Plaza, originally designated for a massive eight-story federal office building, was occupied by the new Federal Building (1967) in the form of a thirty-one story tower, the twenty-story Bond Court office building (1971), and the Bond Court Hotel on St. Clair Avenue. Across St. Clair was the fifteen-story One Erieview Plaza building (1965). Of this group the critical consensus seemed to be that the best architectural design was that of the Bond Court office building planned by Skidmore, Owings & Merrill, the most skillful of the packagers.

At the north end of 12th Street, the proposed mall was begun. On the east side the city erected the $5,600,000 Public Utilities Building. Built in 1969–1971 under the mayoralty of Carl B. Stokes, the first black mayor of a major American city, it was the first new municipal office building in thirty years and was planned by Thomas Tse Kwai Zung Architects. Zung was a former associate of Edward D. Stone,

Public Utilities Building, Lakeside Avenue and East 12th Street, 1971, Thomas T. K. Zung, architect. (*Thomas T. K. Zung*)

one of the foremost exponents of the idea that an ornamental grace could be brought back into architecture to counter the sterility of the glass box. The symmetrical marble-clad structure, a long narrow building with a cantilevered fifth floor, contains an interior atrium rising the full five stories to an aluminum framed skylight. Across the street a motel was built to a standard design, with a projecting deck at the second story level which seems to be intentionally related to the one on the public building.

Visually the most successful part of the project area by 1976 was the square at East 12th Street and Chester Avenue. Built by the city in 1972 and called Chester Commons Park, the square is one of the best genuinely urban pedestrian spaces in Cleveland. Considerable spatial drama is created within a small compass on a stage set of concrete and plantings. The space is divided and made to appear much larger than it is by the use of numerous levels built up of stepped platforms at irregular angles. Some of the concrete parapets take on the shape of imaginary fortified bastions. Trees, wooden benches, brightly colored graphic designs, and a small cascade at the center of the square add variety and freshness, and the ensemble has a distinctly playful quality. However, the urban character of the square is dependent on the backdrop of the older Chester Twelfth Building,

the new Diamond Shamrock and Penton Plaza Buildings, the Chesterfield Apartments, and Park Centre.

Park Centre was an exciting example of the urban concept of a multi-purpose center, comprising housing units built on top of offices and an internal shopping mall, a parking garage, and rooftop recreational facilities. It was considered by some competent observers to be the most important potential catalyst for the downtown revitalization. The $42,500,000 development received the largest FHA loan guarantee in the history of the federal agency. The financial investment was second in Cleveland history only to that for the Terminal group.[8]

Park Centre was planned by the giant Cleveland firm of Dalton-Dalton-Little-Newport, with Norman Perttula as chief designer. The size and placement of the two twenty-story apartment towers was determined by the Erieview plan. The decision to add a two-story shopping mall was made after the initial planning. The architecture exhibited a marked difference from the boxes of the 1950s whose walls were treated as the "skin" of the building. By the time Park Centre was built in 1972–1973, this new manner was known as "Brutalist," referring to the look of weight, massiveness, and solidity. The use of exposed, rough-textured con-

227

Chester Commons Park, and Park Centre, East 12th Street and Chester Avenue, 1973, Dalton-Dalton-Little-Newport, architects. (*Dalton-Dalton-Newport*)

crete (going back to Le Corbusier's Unité d'Habitation) was another characteristic of Brutalism, as were the recesses or slots in the surfaces which created shadows and a more three-dimensional sense of the wall. Two kinds of concrete construction were used, a poured-in-place shear wall system in the apartment towers and precast beams in the parking garage, which is in effect a separate structure between the two towers. The grooved surfaces in the coarse aggregate of the concrete piers were cast in specially made forms. The construction methods and the location of the structural piers in turn determined the nature of the interior spaces of the mall, which consist of two parallel halls linked by cross corridors, with the two levels being connected by a variety of staircases and escalators. The heavy square concrete piers were finished like those on the

exterior. In the stylistic terms of the shopping centers discussed earlier, the space is midway between that of the classic Severance Center and the baroque Randall Park Mall. While the complex spatial articulation is a positive architectural quality, it has a labyrinthine character not always easy for the shopper to grasp immediately, with something of the confined feeling of a subway. Unfortunately, during the first few years of its existence Park Centre failed to attract the anticipated business, social, and recreational activity.[9]

By 1972, over $220,000,000 of construction was committed to the Erieview project. A dozen major buildings had been constructed or were underway in the project area, and with the exception of the block north of St. John's Cathedral, the first phase of the Erieview plan was virtually complete.

Tower East, 20600 Chagrin Boulevard, 1968, The Architects Collaborative and Walter Gropius.

# 1960–1976

## Hough

The sixties and early seventies were overwhelmed by serious events—the war in Vietnam, assassinations, a revolution in social mores, and racial turmoil which erupted in riots. In cities such as Cleveland, declining population and the general decay of the urban fabric created economic and social problems which evaded any clear-cut solutions. Some people have sought to define the changing society of these years in no uncertain terms—as inhuman, self-centered and self-promoting, and violent or escapist. Certainly the social values and the kind of vision which made Cleveland a national leader in the early years of the century had changed. The period saw the construction of a number of notable buildings, but they do not seem to represent any discernible trend. Planning and building efforts were sporadic and of uneven quality, and the ability to conceive visionary or ideal schemes was dissipated. At best, whether built for prestigious clients, the renewal of the ghetto, or the universities, the architecture represented the diversity and the rapid change of the period.

The decline of the inner city and the struggle to regroup its forces and maintain its existence were epitomized by the Hough area on Cleveland's East Side. The area bounded by East 55th and East 105th Streets, Superior and Euclid Avenues was a relatively stable residential neighborhood of mixed ethnic, white middle class, and Negro groups throughout the 1950s. In 1960 the black community made up 74 percent of the population, and during the 1960s the exodus of white residents accelerated. When the University-Euclid urban renewal project was announced, with its promise of land acquisition and clearance, much of the incentive for maintaining property was removed. The city ignored the enforcement of the building code, the density of population increased as single-family dwellings became multi-family, and absentee landlords charged exorbitant rents for increasingly inadequate and substandard housing.

The urban renewal project was unsuccessful for many reasons. According to some observers, these included the conflict between the need for neighborhood rehabilitation and the demands of University Circle expansion plans on urban renewal funds. Before long conditions were established for the mounting frustration which erupted in the riots of midsummer, 1966. The widespread destruction of buildings and property was referred to by some of the inhabitants as "instant urban renewal." During the remainder of the decade, the population of the area declined from 71,000 to 45,000. At the same time, the massive problems of rebuilding were exacerbated by the inability to obtain insurance and mortgage money because of the area's economic and social instability.[10]

In the early 1970s, although there was a continuing need for expanded social services and economical housing, a number of significant building projects gave reason for a somewhat more optimistic view of the future of Hough. One of the first projects and one of the most interesting planning concepts was the Martin Luther King, Jr., Plaza, an innovative small-scale combination of commercial and residential facilities. Built in 1971–1972 by the Hough Area Development Corporation, which had been formed in 1967 to promote the growth of small black-owned businesses, the Plaza was a part of the long-range plans for new offices, apartments, shopping areas,

parks and boulevards. Its program was the first in the nation to be funded directly by the Office of Economic Opportunity under its Special Impact program. These programs were designed "to have a major impact on unemployment, dependency, and community tensions in urban areas having large concentrations of low-income residents." Between 1968 and 1972 the Hough corporation received over $5,000,000 from the federal agency.[11]

Located on Wade Park Avenue at Crawford Road, the Martin Luther King, Jr., Plaza combined a shopping center with roof-top town houses. Because of the ghetto location, the plans for occupancy by black businessmen, and the unusual roof-top

housing concept, there was some initial difficulty in finding tenants to commit themselves to leases. Architecturally, the Plaza was more significant as a functional concept than as an artistic design. The internal shopping mall is reached by entrances from parking lots on two sides of the building, while on the roof level twenty-six town houses grouped around a courtyard are accessible by an entrance separate from the mall.

Apart from housing, other buildings especially important in the renewal of the inner city neighborhood included schools and social service centers. The Martin Luther King, Jr., High School at East 71st Street and Hough Avenue was completed

*above:* Martin Luther King, Jr., Plaza, Wade Park Avenue and Crawford Road, 1972, Madison & Madison, architects.

*right:* Martin Luther King, Jr., High School courtyard, East 71st Street at Hough Avenue, 1973, Madison & Madison, architects.

Giddings Elementary School, 2250 East 71st Street, 1970, Don Hisaka, architect.

in 1973 and designed by Cleveland architects Madison and Madison. The school is a spreading two-story structure typical of the large city and suburban schools required by the complex educational programs of the late 1960s, including large vocational, physical education, and supporting facilities in addition to the academic learning areas. Angular lines and projecting sculptural forms dominate the architectural scheme. More significantly, the building faces inward toward a central court, open to the sky. Glass-walled corridors and the library area open onto the court, whose various levels, plantings, and trees center around a bust of Martin Luther King, Jr., to create a controlled interior landscape. A characteristic common to many of the newer schools, this orientation toward the inside derived from two sources: a change in educational theory which decreed that external

windows were distracting to the students, and the need to prevent vandalism. The net result of the latter consideration was that many inner city buildings of the 1970s came to look like veritable fortresses. As a total architectural design the Martin Luther King, Jr., High School was less successful than some other schools, but the provision of a completely new, functional, and attractive educational setting was an important asset for the Hough area.

A more generally admired example of inward orientation was the Giddings Elementary School, but the function and the architecture of its inner court are very different. All of the rooms are wrapped around a three-story interior space covered by a skylight of steel I-beams and curved plastic panels. The pavement of the court is concrete, and the walls are concrete block painted white. The glass-fronted classrooms on the three stories are stepped back to form balconies. The architectural drama of the space has been widely praised, and the teachers and children have found that the plan works well and provides an open and pleasant atmosphere. The amenity of the interior contrasts with the somewhat forbidding brick masses of the exterior, and the main entrance portal has an atavistic quality, evoking the ancient monuments of Stonehenge, Mycenae, or Egypt. Located outside the Hough area on East 71st Street near Central Avenue and completed in 1970, the school was designed by Don Hisaka & Associates.[12]

In 1973–1974 two of the social service centers in the Hough area were provided with striking but quite different examples of functional architecture. A small community center was built by the City of Cleveland and a group of public agencies on Hough Avenue at East 85th Street. Also designed by Madison and Madison, the Hough Multi Service Center is built around a spacious central common room lighted by a skylight. The atrium-like area is surrounded by a corridor from which the various services, meeting, and activity rooms open. The interior finishing materials of wood, plaster, and masonry are natural, bright, and economical. Both the external shape and the interior plan of the attractive and serviceable structure combine parallel and angled surfaces to create sculptural masses and spaces. Some of these architectural forms are similar to those of the Martin Luther King High School.

In 1974 the Hough Norwood Family Care Center was opened on Hough Avenue at East 82nd Street. It was erected by the Cleveland Neighborhood Health

Hough MultiService Center, Hough Avenue at East 85th Street, 1973, Madison & Madison, architects.

Service Corporation, which was established in 1967 to provide health care for low-income residents and supported by the Office of Economic Opportunity and the Department of Health, Education and Welfare. Designed by Flynn, Dalton & van Dijk, the building is a simple two-story structure whose handsome institutional and almost classical look complements the logic of the interior plan. The planes of dark warm brick at the center section flank a two-story recessed entrance which seems open and inviting. The entrance leads to a main lobby and reception area, where the pharmacy is also located. The plan is a clear expression of the center's team method of operation. Patient care is provided by several teams, each including a general physician, a pediatrician, medical and dental assistants, and administrative coordinators. Outside corridors running the entire length of the building lead to subsidiary reception areas for the consulting rooms of each team. Additional cross corridors give access to the various departments, offices and laboratories. Plain surfaces, brightly colored graphics, and good lighting also give the interior spaces a familiar, inviting appearance.[13]

The year 1968 marked the retirement of Ernest J. Bohn, director since 1933 of the Cleveland Metropolitan Housing Authority, author of the first state housing law in the nation, and a national figure in public housing. During the 1960s and early 1970s the Housing Authority continued to develop inner-city housing for low-income families and elderly residents. Not only did it seek to improve existing housing estates and to expand social programs to assist the residents, it also increased the number of dwelling units by several methods. New housing was built, existing apartment buildings were bought, leased and managed, and housing was built by developers for acquisition by the Housing Authority. Between 1967 and 1969 two-thirds of all the new housing in Cleveland was built by the Housing Authority.

Within the Hough area there were several projects, including sites with both apartment towers and row houses. The Willson project at East 55th Street and Chester Avenue has a twenty-two story tower and seven groups of two-story row houses and was planned by Cleveland architects Visnapuu & Gaede. The Addison Square project at Wade Park Avenue and Addison Road, designed by the Akron firm of James Barbitta & Associates, has a sixteen-story tower and six rows of two and three-story town houses. The latter are separated into individual

*above*: Hough Norwood Family Care Center, Hough Avenue at East 82nd Street, 1974, Flynn, Dalton & van Dijk, architects. (*Dalton, van Dijk, Johnson & Partners*)

*right:* Addison Square public housing project, Wade Park Avenue and Addison Road, 1969, James Barbitta & Associates, architects.

units by masonry party walls which project like fins beyond the facades and roofs. The towers of both projects have a certain architectural character frequently lacking in public housing. The Addison tower in particular, with ranks of recessed balconies alternating with plain walls, has a definite sculptural quality. When these two projects were completed in 1970, the Cleveland Metropolitan Housing Authority was managing housing estates with more than 10,500 dwelling units.[14]

However, by the seventies most observers agreed that building the kind of public housing which placed large numbers of low-income or minority people in huge, identical, densely populated blocks was tantamount to creating new ghettos and slums. This concept, which could be traced directly to Cleveland's pioneer Cedar-Central project of 1935, was by now thoroughly discredited, and most of the problems of inner-city housing seemed as far from solution as ever.

## Urban Campuses

In order to provide educational opportunities for an entirely different segment of society from that served by the traditional four-year college, the uniquely American idea of the two-year college, whether a public community college or a private junior college, came into being. These institutions serve students wanting only two years of higher education; students preferring a commuter college for the first two years of a four-year program; workers improving their vocational training; and housewives and older adults developing new skills or interests. During the 1960s there was a phenomenal increase both in the enrollment and in the number of two-year colleges. The need and the opportunity for such an institution in Cleveland was clearly outlined in a report to the State Community College Board in 1962, and in the same year the Cuyahoga Community College was chartered as the first two-year community college in Ohio. Within five years, the enrollment reached 12,500 students.[15]

The college originally occupied the Brownell School, a nineteenth century elementary school building on East 14th Street, and several nearby office buildings. In 1966 construction began on a downtown Metropolitan Campus in an urban renewal area between Scovill and Woodland Avenues. A five-block long interconnected structure was designed by Outcalt, Guenther, Rode & Bonebrake. As the entire campus was completed in a few years according to the master plan, the architects were able to take advantage of a rare opportunity to achieve an unusual unity. The concept of the urban college as a self-contained, defined, and yet spacious environment determined the way in which the complicated set of physical requirements was unified.[16] The entire campus is situated on a raised platform with parking garages underneath. This scheme enabled the major structures at the center of the campus to be arranged around a landscaped courtyard on the lower level. The inward orientation, arising in part from motives similar to those of the public schools, serves to create spaces suggesting the feeling of a traditional college campus. The covered ambulatories surrounding the courtyard and connecting the buildings actually suggest the medieval university cloister more than the open American quadrangle, although the architecture of the structures themselves makes no pretense of recalling the traditional campus. In fact, the college is virtually a small city of twelve interconnected and interrelated buildings. A uniform roof line, with the exception of the five-story library, together with the steep truncated hip roofs

Cuyahoga Community College, 1969, Outcalt, Guenther, Rode & Bonebrake, architects.

of the various auditorium and lecture halls, gives the campus a distinctive skyline. The consistent use of dark red brick, pebbled concrete panels, gray slate, and seamed metal roofs serves both to unify the structures and to create a sympathetic environment. Concrete pavements and modern light standards, set off by the landscaping in the court and around the buildings, reflect the urban context. After the extreme functionalism of the previous two decades, the design was another indication of a partial return to the symbolic and affective role of architecture. In 1970 the college received an Honor Award in Community and Junior College Design from the American Institute of Architects, whose citation referred to the campus as "an outstanding handling of a very limited site in an urban renewal area."[17]

There were already several branches of the state universities in Metropolitan Cleveland in addition to the Community College. In December, 1963, Fenn College proposed a plan to coordinate public higher education in the county with Fenn as the nucleus of a new comprehensive state university. Among the advantages, Fenn listed its downtown location within an hour's commuting distance of one-fourth of Ohio's population; its excellent relationship with the business and industrial community; its existing accreditation, faculty and staff; its university organization with Schools of Arts and Sciences,

Business, and Engineering; its proximity to a proposed 205-acre urban renewal area adjacent to Erieview on the west; and the availability of federal matching funds for university development. The proposed enrollment by 1980 was 20,000 students, and the estimated cost for site acquisition, planning and engineering, construction, and equipment was over $100,000,000. The approximate boundaries of the resulting campus would be Euclid and Superior Avenues, East 18th Street on the west, and the Innerbelt freeway.[18]

In mid-1964 Fenn College indicated its commitment to the proposal by acting to buy additional land on Euclid Avenue, and later in the year the Ohio Board of Regents created the Cleveland State University with Fenn College as its nucleus. Early in 1965 the trustees authorized the preparation of a master campus plan by Outcalt, Guenther, Rode & Bonebrake. Many of the planning considerations were determined by the urban location, but high on the list was the requirement that "all elements of the campus plan must express the academic and other goals of the University." Further, "the physical design must be warm, dignified, practical and acceptable over a long period of time," and "the physical plant can and will contribute to the process of education and reinforce the interest in learning." While such sentiments might easily be dismissed as

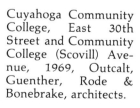

Cuyahoga Community College, East 30th Street and Community College (Scovill) Avenue, 1969, Outcalt, Guenther, Rode & Bonebrake, architects.

Preliminary plan for Cleveland State University, 1966, Outcalt, Guenther, Rode & Bonebrake, architects.

mere declarations of intent, it is significant that it was considered important to formulate them. More practical considerations included optimum land use, adequate parking, flexibility and adaptability of the basic design, easy access, separation of pedestrian and vehicular traffic wherever possible, and the relationship to the planning needs of the city.

As the master plan developed, its fundamental concept was clearly very similar to the same architects' Community College campus. The basic plan included an elevated campus with parking underneath, organized in quadrants with a series of interior courts. Bridges would carry pedestrian traffic over streets and parking areas. In order to maintain a quiet academic environment, the planners sought to provide isolation from the street, human scale, and other campus-like qualities. The suggested facing materials of the buildings were limestone and brick.[19]

As construction proceeded, the architects' concept began to take shape, but the "warm, dignified," academic expression was somehow lost in the translation to actuality. Although five major structures were erected in the first ten years, the employment of several architectural firms inevitably weakened the sense of unity. Only two buildings

were designed by the architects of the master plan—the Science Building, completed in 1969, and the University Tower (1971). The Science Building probably approaches most closely the architects' original intention. Square limestone-faced columns alternate with large brick panels on the facades, but the building is made top-heavy by a massive overhanging masonry fifth story. The twenty-story University Tower contains five floors housing the library, a computer laboratory, audio-visual facilities, and several hundred faculty and departmental offices. The distance between the academic intention and the reality may be gauged by the fact that, despite its educational function, the Tower is indistinguishable in scale and expressive character from other urban high-rise buildings such as the Justice Center complex built in 1975–1976.

The Classroom-Lecture Center, planned by Dalton, Dalton & Little and completed in 1970, is a four-story, block-long structure containing fifty-six classrooms, twenty-two laboratories, lounges and study rooms, a 478-seat auditorium, and two 250-seat lecture halls, making it the largest single classroom building in the state. It rests on giant pilotis which support a concrete waffle slab ceiling and which surround the stairwells faced with purplish brown tile. The Euclid Avenue facade is an expression in masonry of the structural grid, with an overhanging fourth story like the Science Building. None of these buildings has a main facade clearly symbolizing a welcoming entrance. To enter the Classroom-Lecture Center, for example, the students and staff must burrow among the dark forest of pilotis to discover the flights and passages into the warren.

Bridges over East 22nd Street connect the Classroom Center, the University Tower, and University Center. Views of the street and the parking garages may be glimpsed from the plaza level, and the stairways to the parking garage in front of the Tower are sheltered by concrete lotus-pad umbrellas. The University Center, designed by Don Hisaka, is the most immediately appealing of the major new structures. The Euclid Avenue facade is related to that of the Classroom Center, although its open masonry grid is more regular, and the eight-

University Tower, Cleveland State University, 1971, Outcalt, Guenther & Associates architects.

University Center, Cleveland State University, 1974, Don Hisaka, architect.

story court, glassed in on two sides and lined with balconies on the other two, is a visual and spatial tour de force.

Of all the university buildings, the most over-powering structure in sheer physical presence is the Physical Education Building, designed by Dalton, van Dijk, Johnson & Partners and dedicated in 1973. It consists of two rectangular brick blocks with rounded corners, one containing the gymnasium and the other the natatorium, articulated by a three-story high galleria with a series of hipped skylights and fronted by an office unit which is a brutalist sculpture of concrete blocks and silos.

In spite of several excellent buildings, one must conclude that the Cleveland State University campus is far less successful than the Cuyahoga

Physical Education Building, Cleveland State University, Euclid Avenue at East 23rd Street, 1973, Dalton, van Dijk, Johnson & Partners, architects. (*Dalton, van Dijk, Johnson & Partners*)

Community College as an educational environment, at least in symbolic terms. Some of the reasons have been mentioned, including the use of different architectural firms, the intimidating urban scale, and the lack of any feeling of receptiveness or welcome. The similarity of the structures to government buildings may help to explain the unsympathetic character of the campus; so also may the fact that many of their components and forms are those of industrial structures. For a campus conceived as an urban educational environment, the Cleveland State University has been given a set of buildings which are far more expressive of the power of the state and the tyranny of technology.

Meanwhile, at University Circle the Case Institute of Technology and Western Reserve University, the two established institutions conceived as complementary schools almost ninety years before, finally became a federated institution in 1967. In spite of the extensive construction on their campuses in the 1960s, the Adelbert, Case, and Mather greens and the areas around new dormitory complexes maintained a campus-like atmosphere. In 1970-1973 three small university religious centers were set between the Church of the Covenant and University Circle Place (Commodore Hotel) on Euclid Avenue to create a strong urban design.

Combining homes for the University Christian Movement (Protestant), Hillel Foundation (Jewish), and Hallinan Center (Catholic), the ecumenical center was planned as early as 1964. The original concept by Schafer, Flynn & Associates was a single E-shaped building with each organization located in one arm of the "E." It was connected to a 200-car parking garage behind the Commodore Hotel, which was built as planned. An important feature of the design was a pedestrian pathway connecting Euclid Avenue with the north campus.[20]

Although this plan was not realized, the idea of the ecumenical center was renewed in 1968. The Hillel Foundation was completed first. Designed by William Gould & Associates, it was connected to the parking garage and constructed of matching brick. The University Christian Movement was housed in a parish hall addition to the Church of the Covenant that provides indoor and outdoor educational space for the church. Designed by Richard Fleischman, it has sharply faceted forms of concrete that harmonize well with the older stone masonry of the church. The Hallinan Center was also designed by Fleischman with related angular geometric forms. It contains a lounge and counseling area on a small upper level overlooking a large worship and fellowship hall, and the extensive use of glass is

240

inviting to users. The three centers are linked by a raised promenade and multi-level plaza which reflect the diagonal geometry of the buildings. From the elevated walk, which carries out the original idea of a pedestrian pathway, the viewer experiences a constantly changing play of forms, spaces and levels. This architectural linkage was designed to express the ecumenical character of the group, and the ensemble has become a highly successful urban space within the university context.[21]

Case Western Reserve University religious center, looking north toward the parish hall, Richard Fleischman, architect. (*Richard Fleischman*)

## Prestige Architects

During the decade and a half from 1960 to 1976, some of the most successful and influential business and cultural institutions of Cleveland erected important buildings. As the large private commitment to building in the Erieview area developed, several clients enlarged or built new structures on East 9th Street and Superior and Euclid Avenues where, except for the Bond Store, no significant structure had been built for nearly forty years.

The Cleveland Trust Company, needing greatly enlarged office space, decided to preserve its 1908 classical temple at the corner of Euclid and East 9th and to build a tall office tower connected to it. Designed by Marcel Breuer and Hamilton Smith, with local associate architects Flynn, Dalton, van Dijk & Partners, the twenty-eight story tower faced East 9th Street; it was to be balanced by the addition of a second tower on Euclid which has not been built, thus completely framing the original bank. The foundation for the structure was constructed with forty-one caissons sunk over 200 feet to bedrock. The design brought some of the sculptural character of Breuer's later work to the typical sheer facade of the tall office building. The facing consisted of precast concrete panels in a grey Vermont granite aggregate, with curved molded openings—a feature which channeled any precipitation and was described as a self-cleaning design. Coincidentally, the effect of this precast wall came closest of any of the new office buildings to resembling the idealized renderings of towers in I. M. Pei's Erieview plan. The entrance and lobby of the building were faced with polished granite, and the *Architectural Record* concluded that the extensive use of masonry, with its deeply molded surfaces, was in harmony with the architectural character of the older building, and that the new tower preserved this important landmark "while reinforcing and invigorating its urban setting."[22] The restoration of the older domed rotunda by Frazier, Orr, Fairbanks & Quam of Geneva, Illinois, was a fine gesture, elegantly executed, but the modernization of the peripheral rooms of the main floor, accomplished by opening them up into a continuous space, violated the premise of the original clearly defined Renaissance spaces and was less successful.

Charles Luckman Associates were the architects of the Central National Bank Building, the most pleasing of the tall office buildings which began to

Cleveland Trust Company tower, East 9th Street, 1971, Marcel Breuer and Hamilton P. Smith, architects.

transform the south side of Superior Avenue near East 9th Street. Luckman's Los Angeles-based firm, which broke with professional architectural precedent when it joined the Ogden Corporation in 1968, represented the complete development of corporate organization in architectural practice. By becoming part of a giant conglomerate with a wide range of business holdings, it was able to participate in large scale real estate developments while maintaining control of high-quality design.[23] Luckman himself had been the president of Lever Brothers in the 1950s and was a defender of Skidmore, Owings &

Merrill's pioneer glass skyscraper designed for that company. On Luckman's Central National Bank, none of the other possible choices for the facing of a tall building—glass and metal, masonry, or precast panels—would have given the warmth and positive sensuous appeal of the brick piers finally used. Applied to the vertical columns alone, the brick emphasized the dimension of height and clearly functioned only as facing. An unusual design refinement was the truncated top of the major corner piers, giving the screen wall of the topmost floors the appearance of being slightly set back.

Edward Durrell Stone was retained to design the Jewish Community Federation on Euclid Avenue at East 18th Street. Planned in association with Cleveland architects Weinberg & Teare and constructed in 1965, it was contemporary with other Stone buildings in the same manner, such as the National Geographic Society building in Washington, D.C. The Jewish Community Federation could almost be described by Marcus Whiffen's definition of the New Formalism in architecture, which states that buildings are "typically self-contained, free-standing blocks, with strictly symmetrical elevations. Skylines are level, the building often being defined at the top by a heavy projecting roof slab . . . Columnar supports tend to be thicker and more fully modeled than in the International and Miesian styles, while the arch . . . appears in various shapes and may constitute the ruling motif of the design."[24] The arcade arches of the Cleveland building were formed by beveled surfaces continuous with the edges of the columns, which were angled to the surface of the facade rather than parallel. With a plaza in front and a parking lot behind, the building was treated as a handsome isolated object, but it may be questioned whether its temple-like form found the most appropriate setting on a crowded urban street.

The awarding of many of the major architectural commissions to non-Cleveland architects, in spite of the fact that many Cleveland architects enjoyed national and even international reputations, was frequently cause for comment. Even as far back as 1931, architect Charles Schneider had written an article about the future of the profession in Cleveland in which he pointed out the "prodigious" number of local buildings designed by non-Clevelanders in the previous forty years and listed a hundred major buildings done by "outside architectural talent." Part of Schneider's concern at that time was the economic loss to local architects during the

Central National Bank, Superior Avenue and East 9th Street, Charles Luckman Associates, architects.

Depression years, but he emphasized the fact that in 1931 "no other large city in the United States [could] anywhere approach or compare with this unique but unfortunate record of Cleveland."[25] While feelings about keeping local work for local architects were not running so high forty years later, remnants of that concern still persisted. However, a general uncertainty about the stature of its local "prophets" was not unique to Cleveland, and the selection of an architect by financial and institutional interests everywhere was frequently determined by the desire for a "prestige" name.

In addition to the Eric Mendelsohn synagogue, Greater Cleveland has one other building by a master of the first generation of modern architects. The Tower East office building in Shaker Heights was designed by The Architects Collaborative with

Walter Gropius as principal-in-charge. TAC was a sort of architectural corporation which carried on the International Style ideals of social function and anonymous architecture. Gropius, the founder of the Bauhaus school of design who left Germany and came to Harvard University in 1937, completed Tower East the year before his death in 1969. The twelve-story building required a waiver of the local zoning ordinance in order to be constructed at the Chagrin Boulevard-Warrensville Center intersection. A low-rise complex was also designed as an alternative, but the tower was accepted by the planning commission. Gropius stated:

> A major traffic junction of seven streets, a conglomeration of surface parking areas and a maze of overhead wiring, poles and trolley car lines created visual confusion for the pedestrian. A bold proposal was needed and was fortunately accepted, because of the good mutual understanding shared by the owner, the architect and the authorities. The finished building establishes new relationships for the further development of the total neighborhood.[26]

Tower East consists of a two-story element with a lobby, shops, and restaurant beneath a ten-story tower. The columns of the reinforced concrete skeleton are exposed on the lower stories and were sandblasted to give a rough texture. The facades of the upper stories consist of precast panels of white cement and silica, cast in fiberglas forms to give a hard, smooth finish. The slanted shades at each window are an integral part of the cast panels and give a remarkable lightness to the structure. Depending on the angle of the sun, the vertical or horizontal elements of the facades are emphasized. In its final effect the tower has the indefinable sense of fine proportion and taste which mark the work of a master.

The most outstanding structure of the sixties at University Circle was the new addition by Marcel Breuer and Hamilton Smith for the Cleveland Museum of Art. Completing the country's largest integrated museum-art education facility, the new wing had to be joined to the original Neo-Classic building of 1916 and its 1958 addition, but the architects made no attempt to blend the design with the older structures. In fact, Breuer was said to "rather enjoy the tensions" created by the juxtaposition of old and new forms. The orientation of the site separates the two parts visually, and a new main entrance was provided on the north. The new wing consists of a series of massive windowless blocks in a dramatic sculptural arrangement, sheathed with alternating bands of light and dark granite which

Jewish Community Federation, Euclid Avenue at East 18th Street, 1965, Edward D. Stone with Weinberg & Teare, associated architects.

Cleveland Museum of Art, 1971 addition, Marcel Breuer and Hamilton P. Smith, architects.

have been called its "most distinctive aspect." The granite stripes were assembled and affixed to four-foot by six-foot concrete panels at the quarry, thus assuring control over the color gradations. The interior plan was determined to a large extent by circulation patterns and the need for certain areas to be separated or open at certain hours for meetings, films, or concerts. In the galleries, a suspended grid ceiling similar to the one used by Breuer at the Whitney Museum of American Art permits the use of modular partitions for flexible installation. Although the building appears to be completely closed, there are several areas which open onto interior courtyards. The new north entrance is dramatized by a 115-foot long concrete canopy. One journal stated that this feature was "not an architectural conceit but an unmistakable directional sign," but it did not meet with the same general admiration as the rest of the building.[27]

In 1973, for the third time in seventy years, a nationally known planner was commissioned to develop a planning concept for Cleveland. The City of Cleveland, the Greater Cleveland Growth Association, and the Cleveland Foundation contracted with Lawrence Halprin & Associates to develop procedures and guidelines for revitalizing the downtown core of the city. Both sponsors and planners agreed that the planning process should involve members of the community, and a series of public workshops was held to receive comments, develop recommendations, and promote confidence in the project. As finally prepared, the Concept for Cleveland plan treated the entire downtown area in a general fashion and concentrated its recommendations on the core area centered around Euclid Avenue from Public Square to Playhouse Square. In the main proposals for the reconstruction of Public Square, the reorganization of Playhouse Square, and the creation of a pedestrian mall on Euclid Avenue there were very few fundamental ideas which had not been suggested in the Downtown General Plan of 1959. Once again, many obvious and commonsense courses of action were given the cachet of a "name" planner.[28]

A comparison of the three planning documents reveals a great deal about the temper of their times.

The Group Plan report by Burnham, Carrere and Brunner in 1903 is a solemn treatise. The text, three-and-a-half folio-size pages long, has a sonorous and reasoned intellectual tone. It was clearly designed to impress and to inspire. As justification for the concept, it cites the precedents of ancient architecture, classical planning, and the Columbian Exposition. Although it still is, at a distance of seventy years, the most visionary of the three, it balances idealism with hard-headed practicality. The eight plates illustrating the plan were executed in the elegant Beaux Arts drawing style which was once again being appreciated in the 1970s. The report concludes with three pages of photographs of European precedents for the formal classic modes of urban planning.

A page from the *Concept for Cleveland: A Report to the People of Cleveland on Their Downtown*, 1975, Lawrence Halprin & Associates, planners.

The Erieview Plan prepared by I. M. Pei in 1960 begins with a message from Mayor Anthony Celebrezze, thus announcing at the outset that it is a political document. As an urban renewal plan, it had to conform to certain governmental expectations. The text is more restrained and attempts to give the impression that the recommendations were arrived at through scientific analysis. Justification for the proposals is offered in terms of economic statistics. The several maps are precise diagrams showing land use, key development areas, traffic circulation, urban renewal controls, and land disposition. Even the perspective renderings, now in full color, have the immaculate, unapproachable feeling of futuristic science illustration. The final impression created by the document is that it is the most practical and fully realizable of the three.

The Concept for Cleveland plan is journalistic in style. It attempts to compel attention with a "human interest" approach. The pages are composed in the sophisticated graphic techniques of advertising design. Several different type styles are used for headings, and the idiom of Pop Art appears in such images as a literal picture of a half-eaten apple core symbolizing the Core of the city. Specific suggestions for details of streets and buildings are executed in the off-hand sketchpad style of the design school, with hand-lettered notes written with a felt-tip pen. This method was especially suitable for showing how an unsavory alloy could be turned into a street of showy boutiques. The final impression of the report is one of extreme informality and improvisation.

The presentation of each plan reflected the manner in which it was expected to be carried out. The Group Plan was seen as a grand totality which would allow for very little deviation in its execution. The Erieview plan was only slightly less rigid in its recommendations and envisioned a logical, phased development. In contrast, the Concept for Cleveland was presented more as a set of guidelines which could be followed by specific but more piecemeal projects. But even with the calculated human interest appeal and community involvement, the Concept for Cleveland report seems the most patronizing of the three. While the conceptions of Burnham and Pei had been frankly authoritarian, Lawrence Halprin's plan was no less a scheme handed down by the master, despite its emphasis on citizens' workshops and suggestions. In this case, the accepted precedents were the West Coast developments of San Francisco, Portland, and

Seattle. However, the suggestions did not reckon with the fact that open trolleys, "year-round sidewalk cafes," and plaza cascades would be unworkable in northeastern Ohio for five months of the year. Furthermore, the planners were caught up in the 1960s underground predilection for "boutiques," craft shops, and streets with a "festival" atmosphere, elements whose very nature was impermanent. The proposal for the reconstruction of Public Square, with a massive terraced overpass on Superior Avenue, was especially insensitive to the existing urban space and historical sense of place.

In order to carry out the recommendations of the Concept for Cleveland plan, the Downtown Cleveland Corporation, a non-profit tax-exempt organization, was formed. Fortunately, when the first phase of the redevelopment of Public Square was actually undertaken, the specific plan was prepared by Sasaki Associates, landscape architects and urban designers, and Don M. Hisaka & Associates, Cleveland architects. Their plan preserved the four quadrants of the historic square and enhanced the setting of the Soldiers and Sailors Monument instead of subordinating it to the terracing of Superior Avenue. The landscaping of the four quadrants more nearly reflected a discreet interpretation of the classical tradition which, while not so spectacular or flamboyant as Halprin's concept, was more appropriate to and respectful of the existing urban setting.

Union Commerce Bank, interior after restoration, 1975, Peter van Dijk, architect-in-charge. (*Dalton, van Dijk, Johnson & Partners*)

# 1976: The Bicentennial Year

In 1976, unlike the Centennial year, there was no great commemorative exposition. However, the diffusion of the celebration on the state and local levels had the important side effect of intensifying interest in architectural preservation. Preservation in the United States had progressed in a desultory fashion from isolated battles for exceptional landmarks like Mount Vernon to the unprecedented restoration of the entire city of Williamsburg in the 1930s and the first declaration of a national policy on preservation in 1935. The movement had received a great stimulus with the passage of the National Historic Preservation Act of 1966, which authorized an expanded National Register of Historic Places, to be kept by the Department of the Interior as a list of districts, sites, buildings, and structures significant in American history, architecture, and culture. The act also assured that historical values would be considered in federal project planning by establishing an Advisory Council on Historic Preservation with the authority to comment on the effect of any federal undertaking on a historic place.[1]

The 1966 act required each state to appoint a State Historic Preservation Officer to administer the state preservation program and the inventory of historic sites. The Ohio office was located at the Ohio Historical Society in Columbus, and in 1973 a regional office was set up at the Western Reserve Historical Society in Cleveland to supervise the state preservation program in the twelve counties of the original Western Reserve. Ohio was the first state in the nation to begin a system of regional preservation offices, and the Western Reserve area was the first of eleven regions into which the state was eventually divided. Initially the office concentrated on submitting nominations to the National Register, and by the end of 1976 over 220 places in the Western Reserve had been listed—an achievement which contributed largely to the fact that Ohio had more places in the National Register than any other state.[2]

At the municipal level, the Cleveland Landmarks Commission, the first city landmark commission in Ohio, was created by the Cleveland City Council in 1971. According to the city ordinance, "the preservation, protection, perpetuation and use of areas, places, buildings, structures, works of art and other objects having a special historical, community or aesthetic interest or value" was made a matter of public policy. Empowered to designate landmarks, the Commission began with research to determine the eligibility of the nominated sites. It was then necessary to obtain the recommendation of the City Planning Commission, since the designation had to be consistent with the long-range city plan. The property owner was then notified and his consent secured, but if it was not forthcoming, a public hearing could be held on the merits of the designation. Upon the final recommendation of the Landmarks Commission, the City Council officially designated the nominated landmark by ordinance. The significant power of the Landmarks Commission lay in the fact that no alteration or demolition of a designated landmark could be carried out without a Certificate of Appropriateness from the Commission. In the event of a conflict, the Commission was given the power to impose a waiting period of from six months to a year to find a "mutually agreeable method" of completing the change.[3]

Under director John D. Cimperman the Commission concentrated at first on the designation of many

Saint Agnes Roman Catholic Church being demolished, 1975.

of the neighborhood churches of the city's ethnic groups, and by the end of 1976, seventy-six sites had been designated out of 232 nominations. No landmark had been designated without the consent of the owner, but one, St. Agnes Roman Catholic Church, had been razed after a delay to seek alternatives. Although a fund-raising campaign made it possible for the bell tower to be retained, no plan for an alternate use of the church building was found, and it was demolished early in 1976. Along with the razing of the churches of St. Thomas Aquinas and St. Edward, this was part of an alarming policy of the Cleveland Diocese to destroy the buildings of economically unsound parishes.[4]

Among other activities, the Cleveland Landmarks Commission sponsored surveys of the historic resources and potential development of several neighborhoods, including the Miles Park district (originally the Newburgh public square), the

Buckeye Road neighborhood, and the inner city area of Prospect Avenue between East 22nd and East 55th Streets. Working in conjunction with the other organizations and agencies devoted to preservation, the Landmarks Commission spent its early years establishing a sound basis for wielding influence in the cause of preservation and neighborhood revitalization in the city.

In October, 1973, Cleveland was host to the 27th Annual Meeting of the National Trust for Historic Preservation. The only national, nonprofit, private organization chartered by Congress to encourage public participation in preservation, the National Trust provides information and educational services as well as administering several historic properties. The headquarters for the meeting was the Western Reserve Historical Society. Meetings and receptions were held at the City Hall, Playhouse Square, and the Historical Society, and trips and tours were made

250

to the Cuyahoga Valley, the Hale Farm, and various other nearby sites. The consensus of the out-of-town visitors was that Cleveland and the Western Reserve had startling and unsuspected historic resources.[5]

In spite of these events, preservation in a large urban setting often seemed a hopeless task. The forces of uncontrolled growth, commercialization, poor planning, and economic priorities continued to threaten what they had not already destroyed. Nevertheless, a persistent minority of dedicated people worked in various ways to develop a consciousness of the necessity for preserving links with the past.

The most dramatic undertaking was the effort of the Playhouse Square Association to save the unique group of four theaters on Euclid Avenue. Ray K. Shepardson, a young employee of the Cleveland Board of Education, first conceived the possibility of saving the old movie and vaudeville palaces and renewing the theatrical activity of the district. Significantly, it was a non-Clevelander who recognized their value, Shepardson having been a resident of the city for only three years. His ambitious plan projected developing the four theaters—which had a combined capacity and flexibility greater than that of the Kennedy Center in Washington, D.C.—as a group of legitimate playhouses, restaurants, and night clubs. In 1970 the Playhouse Square Association, a nonprofit group, was organized, with membership fees to provide a source of working capital. The owner's threat to raze the State and Ohio Theatres in 1972 spurred community backing more than the two previous years of groundwork had done. With support from the Junior League and other groups, a reorganized Association created a cabaret theater in the lobby of the State Theatre. A projected three-week production of the musical revue *Jacques Brel* turned into a two-year run, the longest running show in Cleveland history, and other productions during the next three years were also well received. In addition, new impetus was given to other commercial and cultural developments in the area, and by 1976 the Playhouse Square renewal had been inspired by several tangible successes.[6]

Various other groups also developed programs of specialized or particular interest. The Downtown Restoration Society was formed in 1972, with the founder, Mrs. Albert Levin, serving as its president and chief inspiration for three years. One of the goals of the group was to develop a revolving fund through financing, restoring, and reselling historic properties. Several potential projects were examined, but it soon became evident that the resources of the organization would not permit such an ambitious program. Renamed the Cleveland Restoration Society to indicate the broader scope of its interest, the group continues to serve an educational role in the community by providing lectures, tours, and publications.[7]

Among other projects, the old Superior Viaduct was the object of study and proposed restoration as a pedestrian mall overlooking the "Flats." The Women's City Club developed a public park near the traditional settlers' landing site on the east side of the Cuyahoga River. For its Designer Showhouse in 1976, the Junior League performed considerable restoration work on a rare group of late nineteenth century row houses on Prospect Avenue. And one month before the Bicentennial day in 1976, the Third Ohio Conference on Historic Preservation was held in Cleveland. Largely organized by architect Robert C. Gaede, who was probably the most active and continuous worker in preservation over a period of many years, the conference offered two intensive days of workshops for professional preservationists, civic officials, and interested citizens from all over Ohio and neighboring states.

Several important preservation projects were initiated by corporate enterprise. Like the Cleveland Trust Company, the Union Commerce Bank decided to renovate its 1924 building. Originally consulted to make recommendations on the space needs of the bank, architect Peter van Dijk proposed that the magnificent vaulted banking room be restored to its original splendor. Unsightly alterations had been made, such as acoustical tile covering the coffered ceilings and partitions concealing the bronze railings of the balcony floor. These accretions were removed, the murals by Jules Guerin were cleaned, and the illumination from the glazed vaulting was enhanced by artificial lighting. This enlightened renovation project by a private bank was completed in 1975 and resulted in a resplendent interior space which made an eloquent argument for the cause of preservation.[8]

On an even more ambitious scale, the Higbee Company announced a plan in 1973 to rebuild a neglected area on the riverfront. The Higbee Development Corporation was created to develop the four-acre site lying between Superior and St. Clair Avenues, West 9th Street and the Cuyahoga

River. A general scheme was developed by Lawrence Halprin & Associates, and Higbee chairman Herbert Strawbridge frankly acknowledged that the source of inspiration was Ghirardelli Square in San Francisco. Called Settlers' Landing, the project envisioned a complex of terraces, shops, restaurants, and entertainment facilities on the sloping land above the river at the traditional landing site of Moses Cleaveland. Strawbridge stated that the "project is a purely commercial venture, but one so unique and historical in its concept that it takes on another function—that of acting as a catalyst for other developments."[9] Several older buildings in the area were to be preserved and renovated, but before work could begin one of them, the National Furniture Warehouse on West 9th Street, burned. Later the Bridge Central Hotel (the old Bethel Union) was found to be structurally unsound and was demolished. Burnham and Root's Western Reserve Building, however, underwent a complete renovation. The original arched entrance with its elaborate foliated ornament, which had been covered with a granite facing, was restored. The

exterior brick was cleaned and waterproofed. The interior was redesigned according to modern office standards, although unfortunately the comment of James Wood on the new brick veneer lobby by Halprin's designer was apposite: "The domes, alcoves and arches are a fatuous addition. The atmosphere is early wine cellar."[10] The renovation of the Western Reserve Building was a significant undertaking, but further plans for the completion of Settlers' Landing were still in abeyance at the end of 1976.

Perhaps the most notable aspect of the preservation movement in the late 1960s and early 1970s was the broadening of the concept of conservation beyond the preservation of outstanding landmarks to include a recognition of the values in older urban neighborhoods which still maintained a livable quality. Such values were "discovered" in the near West Side neighborhood which had been a part of old Ohio City. Bounded roughly by West 25th and West 45th Streets and Detroit and Monroe Avenues, the area conveyed the atmosphere of a nineteenth century middle and working class neighborhood.

Settlers' Landing, 1973. The Higbee Development Corporation site. At the head of Old Superior, the Western Reserve Building. (*Cleveland Press*)

There were a few key landmark structures, such as the West Side Market, St. Ignatius School, the Carnegie West Library, and the churches, and some of the better mansions on Franklin Avenue remained. But the character of the neighborhood came largely from the original radiating street plan, the compactness and architectural variety of the small wooden and brick vernacular houses, and the diversity of the residents. The Ohio City area was the subject of city planning studies several times during the 1960s. However, the planners' suggestions, as Carol Poh Miller has pointed out, included all of the "urban planning clichés" of the period.[11] Revitalization would be accomplished by providing new traffic arteries, parking lots, and "open space" with landscaped institutional buildings. The planners applied their definition of "urban blight" and assumed the total clearance of the area. The very aesthetic and social qualities which made the area desirable would be obliterated, as if no neighborhood had ever existed.

Fortunately, the plans were never adopted. Instead, the Ohio City Community Development Association was formed in 1968, under the leadership of Bruce Hedderson, to encourage investors to restore and rehabilitate the old houses and to move into the neighborhood. A development corporation formed by the West Side Federal Savings and Loan purchased properties for resale on condition that they would be rehabilitated, and later made mortgage financing available. By 1976 over a hundred properties had been purchased and restored. Some community opposition developed among those who felt that the younger professional people who could afford to buy properties might drive out the older residents who gave Ohio City the heterogeneous character which made it worth preserving. Nevertheless, in the Bicentennial year considerable progress had been made toward the conservation of the neighborhood. (The term "conservation" was preferred because it implied the recognition of the older values without suggesting a completely historic restoration.) The social and physical environment was not yet completely stabilized, however, and vandalism, arson, deterioration, and demolition still occurred on a regular basis.

As Cleveland entered the nation's third century, the justness of David Bailey's remark, "And in a hundred years from now? God knows," was apparent. Almost nothing of Charles Heard's Cleveland of 1876 remained. As the normal forces of urban change and the drive for civic improvement so often conflicted with those of conservation, what had survived?

What survived was a city whose profile had been determined early by the exigencies of industry and railroads; a town of New England settlers enriched by the ethnic and racial variety of its later immigrants; a town center with a unique urban configuration; and the ruin of "the most beautiful street in the world."

What survived was the lore of the princely builders of oil, steel, and railroads; a celebration of the wedding of commerce, engineering, and art in an iron-webbed bazaar which afforded that genuine rarity, an authentic architectural experience; and a community with a progressive social consciousness.

What survived was a city with an insatiable appetite for making plans; the memory of a brief mastery of the proper relationship between city and suburb; the most completely realized civic plan to follow the Columbian Exposition; and a cultural center second to none in its concentration of artistic and educational institutions.

What survived was the record of the architects, local and national, exceptional and typical; a monument to the ambition to raise for a moment the second highest tower in the world and a commerce and transportation center rivalling any other in its concept; a tenacious dream of the spectacular garden suburb; and a city where the display of wealth was quiet and not ostentatious.

What survived was early public housing which embraced the International Style in its social meaning as well as its formal style; the torn fabric amid the freeways; the displacement resulting from the promises, successes, and failures of urban renewal; the evidence of traumatic violence and of the desire and will to rebuild.

What survived above all was a Cleveland whose detractors and failures could never compete with the optimism and the vigor and the persistence of its builders and its plans.

## NOTES

### 1876

1. David Bailey, *Eastward Ho! or Leaves from the Diary of a Centennial Pilgrim* (Hillsboro, Ohio, 1877), 40, 48.

2. *Final Report of the Ohio State Board of Centennial Managers* (Columbus, 1877), 8–11.

3. James D. McCabe, *The Illustrated History of the Centennial Exhibition* (Philadelphia, 1876; reprinted 1975), 224.

4. Eric Johannesen, "Charles W. Heard, Victorian Architect," *Ohio History*, Autumn, 1968, 130–142.

5. Edmund H. Chapman, *Cleveland: Village to Metropolis* (Cleveland, 1964), 97–107.

### 1876–1890

6. William Ganson Rose, *Cleveland: The Making of a City* (Cleveland, 1950), 427–435; *Cleveland Board of Trade Report* (1881), 96.

7. *Cleveland 1888: Its History and City Government* (Cleveland, 1888), 138 ff., 170 ff.

8. *Ibid.*, 190–193.

9. *Leading Manufacturers and Merchants of the City of Cleveland and Environs* (New York, 1886), 39–40.

10. *Ibid.*, 154. The hospital was demolished in 1977.

11. *Cleveland Architectural Club, Catalogue of Its Third Exhibition* (1900), 11.

12. Rose, *Cleveland*, 455; *Some Selections from the Work of Coburn and Barnum, Architects* (Cleveland, 1897), 5.

13. Edward Schwabe, in *Leading Manufacturers*, 155.

14. Donald Egbert and Paul Sprague, "In Search of John Edelman, Architect and Anarchist," *AIA Journal*, February, 1966, 35–41.

15. *Work of Coburn and Barnum*, 36.

16. *Leading Manufacturers*, 133; Rose, *Cleveland*, 217.

17. *The Cleveland Directory* (1883); *Leading Manufacturers*, 133; E. M. Avery, *Cleveland and Its Environs* (Chicago and New York, 1918), III, 383.

18. *The Cleveland Directory* (1885); *Leading Manufacturers*, 190.

19. *Leading Manufacturers*, 75.

20. *American Architect and Building News*, November 19, 1887; Rose, *Cleveland*, 471–472.

21. Rose, *Cleveland*, 492; *Cleveland City Directory* (1888–1890).

22. The Perry-Payne has erroneously been claimed to have the first steel frame in Cleveland. The iron posts are shown in Sanborn's *Insurance Maps of Cleveland, Ohio* (New York, 1896).

23. *The Cleveland Directory* (1863–1872).

24. Scofield's career is outlined in William J. Gleason, *Soldiers and Sailors Monument* (Cleveland, 1894), 572–576. The Winslow house is described in the *Sunday Morning Voice*, April 14, 1878. The drawing is from the Levi Scofield papers (Western Reserve Historical Society manuscript collection).

25. A complete account of Schweinfurth's life and work is contained in Regenia Perry's "The Life and Works of Charles Frederick Schweinfurth, Cleveland Architect 1856–1919" (Ph. D. dissertation, Western Reserve University, 1967).

26. Charles A. and Mary A. Beard, *A Basic History of the United States* (New York, 1944), 303–311.

27. Samuel P. Orth, *A History of Cleveland, Ohio* (Chicago, 1910), 607–609.

28. Grace Goulder, *John D. Rockefeller: The Cleveland Years* (Cleveland, 1972), 135–136; Ella Grant Wilson, *Famous Old Euclid Avenue* (Cleveland, 1932), 321–323.

29. "An American Palace," *Irish Builder* (Dublin), September 1, 1883, 273.

30. *"The World's" History of Cleveland* (Cleveland, 1896), 330–333; Rose, *Cleveland*, 440, 866.

31. F. Washington Jarvis, *St. Paul's Cleveland, 1846–1968* (Cleveland, 1968), 18–21.

32. Arthur C. Ludlow, *The Old Stone Church: The Story of a Hundred Years, 1820–1920* (Cleveland, 1920), 245–261.

33. Rose, *Cleveland*, 462.

34. *Twenty-Five Years 1892-1917* (The Calvary Presbyterian Church, 1917), 9–10; *Annals of the First Presbyterian Church of Cleveland, 1820-1895*, 236-237.

35. *The Cleveland Directory* (1880, 1908, 1923).

36. *21st Annual Report of the Board of Trustees and Directors of the Orphan Asylum* (Cleveland, 1889), 42–43, 45.

37. Rose, *Cleveland*, 351.

38. Orth, *History of Cleveland*, III, 642; David Lowe, *Lost Chicago* (Boston, 1975), 26, 33, 107; Registrar of Births, Herzogenrath, Germany.

39. *Parishes of the Catholic Church, Diocese of Cleveland* (Cleveland, 1942), 133–134. Michael J. Hynes, *History of the Diocese of Cleveland* (Cleveland, 1953), 70-71; Cleveland *Leader*, October 23, 1871.

40. *Souvenir of the Golden Jubilee of St. Stephen's Church (1870–1920)* (Cleveland, 1920), n. p.

41. Alanson Wilcox, *An Autobiography* (Cleveland, 1912) 69–70; Rose, *Cleveland*, 185–186.

42. Cuyahoga County tax records. *The Cleveland Directory*

(1881–1883); Rose, *Cleveland*, 430, 458; *Cleveland Plain Dealer*, May 11, 1975, 25.

43. Carol Poh Miller, "Ohio City: A Proposal for Area Conservation in Cleveland" (M. A. thesis, George Washington University, 1975), 40–45.

44. Hynes, *Diocese of Cleveland*, 139–140. *75th Anniversity, St. Ignatius High School, Cleveland, Ohio* (Cleveland, 1961), n. p. There is an undocumented tradition that the dimensions of the building were planned in the metric system because the Fathers were German. However, measurements of the existing fabric are in whole inches and fractions, not in centimeters.

45. Diane Newell, "With Respect to Breweries," *Historic Preservation*, January-March 1975, 24–27.

46. *One Hundred Years of Brewing*, as quoted in Bruce R. Leisy, *A History of the Leisy Brewing Corporation* (Witchita, 1975), 20.

47. Leisy, *Leisy Brewing*, 19–20.

48. *Leading Manufacturers*, 142.

49. Leisy, *Leisy Brewing*, 28–30.

50. *The Architecture of Cleveland, Twelve Buildings* (Cleveland and Washington, 1973), 35–38.

51. Charles W. Coulter, *The Poles of Cleveland* (Cleveland, 1919), 9–11.

52. *A People 100 Years, St. Stanislaus 1873–1973* (Cambridge, Md., 1973); *Plain Dealer*, November 15, 1891.

53. William J. Akers, *Cleveland Schools in the 19th Century* (Cleveland, 1901), 185–186; Rose, *Cleveland*, 419.

54. Akers, *Cleveland Schools*, 196; Leonard P. and May Ayres, *School Buildings and Equipment* (Cleveland, 1916), 28–29; Orth, *History of Cleveland*, I, 521.

55. Rose, *Cleveland*, 453, 540.

56. Orth, *History of Cleveland*, I, 556 ff; Case Western Reserve University Archives.

57. Frederick C. Waite, *Western Reserve University, The Hudson Era* (Cleveland, 1943), 448–465; Rose, *Cleveland*, 454–455.

58. *The Cleveland Directory* (1865–1885); *Cleveland Leader*, January 6, 1865, September 28, 1866, November 14, 1876; *Specification of Work and Materials for Proposed new National Bank Building* (Cleveland, 1867).

59. Frederick C. Waite, *Western Reserve Centennial History of the School of Medicine* (Cleveland, 1946), 174, 222–223.

60. W. Scott Robison, *History of the City of Cleveland* (Cleveland, 1887), 222–223.

61. Waite, *School of Medicine*, 223–226.

62. Faculty Minutes, Western Reserve University, January 5, January 21, and February 12, 1885; James F. O'Gorman, *H. H. Richardson and his office, a centennial of his move to Boston, 1874: selected drawings* (Boston, 1974), 115.

## 1890

1. *American Victorian Architecture* (New York, 1975: reprint of *L'Architecture Americaine*), pl. III, 32, and pl. II, 33.

2. *Exhibitive of the Features and Attractions of the Arcade Building, Cleveland* (New York, 1891), n.p.; Goulder, *Rockefeller*, 188.

3. I am indebted in the following discussion to the excellent aesthetic and structural analysis of The Arcade contained in Mary-Peale Schofield's "The Cleveland Arcade," *Journal of the Society of Architectural Historians*, December, 1966, 281–291.

4. *Ibid.*, 289–290.

## 1890–1903

5. This quotation and the following one, plus a beautifully detailed description and analysis of the building, are contained in *Society for Savings Building* (New York, 1891), n.p.

6. Donald Hoffman, *The Architecture of John Wellborn Root* (Baltimore, 1973), 121.

7. Rose, *Cleveland*, 489; Charles Moore, *Daniel H. Burnham: Architect—Planner of Cities* (Boston, 1921), II, 210; Cleveland building permit, May 15, 1891. This and all subsequent building permits are located in the building department, Cleveland City Hall.

8. Rose, *Cleveland*, 541, 610; Moore, *Burnham*, II, 210; *Cleveland News*, September 19, 1926; Cuyahoga County property records, County Administration Building.

9. Among these booklets are: *Glimpses of Greater Cleveland*, issued by Henry Leopold, Artistic Furniture (Cleveland, 1896); *Glimpses of Greater Cleveland* (Cleveland, 1899); *Cleveland Illustrated* (Cleveland, ca. 1900).

10. Rose, *Cleveland*, 547, 799; Cleveland building permit, February 7, 1894.

11. *New England Building*, description and floor plans (Cleveland, 1895); Rose, *Cleveland*, 565, 723; Henry F. and Elsie R. Withey, *Biographical Dictionary of American Architects (Deceased)* (Los Angeles, 1970), 136, 551.

12. Rose, *Cleveland*, 567, 627; Withey and Withey, *Dictionary of Architects*, 543.

13. Rose, *Cleveland*, 610; *Dictionary of American Biography* (New York, 1935), XV, 118.

14. Rose, *Cleveland*, 521; newspaper clipping, December 26, 1891, in Scrapbook of items relating to Ravenna (Ohio), (Western Reserve Historical Society, hereinafter referred to as W. R. H. S.).

15. S. Winifred Smith, "Alexander E. Brown and George H. Hulett," *Museum Echoes*, September, 1955, 67–70.

16. *The Ohio Architect and Builder*, July, 1903, 21; *The Brown*

*Hoisting Machinery Company,* Catalog (Cleveland, 1919).

17. Orth, *History of Cleveland,* I, 744; Cleveland building permit, September 7, 1897.

18. Rose, *Cleveland,* 476; "National Carbon Company," *Historic American Engineering Record Inventory,* August, 1976; *The Hunkin-Conkey Construction Company* (Cleveland, n.d.), 48.

19. Bay Village Historical Society, *Bay Village: A Way of Life* (Bay Village, 1974), 74–79; *The Cleveland Directory* (1897–1900); Rose, *Cleveland,* 564.

20. Rose, *Cleveland,* 470.

21. Harold U. Faulkner, *Politics, Reform and Expansion 1890–1900* (New York, 1959), 203–206, 261–262.

22. Cleveland *Press,* Home magazine, December 11, 1976, 6–7.

23. *The Cleveland Blue Book, Social Register and Elite Directory* (Cleveland, 1907), 230–231; C. F. Schweinfurth, plans of the Cox-Prentiss house, dated July, 1898 (W. R. H. S. ms. 3272).

24. Perry, *Life and Works of Schweinfurth,* 144.

25. *The Cleveland Directory* (1898); Levi T. Scofield, plans of the L. T. Scofield house (W.R.H.S. ms., collection in process).

26. My discussion in this and the following four paragraphs is indebted to Faulkner's chapter on the cities in *Politics, Reform and Expansion,* 24–26.

27. That these ideals were by no means universally appreciated is shown by this extract from the diary of Kathleen Matchell Smith, who would become the mother of Christopher Isherwood: "November 12, 1896. Heard Mr. Lethaby on *Beautiful Cities,* which was very charming and fantastical and romantic and utterly impracticable and received with immense applause. London without telegraph wires, which were after all put up for men's amusement! With no buses in the chief thoroughfares, which should be lined with trees and grouped with fountains and statues. That a girdle should bound the limits of London in the form of a lovely park, etc." Christopher Isherwood, *Kathleen and Frank* (New York, 1971), 43.

28. *Historical Sketches of Our Twenty-five Churches and Missions* (Cleveland, 1896), 90–97; *Our First One Hundred Years–Pilgrim Church* (Cleveland, 1959), 5–8.

29. *Ohio Architect and Builder,* August, 1903, 23–28.

30. *Ibid.,* 26–27; *Epworth Memorial Church: A Monument and a Movement* (Cleveland, 1903).

31. C. A. Urann, *Centennial History of Cleveland* (Cleveland, 1896), 109–110.

32. Orth, *History of Cleveland,* I, 373; Hynes, *Diocese of Cleveland,* 214.

33. Orth, *History of Cleveland,* I, 378–379.

34. Rose, *Cleveland,* 501, 572, 578–579, 583, 596; *Work of Coburn and Barnum.*

35. Carl J. Reifsnider, *Alta House* (Cleveland, 1953), n.p.; Goulder, *Rockefeller,* 185.

36. *Exercises in Dedication of the Jones Home* (Cleveland, October 8, 1903); Rose, *Cleveland,* 482.

37. Rose, *Cleveland,* 406; List of buildings by Mitermiler in letter, Frances Sverina to Mary-Peale Schofield, in possession of recipient.

38. Eleanor Ledbetter, *The Czechs of Cleveland* (Cleveland, 1919), 7–11, 25–27; *Diamond Jubilee, Bohemian National Hall* (Cleveland, 1973), n.p.; Robert J. Liederbach, *Cleveland Past* (Cleveland, 1975), 62; *The History of the Bohemian Communities in Cleveland* (Cleveland, 1895), 180; *Inland Architect,* October, 1896, 30.

39. Rose, *Cleveland,* 452, 543, 548, 554, 573, 621; Park Administration, "History of the Acquirement and Development of the Municipal Park System of Cleveland," typescript, n.d., 3–4.

40. Goulder, *Rockefeller,* 186–188; Rose, *Cleveland,* 609.

41. C. H. Cramer, *Case Western Reserve, A History of the University 1826–1976* (Boston, 1976), 86–103; Western Reserve University Building Committee minutes, January 1, 1891.

42. *In Memoriam, Flora Stone Mather* (Cleveland, 1910; privately printed); Cleveland *Leader,* January 20, 1909.

43. Case Western Reserve University Archives.

44. Cramer, *Case Western Reserve,* 306–308.

45. *Manual of the Western Reserve Historical Society,* W.R.H.S. Tract No. 91 (Cleveland, 1907); Rose, *Cleveland,* 343, 534, 566, 589.

46. *The Man and the Mausoleum* (Cleveland, 1890), 32–42; Withey and Withey, *Dictionary of Architects,* 334–335; *Historic and Descriptive Sketch of the Garfield Memorial* (Cleveland, 1889), 17.

47. Gleason, *Soldiers and Sailors Monument.*

48. Rose, *Cleveland,* 154, 506, 545, 562, 574.

49. *Cleveland The Forest City* (Cleveland, 1907), n.p.; Rose, *Cleveland,* 506, 548, 572–575.

50. *Official Report of the Centennial Celebration of the Founding of the City of Cleveland* (Cleveland, 1896). 27; Cleveland Architectural Club, *Catalogue of the Second Annual Exhibition* (Cleveland, 1897), 31.

51. *In Memory of Jeptha H. Wade* (n.d.; privately printed), n.p.

52. *The Cleveland Chamber of Commerce Annual Report* (1897), 63–65, (1898), 46–49, (1899), 55–56. Cleveland Architectural Club, *Catalogue* (1897), 71.

53. Charles A. Post, "Cedar Road Proves Key to Growth of City on Heights," news clipping, August 19, 1932, in Records of the Women's Civic Club of Cleveland Heights (W.R.H.S. Library).

54. Cleveland building permit, October 14, 1901; Withey and Withey, *Dictionary of Architects,* 636.

55. R. Furneaux Jordan, *A Concise History of Western Architecture* (London, 1969), 312–313.

56. "Recollections of Homer H. Johnson," November 15, 1929, in Records of the Women's Civic Club of Cleveland Heights; Joseph Weinberg, letter to Alex

C. Robinson, December 27, 1976 (W.R.H.S. Library); Cleveland building permits, March 6, 1913, and October 7, 1916.

57. *Ohio Architect and Builder*, June, 1903, 13–15.

## 1903

1. *Report on the Group Plan of the Public Buildings of the City of Cleveland, Ohio* (1903); a copy of this rare document is in the Western Reserve Historical Society Library.

2. Cleveland Architectural Club, *Catalogue of its Third Exhibition* (1900), 20–26; Rose, *Cleveland*, 549, 559, 629–630. Professor Olney had opened the Olney Art Gallery in 1893 in a beautiful classic building by Coburn and Barnum which still stands on West 14th Street near Fairfield. At the time of his death in 1907, his valuable collection was given to Oberlin College.

3. Thomas S. Hines, *Burnham of Chicago* (New York, 1974), 158.

4. Chapter 8, "The Paradox of Progressive Architecture," in Hines' *Burnham of Chicago*, gives a succinct and well-balanced description of the details of the Plan.

5. The Cleveland Chamber of Commerce, *The Union Station, On the Lake Front? or On the Public Square* (Cleveland, 1918), 34.

6. Frederic C. Howe, "Plans for a City Beautiful," *Harpers Weekly*, April 23, 1904, 624–626.

7. F. E. Cudell, *The Grouping of Cleveland's Public Buildings*, brochure, September 1, 1903, n.p.; F. E. Cudell, *The Columns Upon Which to Support Our Republic* (Cleveland, 1905); F. E. Cudell, *The Proposed Revised Plan of 1903 to Fit Present Conditions* (Cleveland, 1916).

8. *Architectural Record*, March, 1911, 201.

9. Rose, *Cleveland*, 700, 705, 743, 831; Joseph Weinberg, architect, "Recollections" (Cuyahoga County Archives).

10. Rose, *Cleveland*, 810, 815, 887, 918; Archer H. Shaw, *The Plain Dealer, One Hundred Years in Cleveland* (New York, 1942), 309–311.

11. Hines, in *Burnham of Chicago*, quotes this version of Burnham's credo, p. xxiii, and discusses its origins in note 8, p. 401.

## 1903–1911

12. "The Work of Mr. J. Milton Dyer," *Architectural Record*, November, 1906, 403.

13. Richard N. Campen, "The Ups and Downs of J. Milton Dyer," *Plain Dealer* Sunday magazine, November 14, 1965, 22–23, 40–41; Cleveland building permit, 1904.

14. Rose, *Cleveland*, 540.

15. *Dedication Services of First Methodist Episcopal Church, March 26–April 2, 1905* (Cleveland, 1905); Rose, *Cleveland*, 649.

16. *The Architecture of Cleveland: Twelve Buildings, 1836–1912* (Washington and Cleveland, 1973), 80–87; Rose, *Cleveland*, 797, 895.

17. *The New York Architect*, May, 1910, n.p.; Rose, *Cleveland*, 171, 201, 673.

18. *Souvenir Book of the Cleveland Industrial Exposition* (Cleveland, 1909), 5–8, 46–47.

19. *The Cleveland Athletic Club*, description and plans for the new club (1910); *C.A.C. Bulletin*, May, 1910–December, 1911; Rose, *Cleveland*, 704.

20. Campen, "Ups and Downs of J. Milton Dyer," 40–41.

21. *Ordinances No. 46388-A and No. 44404-A, The Building Code of the City of Cleveland, Ohio* (Cleveland, 1904).

22. John Eisenmann, "How Cleveland Obtained its Code," *Ohio Architect and Builder*, May, 1906, 23–31.

23. *The Architecture of Cleveland: Twelve Buildings*, 61–70; Ralph T. Coe, *The Rockefeller Building of Cleveland* (Cleveland, 1951?).

24. *Plans, Perspectives, Details and Specifications of the Caxton Building*, pamphlet (The Caxton Building Company, 1903), n.p.; Rose, *Cleveland*, 617, 650.

25. *The Cleveland Trust Company, An Epitome of the Past, A Chronicle of the Present, A Promise of the Future* (Cleveland, 1908), 9–28.

26. Mrs. Edward A. Merritt to Myron T. Herrick, June, 1912 (W.R.H.S. ms. 2925).

27. Rose, *Cleveland*, 689.

28. *Dictionary of American Biography* (New York, 1935), XV, 117–118.

29. Nathaniel R. Howard, *The First Hundred Years: A History of the Union Club in Cleveland* (Cleveland, 1972), 49–57.

30. *Trinity Cathedral, Cleveland, Historical and Architectural Guide* (Cleveland, 1912), 9–11, 20, 27–30; *The Architecture of Cleveland: Twelve Buildings*, 55–59.

31. Withey and Withey, *Dictionary of Architects*, 146; Marcus Whiffen, *American Architecture Since 1780* (Cambridge, Mass., 1969), 173.

32. Rose, *Cleveland*, 513; Charles F. Schweinfurth, "The New Trinity Cathedral, Cleveland, Ohio," *The New York Architect*, May, 1910, n.p.; Ella Grant Wilson, *Famous Old Euclid Avenue* (Cleveland, 1937), II, 77–78.

33. Rose, *Cleveland*, 659; *The Explorer* (Cleveland Museum of Natural History), no. 97, 1948, 2–3; Richard Campen, *Architecture of the Western Reserve* (Cleveland, 1971), 46–47, 242.

34. Cleveland Architectural Club, *Catalogue* (1900), 14.

35. Rose, *Cleveland*, 235; *The Cleveland Directory* (1891); Cleveland building permit, 1898.

36. Cleveland building permit, 1902.

37. Cleveland building permit, 1905.

38. *The Cleveland Directory* (1905); Hubbell & Benes, rendering of Equity Savings & Loan building (W.R.H.S. Library).

39. Rose, *Cleveland*, 442, 739, 916; *Parishes of the Catholic*

Church, 70–71; Hynes, Diocese of Cleveland, 258, 316; Withey and Withey, Dictionary of Architects, 428.

40. Rose, Cleveland, 418.

41. Huldah Cook, The Magyars of Cleveland (Cleveland, 1919), 21–22; Rose, Cleveland, 642; Book of Clevelanders (Cleveland, 1914), 270.

42. Rose, Cleveland, 336, 357, 643, 646, 810, 813.

43. Ibid., 637.

44. Ayres and Ayres, School Buildings and Equipment, 33; Marshall Everett, Collinwood School Disaster (Cleveland, 1908).

45. Cleveland Architectural Club, Catalogue (1900), 12.

46. Lewis Mumford, The City in History (New York, 1961), 428.

47. Plat Book of the City of Cleveland, Ohio, and Suburbs (Philadelphia, 1912).

48. Perry, Life and Works of Schweinfurth; "The Buildings of the Cleveland Music School Settlement," mimeographed sheet (Cleveland Music School Settlement).

49. "Autobiographical Sketch of Abram Garfield," typescript (W.R.H.S. Library); Abram Garfield, sketches and blueprints for Mrs. John Hay house (W.R.H.S. Library).

50. Cramer, Case Western Reserve, 354–355; "A Catalogue of the Books in the Library of Samuel Mather," bound typescript, 1911 (W.R.H.S. Library), 24–26, 151.

51. Henry E. Bourne, The Church of the Covenant, The First Hundred Years (Cleveland, 1945), 32–37.

52. Ibid., 38; "The Remodeled Williamson Chancel," pamphlet (Cleveland, 1931); Cleveland Leader, April 3, 1911.

53. Mary Emma Harris and Ruth Mills Robinson, The Proud Heritage of Cleveland Heights (Oberlin, 1966), 20–23, 45; "Cedar Road Proves Key to Growth of City on Heights," news clipping, August 19, 1932, and "Recollections of Homer H. Johnson," typescript, November 15, 1929, in Records of the Women's Civic Club of Cleveland Heights (W.R.H.S. Library); Rose, Cleveland, 575.

54. Otto Miller, Jr., "A History of the Growth and Development of the Van Sweringen Railway System" (B.A. Thesis, Harvard College, 1924), 1–2. Harry Christiansen, Northern Ohio's Interurbans and Rapid Transit Railways (Cleveland, 1965), 105–111.

55. Blythe Gehring, Vignettes of Clifton Park (Cleveland, 1970).

56. "Cedar Road Proves Key to Growth of City on Heights"; Withey and Withey, Dictionary of Architects, 247.

57. Gehring, Clifton Park, 17, 73, 79, 105. George F. Hammond, A Treatise on Hospital and Asylum Construction (Cleveland, 1891); Phillip R. Shriver, The Years of Youth: Kent State University, 1910–1960 (Kent, 1960), 31–32; Cleveland Landmark Commission, 1975 Annual Report, 8.

58. Withey and Withey, Dictionary of Architects, 475–476; Walter C. Kidney, The Architecture of Choice: Eclecticism in America 1880–1930 (New York, 1974), 33.

59. Samuel Howe, American Country Homes of ToDay (New York, 1915), 132–135.

60. McKim, Mead & White, plans for Howard M. Hanna, Jr., house; photocopies are located in the W.R.H.S. Library.

61. The Architecture of Cleveland: Twelve Buildings, 88–95; Frederic Wm. Striebinger, brochure (Cleveland, 1914), n.p.

62. Ohio Architect, July, 1904, and April, 1908.

63. There is reason to believe that the Canfield house was planned by Cleveland architects William Bohnard and Raymond Parsson, based on its close resemblance to a residence designed by them and built in 1911 at 715 East Main Street, Ravenna, Ohio.

64. Aymar Embury II, One Hundred Country Houses (New York, 1909), 3–15.

65. Withey and Withey, Dictionary of Architects, 415; I. T. Frary, Early Homes of Ohio (Richmond, 1936), 295; Country Club News, various articles, 1925–1927; Town and Country Club News, various articles, 1927–1928.

66. Mary-Peale Schofield, "The Traditional House for Modern Living: The Work of Meade and Hamilton, Cleveland, 1900–1919," unpublished paper in possession of the author.

## 1911

1. Hollis L. Townsend, A History of Nela Park 1911–1957 (Cleveland, 1957), 14. Townsend's history gives a remarkably complete description of the planning and construction of the park and its buildings. Most of the detail in the following discussion is from this book.

2. Robert D. Kohn, "Architecture and Factories," The Architectural Record, February, 1909, 131–136.

3. Withey and Withey, Dictionary of Architects, 627.

4. Florence Dempsey, "Nela Park, a Novelty in the Architectural Grouping of Industrial Buildings," The Architectural Record, June, 1914, 469–503.

5. Montgomery Schuyler, "A New Departure in 'Big Business'," The Architectural Record, June, 1914, 507.

6. Ibid.

## 1911–1920

7. Arthur S. Link, Woodrow Wilson and the Progressive Era (New York, 1954), 168.

8. Rose, Cleveland, 703; Cleveland City Directory (1915–1921); Book of Clevelanders (1914), 168.

9. Rose, Cleveland, 536, 783, 818; Withey and Withey, Dictionary of Architects, 601.

10. Cleveland building permit, 1909. The architect of the Church of the Holy Ghost was Marion E. Wells of Cleveland.

11. St. Theodosius Russian Orthodox Greek Catholic Cathedral,

booklet (Cleveland, 1962), n.p.; Theodore Turak, "A Celt Among Slavs: Louis Sullivan's Holy Trinity Cathedral," *The Prairie School Review*, IX, no. 4, 1972, 8–9.

12. *Cleveland City Directories* (1911–1920).

13. Cleveland building permit, 1913.

14. Orth, *History of Cleveland*, II, 1078–1081; *Progressive Men of Northern Ohio* (Cleveland, 1906), 217.

15. Benjamin S. Hubbell, address given at Builders' Luncheon, October 14, 1910 (W.R.H.S. Library).

16. Orth, *History of Cleveland*, II, 1078–1081.

17. Withey and Withey, *Dictionary of Architects*, 50–51; Cleveland building permit, 1922.

18. Hubbell, Builders' Luncheon address; I. T. Frary, "The Cleveland Museum of Art," *Architectural Record*, September, 1916, 194–211.

19. Frary, "Cleveland Museum of Art," 195.

20. Ibid., 211; Cleveland Chamber of Commerce, *Annual* (1916), 113; Hubbell and Benes, Wade Park drawings (W.R.H.S. Library).

21. University Improvement Company Records, Benjamin S. Hubbell Collection (W.R.H.S. Library); Hynes, *Diocese of Cleveland*, 296.

22. Hubbell and Benes, University of Cleveland plans and drawings (W.R.H.S. Library).

23. *The Architecture of Cleveland: Twelve Buildings*, 91; Church archives, First Church of Christ Scientist, Lakewood.

24. Hynes, *Diocese of Cleveland*, 266–268, 288–291.

25. *Parishes of the Catholic Church*, 79–80; Cleveland building permit, 1911; *Akron City Directories* (1875–1933).

26. *Parishes of the Catholic Church*, 106–107.

27. Ibid., 113–115; *Our Hero (Visit of Cardinal Mindszenty to Cleveland, 1974)* (Cleveland, 1974), n.p.

28. Anne O'Hare McCormick, *Story of St. Agnes Parish, 1893 to 1937* (Cleveland, 1937).

29. I.T. Frary, "St. Agnes' Church, Cleveland, Ohio," *Architectural Record*, July, 1917, 43; McCormick, *Story of St. Agnes*, 3, 31; Anne O'Hare McCormick, *St. Agnes' Church, Cleveland, Ohio, An Interpretation* (Cleveland, 1920), 5.

30. Unless otherwise noted, the following sources were used throughout this section. All give the same basic account of the Van Sweringen developments. Taylor Hampton, "Cleveland's Fabulous Vans," *The Cleveland News*, August 2, 1955—August 20, 1955; Joseph G. Blake, "The Van Sweringen Developments in Cleveland" (Senior thesis, University of Notre Dame, 1968); Christiansen, *Northern Ohio's Interurbans and Rapid Transit Railways*, 105–109; Miller, "Van Sweringen Railway System"; Rose, *Cleveland*, 529, 707, 730, 738, 767, 769, 788.

31. I. T. Frary, "Suburban Landscape Planning in Cleveland," *Architectural Record*, April, 1918, 371–384.

32. Van Sweringen Company, *The Heritage of the Shakers* (Cleveland, 1923).

33. *The Union Station, On the Lake Front? or On the Public Square* (Cleveland, 1918).

34. Building contract, in *Record, The Terminal Hotels Company, The Terminal Building Company, in Re Hotel Cleveland and Sub-Structure (1917)*, 708.

35. Wilbur J. Watson, *Bridge Architecture* (New York, 1927), 200–208, illus., 250–251.

36. Ibid., 201–202; *Plain Dealer*, October 12, 1910, 3; "Detroit Avenue (Rocky River) Bridge," Historic American Engineering Record Inventory, May 15, 1975.

37. *Bridges of Cleveland and Cuyahoga County* (Cleveland, 1918), 7–13; "A Half-Mile Double-Deck Concrete Bridge," *Scientific American*, April 15, 1916, 403; Rose, *Cleveland*, 615, 681, 758.

38. *Plain Dealer*, August 6, 1914; Allan Nevins and Frank E. Hill, *Ford: Expansion and Challenge 1915–1933* (New York, 1957).

## 1921

1. Rose, *Cleveland*, 745.

2. Harvey Wish, *Contemporary America* (New York, 1955), 26–29.

3. *Plain Dealer*, February 5, 1921; *Playhouse Square* (Cleveland, 1975), n.p.; Rose, *Cleveland*, 800–801.

4. Talbot F. Hamlin, *The American Spirit in Architecture* (New Haven, 1926), 306; Rose, *Cleveland*, 801–802, 804.

5. Wolf Von Eckardt, excerpt from the Washington *Post*, February 9, 1972, quoted in *Playhouse Square*.

6. I. T. Frary, "The Hanna Building and the Hanna Building Annex," *Architectural Record*, January, 1922, 16–32.

7. Archie Bell, *A Little Journey to B. F. Keith Palace, Cleveland* (no publisher, n.d.), 1–4, 41–45.

8. *Plain Dealer*, January 22 and 23, 1921; Rose, *Cleveland*, 799.

## 1921–1930

9. George H. Mayer and Walter O. Forster, *The United States and the Twentieth Century* (Boston, 1958), chapter 17, "The Politics of Prosperity"; Wish, *Contemporary America*, chapter 11, "Triumph of Mature Capitalism."

10. Rose, *Cleveland*, 795–796; *Plain Dealer*, May 19, 1924, 1, 3.

11. *Through the Ages*, May, 1927, 25; Rose, *Cleveland*, 825; "The Story of the New Union Depot," brochure (1919), n.p.

12. Wilfred Henry Alburn, *This Cleveland of Ours* (Chicago and Cleveland, 1933), III, 85–90; Withey and Withey, *Dictionary of American Architects*, 624, 640.

13. John D. Baker, "Anonymity and American Architecture," *Historic Preservation*, July–September, 1972, 15–17; Rose, *Cleveland*, 171, 182, 644–645.

14. Rose, *Cleveland*, 547, 565, 723, 799.

15. *Architectural Revue of the Mississippi Basin*, I, no. 1, Summer, 1930, 13–15.

16. *Ibid.*, 3, 21, 36.

17. Sheldon Cheney, *The New World Architecture* (New York, 1930), 120–154.

18. *A Temple of Telephony*, brochure (1927), n.p.; Hubbell and Benes, renderings for the Ohio Bell Telephone Building (W.R.H.S. Library).

19. "The Modern Club" and "The Significance of the National Town and Country Club," brochures, n.p.; G. B. Post & Sons, architects' drawings (W.R.H.S. Library).

20. G. Brooks Earnest, *A History of Fenn College* (Cleveland, 1974), chapters 1 and 4.

21. Thomas F. Campbell, *Daniel E. Morgan, 1877–1949, The Good Citizen in Politics* (Cleveland, 1966), 98; Rose, *Cleveland*, 829, 832–833.

22. *Official Souvenir, Cleveland Public Auditorium* (Cleveland, 1922); *Through the Ages*, June, 1923, 37–41.

23. Russell Allen Hehr, *Architecture and Allied Arts of the Cleveland Public Library Landmark Main Building* (Cleveland, 1975). John Russell Pope is best known as the architect of the Jefferson Memorial and the National Gallery of Art in Washington, D.C.; Edward L. Tilton designed the Ellis Island Immigration Station and Cleveland's Carnegie West Library; Robert D. Kohn was the architect of the Black factory and the Lindner store in Cleveland; Allen & Collins' most noted works include Riverside Church and Union Theological Seminary in New York; and Holabird & Roche were among the pioneers of Chicago skyscraper design in the 1880s. These were formidable competition for Walker & Weeks.

24. *The Open Shelf*, May, 1925, entire issue: "The New Main Library."

25. Wish, *Contemporary America*, 322–323.

26. *Plain Dealer*, July 3, 1931, 1, 6, 32.

27. Martha A. (Parsons) Williams, "The truth about the opening of Carnegie Avenue and Lorain Street and the building of the Lorain Street Bridge. . .," typescript (1955?); Map issued by the Carnegie Extension Association, 1911; City of Cleveland, City Plan Commission, *Lorain-Carnegie Bridge and River Improvement* (Cleveland, 1926); Wilbur J. Watson, *A Decade of Bridges, 1926–1936* (Cleveland, 1937), 11–16.

28. Wilbur J. and Sara Ruth Watson, *Bridges in History and Legend* (Cleveland, 1937), 223.

29. Also located in the Western Reserve Historical Society Library are blueprints for the stonework by the Ohio Cut Stone Company, drawn by Herman Deneke.

30. *Plan for the Future Development and Enlargement of the Water Supply System of Cleveland* (Cleveland, 1920), 32–33.

31. Thodur M. Bavanarayanan, *The Cleveland Water History and Details of Baldwin Filtration Plant* (City of Cleveland, Department of Public Utilities, Division of Water, 1975), 6–10; Elbert Peets, "The Cleveland Reservoir," *The Nation*, February 9, 1927, 145.

32. The architect's drawings by Herman Kregelius are located in the City of Cleveland Sewer and Water Design Offices.

33. James S. Ackerman, *Palladio* (Baltimore and Harmondsworth, 1966), 160–182. In Palladio's *Second Book of Architecture*, Plate XXXVIII in particular suggests the organization of the Baldwin plant.

34. "Anshe Emeth, Beth Tefilo," WPA Survey of State and Local Historical Records, Ohio (1936), (W.R.H.S. Library); Cleveland building permit, 1921.

35. *The Temple*, booklet, n.d., n.p.; "Tifereth Israel," WPA Survey of State and Local Historical Records, Ohio (1936), (W.R.H.S. Library).

36. George R. Collins, "The Transfer of Thin Masonry Vaulting from Spain to America," *Journal of the Society of Architectural Historians*, October, 1968, 183, 199.

37. Epworth-Euclid Church records; Rose, *Cleveland*, 126, 407, 838.

38. Charles E. Whitaker, ed., *Bertram Grosvenor Goodhue—Architect and Master of Many Arts* (New York, 1925), 27; Eric McCready, "The Nebraska State Capitol: Its Design, Background and Influence," *Nebraska History*, Fall, 1974.

39. *Who's Who in America*, IXX, 1936–1937 (Chicago, 1936), 929.

40. *Plain Dealer*, February 6, 1931, 3; *The Bystander*, February 7, 1931, 10–11; Rose, *Cleveland*, 736, 767, 893.

41. William F. McDermott, in *Plain Dealer*, February 6, 1931, 1.

42. *The Bystander*, February 7, 1931; Alburn, *This Cleveland of Ours*, II, 1133–1134.

43. Alburn, *This Cleveland of Ours*, II, 1125, 1129. *Plain Dealer*, February 6, 1931, 3.

44. Withey and Withey, *Dictionary of Architects*, 289.

45. *Plain Dealer*, Wade Park Manor Section, December 24, 1922; Withey and Withey, *Dictionary of Architects*, 621–622.

46. The following sources were used throughout the discussion of the Play House: "The New Play House," in *The Cleveland Year Book, 1927* (Cleveland, 1928), 117–127; Frederic McConnell, "The Cleveland Playhouse," *Architectural Record*, August, 1927, 81–94; Charles S. Brooks, "The Cleveland Play House," *Theatre Arts Monthly*, August, 1926, 517–522.

47. Harold E. Atkinson, "The Cultural Gardens of Cleveland," *Parks and Recreation*, November, 1937; Leo Weidenthal, "Cleveland's Cultural Gardens, A Symbol of Unity," *The Clevelander*, August, 1952, 4–5.

48. Clara Lederer, *Their Paths Are Peace* (Cleveland, 1954).

49. Letter, Charles J. Wolfram, president, Cultural Garden League, to Harmonia Chopin Singing Society, October 10, 1940, with autograph notation by Abram Garfield (Weidenthal Collection, W.R.H.S. Library).

50. The Van Sweringen Company, *The Heritage of the Shakers* (Cleveland, 1923), 29; The Van Sweringen Company, *Peaceful Shaker Village* (Cleveland, 1927); Howard Whipple Green, *Population Characteristics by Census Tracts* (Cleveland, 1930), 55.

51. Augusta Owen Patterson, *American Homes of To-Day* (New York, 1924), 8, 86.

52. William K. Hellmuth and William E. Oberndorf, "The Van Sweringens' Development of Shaker Heights (1906–1930)," typescript (Senior Project Report, Western Reserve University, n.d.); *Cleveland City Directories* (1921–1930).

53. *Plymouth Church of Shaker Heights* (Cleveland, 1923), n.p.

54. Withey and Withey, *Dictionary of Architects*, 541.

55. Jarvis, *St. Paul's Cleveland, 1846–1968; Architectural Revue of the Mississippi Basin*, Summer, 1930, 52–56.

56. The Van Sweringen plan also provided sites for three private preparatory schools. The Hathaway Brown, University, and Laurel Schools all moved to Shaker Heights from older locations in Cleveland in 1926–1927. The three sites, north of Shaker Boulevard and east of Courtland Boulevard, Warrensville Center Road, and Green Road respectively, were islands in the residential tracts. The Walker & Weeks firm produced a Tudor building for Hathaway Brown and a Georgian Revival group for University School. John H. Graham was the architect for Laurel School.

57. "Moving a Neighborhood," *The Architectural Exhibitor*, April, 1929, 3, 10; *Cleveland City Directories* (1929–1931); Cleveland building permits.

58. Cleveland *News-Leader*, March 26, 1922, 1, 10.

59. Rose, *Cleveland*, 816; Diary of Alfred W. Harris, 1923–1924, in the possession of Alfred W. Harris, Jr.

60. "A New and Convenient Neighborhood," *The Bystander*, June 22, 1929, 10.

61. Whiffen, *American Architecture Since 1780*, 164.

62. *Plain Dealer*, December 19, 1937, C–11; Lowe, *Lost Chicago*, 192, 203; Geoffrey Baker and Bruno Funaro, *Shopping Centers: Design and Operation* (New York, 1951), 184–185.

63. The Van Sweringen Company, "Plan of the Van Sweringen Company's Shaker Country Estates, East of Green Road" (Cleveland, 1926).

64. Alburn, *This Cleveland of Ours*, II, 861.

65. For easy reference, newspaper clippings pertaining to this entire development, 1923–1930, are collected in Virginia Taylor Hampton's "Material on the Nickel Plate Road, 1869–1960" (W.R.H.S. Library).

## 1930

1. "A Great Passenger Terminal," *Railway Age*, June 28, 1930, 1549.

2. Most of the descriptive and construction details in the following section are from Walter S. Lacher's "Dedicate New Cleveland Station Today," *Railway Age*, June 28, 1930, 1553–1580.

3. *The Cleveland Union Station, A Description of the New Passenger Facilities and Surrounding Improvements* (Cleveland, 1930).

4. Henry-Russell Hitchcock, *Architecture, Nineteenth and Twentieth Centuries* (Harmondsworth and Baltimore, 1958), 401.

5. James Marston Fitch, *Grand Central Terminal and Rockefeller Center, A Historic-Critical Estimate of their Significance* (New York, 1974).

6. Winston Weisman, "The First Landscaped Skyscraper," *Journal of the Society of Architectural Historians*, May, 1959, 54.

7. Graham, Anderson, Probst & White had already worked another variation on this tower scheme with Chicago's Wrigley Building in 1921–1924.

## 1930–1950

8. Rose, *Cleveland*, 965.

9. *Architectural Forum*, March, 1936, 187–188, and October, 1937, 90; Brecksville Historical Association, *A Reminiscent History of Brecksville* (Berea, 1961), 73. The Brecksville Congregational Church was destroyed by arson in 1965.

10. S. Prentiss Baldwin, "Remaking a Village," *The Country Calendar*, October, 1905, 546–549; Gates Mills Historical Society, *A Pictorial History of Gates Mills 1826–1976* (Gates Mills, 1976).

11. Alan Gowans, *Images of American Living: Four Centuries of Architecture and Furniture as Cultural Expression* (Philadelphia, 1964), 383.

12. Walter McCornack, "Cleveland Housing Studies," *Architectural Record*, March, 1933, 150–153.

13. Rose, *Cleveland*, 934–935; Abram Garfield, "Growth of Regional Planning," *Architectural Record*, September, 1938, 67–69.

14. W. A. Stinchcomb, "The Cleveland Metropolitan Park System," *Cleveland Engineering*, March 21, 1929, 3–7.

15. *The Emerald Necklace*, May, 1952.

16. "The Finish *Must* Be Modern," *The Architectural Exhibitor*, February, 1930, 3.

17. Gowans, *Images of American Living*, "From Europe to America," 429–434.

18. Gowans, *Images of American Living*, "New Deal, New Order, New Architecture," 435–444; *Le Corbusier Talks With Students* (New York, 1961), 25–26.

19. Alfred H. Barr, Jr., Henry-Russell Hitchcock, Jr., Philip Johnson and Lewis Mumford, *Modern Architects* (New York, 1932).

20. *Plain Dealer*, July 3, 1932, 2-C, and July 10, 1932, 2-C.

21. *Ibid.*, July 10, 17, 24, 31, 1932; *Architectural Record*, January, 1934, 25; "Here's the World's First Porcelain House," *Popular Science Monthly*, November, 1932, 44.

22. *Plain Dealer*, July 2, 1932, 8.

23. Harold Burdick obituary, Cleveland *News*, May 26, 1947; Interviews with Stephen Esrati, owner of the Burdick house since 1971.

24. *Plain Dealer*, December 31, 1938, 14, March 11; 1939, 11, and March 12, 1939, 24. F. L. Wright claimed that "Fallingwater" had the first domestic installation of flourescent lighting. It was contemporary with the Burdick house at best. The Wright house was begun in 1936 and completed a year and a half later. The lighting was the last thing installed. The location of General Electric's Nela Park in Cleveland makes a local initial trial much more plausible. The first public announcement of flourescent lighting was made in March, 1936.

25. Unless otherwise noted the factual material on the Exposition is from Herbert G. Fickes, "General Story on Great Lakes Exposition," mimeographed publicity release (1936), and *Great Lakes Exposition, Official Souvenir Guide* (Cleveland, 1936).

26. "The Mall Progresses," *The Clevelander*, August, 1931, 11; Rose, *Cleveland*, 876–878, 918, 929.

27. "Cleveland Building Employs First Wood Rigid Frames," *Architectural Record*, December, 1937, 31.

28. For a description of the Nuremberg Rally lighting, see Albert Speer's *Inside the Third Reich* (New York, 1970), 58–59.

29. "Lighting the Great Lakes Exposition," *The American City*, July, 1936, 113–115; "A Fountain at the Great Lakes Exposition," *The American City*, September, 1936, 139.

30. *Plain Dealer*, August 11, 1940; Rose, *Cleveland*, 987. The Coast Guard Station has often been compared with Eric Mendelsohn's Einstein Tower (1920), but apart from the coincidental existence of a tower, the design bears little relationship to the plasticity of that early Expressionistic landmark.

31. Gowans, *Images of American Living*, 447.

32. *Plain Dealer*, October 13, 1947, 1, 6.

33. William E. Leuchtenburg, *Franklin D. Roosevelt and the New Deal* (New York, 1963), 133.

34. *Plain Dealer*, June 26, 1931, 1, July 22, 1931, 4, February 17, 1933, 11, February 19, 1933, 12, September 4, 1934, 1, October 20, 1934, 17.

35. Rose, *Cleveland*, 908–909, 1044.

36. *Plain Dealer*, October 28, 1932, 16.

37. The following discussion of housing in Cleveland and Lakeview Terrace is based on Helen A. Harrison's "Lakeview Terrace: Architecture as Housing," typescript paper (n.d.), and Wallace G. Teare's "Brief Description of Lakeview Terrace, Cleveland, Ohio," typescript paper (ca. 1941–1945).

38. Karal Ann Marling, *Federal Art in Cleveland 1933–1943* (Cleveland, 1974).

39. Lewis Mumford, *The Culture of Cities* (New York, 1938), 373.

40. Harrison, "Lakeview Terrace," 20–21.

41. Rose, *Cleveland*, 951.

42. *Ibid.*, 928, 945; *Plain Dealer*, May 9, 1936, 1, and August 27, 1936, 1.

43. Rose, *Cleveland*, 961-962; *Plain Dealer*, October 7, 1939.

44. Rose, *Cleveland*, 973, 984, 989, 1018–1019.

45. *Plain Dealer*, May 20, 1943; Rose, *Cleveland*, 991–992, 1013.

46. Rose, *Cleveland*, 998, 1009, 1013; Interview, Mr. Koppelberger, Brookpark, July 28, 1977.

47. Schofield, "The Cleveland Arcade," 283, 288.

48. Hynes, *History of the Diocese of Cleveland*, 59, 469–473.

49. Kenneth L. Kusmer, *A Ghetto Takes Shape* (Urbana, Ill., 1976), 165–170, population distribution maps between 146–147.

50. Rose, *Cleveland*, 124, 217–218, 667, 810; Cleveland Landmark Commission, *1975 Annual Report*, 9.

51. Kusmer, *A Ghetto Takes Shape*, 149–151, 257–259.

52. *Ibid.*, 216–218.

53. A trenchant indictment of the effects of the government-industrial complex on the cities is contained in Robert Goodman's *After The Planners* (New York, 1971).

## 1950

1. Arnold Whittick, *Eric Mendelsohn* (London, 1956), 162.

2. Whittick, *Eric Mendelsohn*, 70, 196–197.

3. Wolf Von Eckardt, *Eric Mendelsohn* (New York, 1960), 23.

4. Quoted in Von Eckardt, *Eric Mendelsohn*, 11.

5. Rose, *Cleveland*, 813–814. Recollections of Rabbi Cohen concerning the planning process are quoted in Whittick's *Eric Mendelsohn*.

6. As quoted in Faulkner, Ziegfeld and Hill, *Art Today* (New York, 1949), 89–90, 99.

7. Whittick, *Eric Mendelsohn*, 167.

8. Charles C. Colman, "Some of the Construction Problems of Park Synagogue," *The Ohio Architect*, July, 1950, 6–7; Whittick, *Eric Mendelsohn*, 183–184.

9. "The Last Work of a Great Architect," *Architectural Forum*, January, 1955, 106–109.

## 1950–1960

10. Paul S. Holbo and Robert W. Sellen, ed., *The Eisenhower Era* (Hinsdale, Ill., 1974).

11. Frederick Lewis Allen, *The Big Change: America Transforms Itself, 1900-1950* (New York, 1952).

12. Cleveland City Planning Commission, *The General Plan of Cleveland* (1950).

13. Hermann H. Field, "Coordinating a College Building Program with a City's Civic Center," *The American City*, September, 1949, 108–110.

14. "An Investment in the Better Things of Life," *The Clevelander*, June, 1955, 20–21.

15. Adams, Howard & Greeley, *University Circle, Technical Report on a General Plan for the Future Development of the Area* (Cambridge, 1957); University Circle Development Foundation, *The First Five Years* (Cleveland, 1962).

16. "Cleveland: City with a Deadline," *Architectural Forum*, August, 1955, 130–139; Cleveland City Planning Commission, *Downtown Cleveland 1975, the Downtown General Plan* (1959).

17. "Cleveland's Illuminating Building," *Architectural Record*, June, 1958, 153–162.

18. "Cleveland's New Airport," *The Clevelander*, March, 1956, 6.

19. *Architectural Forum*, November, 1952, 136–137.

20. "Cleveland's New Airport," *The Clevelander*, 7, 48, 50; see also *Cleveland Hopkins Airport, Official Dedication Program* (April 28–29, 1956).

21. *The American City*, March, 1951, 133; *Cleveland Transit System Annual Reports* (1954, 1955); *Plain Dealer*, March 15 and August 14, 1955.

22. *Rapid Transit to Airport*, Demonstration Project Proposed by City of Cleveland (August, 1961); *Proceedings of the Modal Choice and Transit Planning Conference (March 17–18, 1966)*, 287–289.

23. Christiansen, *Northern Ohio's Interurbans and Rapid Transit Railways*, 135–154.

24. *Plain Dealer*, May 5, 1959, 33, and December 6, 1961, 28.

25. Russell Lynes, *The Domesticated Americans* (New York, 1963), 274.

26. *Ibid.*, 266.

27. *Plain Dealer*, December 15, 1961, 45.

28. "Branch Store Breaks Modern Design Blockade in Cleveland," *Architectural Forum*, February, 1950, 96–101; Robert A. Little, lecture, October 23, 1977.

29. Much of this exposition of the development of the shopping center is based on Victor Gruen's *Centers for the Urban Environment* (New York, 1973).

30. Heinrich Wölfflin, *Principles of Art History*, trans. by M. D. Hottinger, 1932 (New York, n.d.).

## 1960

1. *Erieview, Cleveland, Ohio, An Urban Renewal Plan for Downtown Cleveland* (Cleveland, 1961), 2.

2. "Downtown's Dramatic Comeback," *Architectural Forum*, February, 1964, 99–100.

3. *Plain Dealer*, November 23, 1960, 2.

4. *Architectural Forum*, February, 1964, 100.

5. Philip W. Porter, "The Mistake That Ruined Downtown," *Cleveland* magazine, November, 1976, 68 ff.

6. *Erieview Plaza*, A Galbreath-Ruffin Project, brochure (n.d.), n.p.

7. "Erieview Plaza," *Architectural Record*, March, 1967, 153–156.

8. *The Stokes Years*, brochure (Cleveland, 1971), n.p.

9. Interview, Norman Perttula, Dalton-Dalton-Little-Newport, September 22, 1977.

## 1960–1976

10. Amos A. Kermisch and Richard M. Peery, "Hough: An Urban Struggle," *Plain Dealer*, December 17–22, 1972.

11. Comptroller General, Report to the Congress, *Development of Minority Businesses and Employment in the Hough Area of Cleveland, Ohio, Under the Special Impact Program* (Washington, 1971).

12. "Urban School Turns Inward," *Progressive Architecture*, February, 1971, 86–87.

13. Cleveland Neighborhood Health Services, *Open House Health Fair*, program (May 17, 1977).

14. Cleveland Metropolitan Housing Authority, *Annual Reports* (1968, 1969).

15. *Cuyahoga Community College: A New College for a New Society*, A Report by The East Ohio Gas Company (Cleveland, 1965).

16. *Official Plan for Cuyahoga Community College* (Cleveland, 1962).

17. "1970 Community and Junior College Design Awards," *AIA Journal*, March, 1970, 37.

18. *The Fenn Plan* (Cleveland, 1963).

19. *Plain Dealer*, May 30, 1964, 1, 7; *Cleveland State University—Preliminary Report—Campus Planning Study—1966* (Cleveland, 1966).

20. *Plain Dealer*, May 19, 1964, 1, 8.

21. "Campus Ecumenical Center," *Architectural Record*, September, 1974, 136–138.

22. "Three precast buildings from the office of Marcel Breuer and Associates," *Architectural Record*, March, 1973, 124–126.

23. "The Architects Want a Voice in Redesigning America," *Fortune*, November, 1971, 144, 203.

24. Marcus Whiffen, *American Architecture Since 1780: A Guide to the Styles* (Cambridge, Mass., 1969), 257.

25. Charles Schneider, "Mr. Architect—What About Your Future in Cleveland?," *The Architectural Exhibitor*, April, 1931, 3.

26. "A Suburban Office Building by TAC—Designed as Focal Point and Landmark," *Architectural Record*, March, 1969, 129.

27. "Education in the Arts," *Architectural Forum*, September, 1971, 20–25.

28. *Concept for Cleveland: A Report to the People of Cleveland on Their Downtown* (Cleveland, 1975).


**1976**

1. Ohio Historic Preservation Office, *Program Guide* (Columbus, 1975), 1–7.

2. The Western Reserve Historical Society, *Annual Reports* (1973–1976).

3. City of Cleveland ordinances, June 23, 1971, June 23, 1972, and March 20, 1973.

4. The Cleveland Landmarks Commission, *Annual Reports* (1974–1976).

5. *Preservation in Your Town*, The 27th Annual Meeting and Preservation Conference of the National Trust for Historic Preservation, Cleveland, October 10–14, 1973.

6. *Playhouse Square* (Cleveland, 1975), n.p.

7. Cleveland Restoration Society (formerly Downtown Restoration society), *Annual Reports* (1973–1975).

8. Carol Poh Miller, "Good News and Bad for Cleveland Architecture of the 20's," *WCLV Cleveland Guide*, August, 1975, 8–9.

9. Cleveland *Press*, July 2, 1973, A-12.

10. *Plain Dealer*, November 14, 1976, V-2.

11. Carol Poh Miller, "Ohio City: A Proposal for Area Conservation in Cleveland" (M. A. thesis, George Washington University, 1975), 78–83, 87 ff.

# INDEX

This is a selective index listing the principal buildings discussed and illustrated, their architects, major clients, and selected topics.